Building Parsers with Java™

Building Parsers
with Java™

Steven John Metsker

Addison-Wesley

Boston • San Francisco • New York • Toronto • Montreal
London • Munich • Paris • Madrid
Capetown • Sydney • Tokyo • Singapore • Mexico City

The publisher offers discounts on this book when ordered in quantity for special sales. For more information, please contact:

Pearson Education Corporate Sales Division
One Lake Street
Upper Saddle River, NJ 07458
(800) 382-3419
corpsales@pearsontechgroup.com

Visit AW on the Web: www.awl.com/cseng/

Library of Congress Cataloging-in-Publication Data

Metsker, Steven John
    Building parsers with Java / Steven John Metsker.
        p. cm.
    Includes bibliographical references and index.
    ISBN 0-201-71962-2
    1. Java (Computer program language) I. Title.

    QA76.73.J38 M48 2001
    005.13'3—dc21
                                    00-068916

ISBN 0-201-71962-2

Text printed on recycled paper
1 2 3 4 5 6 7 8 9 10—MA—0504030201
First printing, March 2001

On behalf of their ancestors
Especially my beloved Alison
To our descendants
Especially our darlings
Emma Kate and Sarah Jane

Contents

Foreword

I never used to like parsing, either in theory or in practice. For one thing, all the parsing theory I've studied suffers from an overabundance of funny characters and symbols. I'm all for rigor, but not at the expense of clarity or the typesetter's sanity. Whatever concrete examples there have been, moreover, tend to be obscure and ignore the problems of modern programming. In fact, most texts on parsing reflect decades-old perspectives on software design and development. And most explanations, it seems, come encased in wooden prose.

The practice of parsing has fared no better. Traditional parsing tools are overkill at best, antiquated and unusable at worst. The result? Ad hoc has become the parsing approach of choice.

But when I read this book, I had a change of heart.

Steve Metsker's up-to-date take on parsing is as accessible as anything I've read on the subject. I even venture that this is *the* most accessible book-length work, both for its foundation on widely appealing technologies like Java and XML and for its clear, simple, engaging presentation.

This book's appeal cannot be limited to a small cadre of language developers and implementers. Sooner or later, every programmer worth his or her salt will need to parse something. When that time comes, said programmer can turn to this book and be enlightened, as opposed to being intimidated or bored to tears. Now you too can understand when to use XML versus building your own parser, what to tokenize versus parse, and when to settle for regular expressions versus a query, imperative, or logic language. And that's just for starters. Indeed, the concepts explained here are so handy and fundamental that all developers should learn them. You might know about tokenizing and grammars and eliminating left recursion without claiming to be a software professional, but the reverse doesn't hold.

Steve has made parsing downright enjoyable. Keep reading and you'll agree.

John Vlissides
IBM T.J. Watson Research

Preface

The premise of this book is that by learning how to work with parsers, you can create new computer languages that exactly fit your domain. When you create a language, you give your language users a new way to control their computers. By learning about parsers, you learn to define the way your users interact with computers using text.

Who Should Read This Book

This book assumes you have a good understanding of Java and would like to learn how to do the following:

- Use a handful of tools to create new computer languages quickly.

- Translate the design of a language into code.

- Create new computer languages with Extensible Markup Language (XML).

- Accept an arithmetic formula from your user and compute its result.

- Accept and apply matching expressions such as th* one.

- Create query languages that fire an engine.

- Program in logic and create a logic language parser.

- Make rules-based programming available to your users from within a Java application.

- Program in Sling, a new computer language that plots the path of a sling.

- Create computer languages that fill niches in the work you do.

Using the Toolkit Code and the Sample Code

This book comes with a CD that contains all the code.

Contents of the CD

The CD includes all the code of the fundamental parser classes, the logic engine, and all the examples. The CD also contains the javadoc documentation from the code, which explains class by class how the code works.

Applying the Code on the CD

The code on the CD is free. It is copyrighted, so you may not claim that you wrote it. Otherwise, you may use the code as you wish.

Hello World

The following program is a sufficient test to verify that you can use the code from the CD. Load the code from the CD into your development environment. Type in the following program, or load it from ShowHello.java on the CD.

```java
package sjm.examples.preface;

import sjm.parse.*;
import sjm.parse.tokens.*;

/**
 * This is a "Hello world" program. Once you get this
 * working on your computer, you can get any example in this
 * book to work.
 */
public class ShowHello {

/**
 * Create a little parser and use it to recognize
 * "Hello world!".
 */
public static void main(String[] args) {
    Terminal t   = new Terminal();
    Repetition r = new Repetition(t);

    Assembly in  = new TokenAssembly("Hello world!");
    Assembly out = r.completeMatch(in);

    System.out.println(out.getStack());
}
}
```

Compiling and running this class prints the following:

```
[Hello, world, !]
```

Once you get this running in your environment, you will be able to use all the fundamental classes and all the examples in this book.

Coding Style

Some features of the coding style in this book may seem unusual. First, this book does not indent method signatures. This practice stems from the fact that the VisualAge development environment exports classes this way, resulting in a pair of curly braces at the end of a class. This convention has the happy effect of allowing a little more space before statements are wrapped within the narrow margins of this book.

Another feature of the coding style in this book that may give you pause is the use of extremely short variable names. Methods in this book nearly always perform a single service and thus are short. Temporary variables are never far from their declarations, and there is usually no need for names longer than one character. For example, it is not difficult in the preceding program to discern that the variable t refers to a Terminal object. In the rare event that two variables of a given type occur in one method, they receive meaningful names, such as in and out in the preceding example.

Comments in the code use javadoc tags such as @param and @exception, but the text usually omits these to save space. Comments for public methods begin with /**, which indicates that the comment is a "doc comment."

Related Books

This book requires that you have a good knowledge of Java. It will help to have available a good resource on Java, particularly *The Java Programming Language*, by Ken Arnold and James Gosling.

This book makes many references to design patterns. Although this book explains the basics of each pattern as it is introduced, it will help to have at hand *Design Patterns*, by Erich Gamma, Richard Helm, Ralph Johnson, and John Vlissides.

This book uses the Unified Modeling Language as a notation for describing object-oriented design. This book includes an appendix on this notation, but it will help to have available *The Unified Modeling Language User Guide*, by Grady Booch, James Rumbaugh, and Ivar Jacobsen.

These books and others are listed in the References section.

Theoretical Context

This book does not assume that you understand compilers and language theory. But if you *are* well grounded in these topics, you may want to know where this book sits within established theory. This section explains the type of parsers that this book covers and describes how this book differs from others in terms of conventions regarding grammars and abstract syntax trees.

All parsers in this book are nondeterministic recursive-descent parsers. If you are interested in learning about other types of parsers, the classic source on this topic is *Compilers: Principles, Techniques, and Tools* [Aho et al.]. The choice of nondeterministic recursive-descent parsers springs from two objectives. The first is to empower a developer of a new little language to easily transition from language design to the implementation of a parser. The second objective is to answer the Extreme Programming question, "What is the simplest thing that could possibly work?" [Beck, page 30].

To simplify the coding of a parser from its design, a parsing technique should let a developer translate a grammar directly into a parser. The sequences, alternations, and repetitions in a grammar must correspond directly to instances of Sequence, Alternation, and Repetition classes. Furthermore, the developer should face few restrictions in the allowable attributes of an input grammar. Nondeterministic recursive-descent parsing provides a comparatively simple approach to meeting these objectives.

Nondeterminism is a central problem of parser construction; parsers do not always know which path to take as they recognize text. Nondeterministic recursive-descent parsing solves this problem by using *sets* to allow all possible parser paths to proceed. This approach used to be too slow, but modern computers make it sufficient for small languages, including all the languages in this book. An advantage of this approach is that the parsers accept any context-free grammar as long as the developer removes left recursion, by using a technique explained in this book. Nondeterministic recursive-descent parsers provide a broadly applicable and simply implemented approach to empowering developers of new languages.

The conventions in this book also differ from some conventions for writing grammars. Specifically, grammars in this book use class names to represent terminals and use semicolons to mark the end of rules. These standards support the simplicity of the translation from grammar to code.

Finally, this book is unusual in the little treatment it gives to abstract syntax trees (ASTs). It is common practice to parse input, create an AST, and then walk the tree. This book argues that it is more effective to build a target object as a parse completes, working on the result as each grammar rule succeeds. Most of the examples in this book build a useful result while parsing an input string, but none of the examples constructs an AST.

Yacc and Lex and Bison and Flex

A variety of tools that facilitate parser building are freely available on the Internet. The tools *yacc* and *bison* accept the design of a language (its *grammar*) and generate a parser. The tools *lex* and *flex* help to collect characters into words, numbers, or *tokens*. All these tools generate C code, but there are newer tools that are oriented toward Java, such as the *javacc* tool.

All these tools require a developer to design a parser in one language and then generate it in another language. For example, to use javacc you must enter a grammar according to the rules of javacc. Then you can feed these rules to the tool to generate the Java code of a parser.

The use of a generator forces you to work in two languages: the language of the generator and the target language, C or Java. This book does not use generators, advocating instead that you enter Java code directly from the grammar. Sequences, alternations, and repetitions in the grammar become Sequence, Alternation, and Repetition objects in your code. The advantage is that the only language you need to know to start creating parsers is Java.

An advantage of using generators such as yacc is that they produce parsers that are much faster than parsers built with the techniques used in this book. The value of this speed depends on the length of the language elements your parser must face. If you create a parser using the techniques in this book and find that you want more speed, you can consider porting your parser to use a tool such as yacc. At that point, you will be comfortable with the rules and meaning of your language, and that will make implementation in yacc much easier.

If you have used yacc or other parser generators, you will find the material in this book familiar territory. Similarly, learning the techniques in this book will prepare you to use parser generators. All parser tools share the aim of helping you to become a language developer.

About the Cover

The cover illustration is original artwork by Steve Metsker. The art form is known as "ASCII-art" and calls for the artist to draw upon a limited set of characters. ASCII is a standard that, like Unicode, specifies a set of characters and their approximate appearance. The artist applies this palette to express meaning that transcends the value inherent in the characters.

The ASCII artist and the computer programmer summon meaning from the keyboard for differing purposes. Adherents of either art may seek and may achieve mastery over their characters, learning to conjure powerful objects from a primitive source. The dragon rider on the cover extends the mastery theme, depicting the knight's mastery over the dangerous and powerful dragon. The dragon represents the complexity of creating new computer languages; the knight represents you, who can master the dragon for your own purposes.

Acknowledgments

This is a much better book because of the efforts of many reviewers. I would like to thank William C. Wake, who, as the initial reviewer of the book, wielded both axe and scalpel deftly, correcting everything from improper terminology to spelling errors. Eric Freeman was another early reviewer who offered many insights, foremost of which was the value of adding a chapter on imperative languages. This suggestion led to Sling, the most innovative language in the book.

I would like to thank Guy L. Steele Jr. for helping to align this book with standard terminology, and for his many other catches of problems large and small. I would also like to thank Erik R. Knowles, Howard Lee Harkness, and Tim Lindholm for their insightful, thorough, and helpful reviews.

Joshua Engel helped this book immensely, both in early reviews and later "user" reviews. He prompted dozens of changes of content, caught many errors and rough points in the text, and helped to drive the book to be faster, lighter, and smaller. I could not ask for a better reviewer.

Although I was constantly surprised at the thoroughness of the reviewers, I was also impressed at each reviewer's ability to catch mistakes and find improvements that neither I nor the other reviewers had yet discovered. I would particularly like to thank Mary Dageforde, Carl Burnham, Lantz Moore, Adam Bradley, Thanh Giang, and David Thomas for helping to make this a better book.

I cannot thank John Vlissides enough for his improvements to the text, from grammar corrections to his insights on my commentaries on design patterns. Dr. Vlissides and the other technical reviewers are part of the wonderful culture of computer science wherein those who have already moved the field forward happily encourage and assist humble efforts such as this book.

The many excellent reviews of this book would not have been possible without the orchestration of the editors and other staff at Addison-Wesley. I would especially like to thank Julie DiNicola, who has been cheerful, upbeat, prompt, insightful, and a pleasure to work with for many months.

CHAPTER 1

Introduction

The objective of this book is to empower you to create new computer languages. This book pursues its goal even though hundreds of vital computer languages are alive today, many having displaced their ancestors. New and important languages are always on the horizon, and developers find themselves encountering and learning new languages every year. Yet none of these languages is ideal for every application.

In every domain where computer programs run, there is an opportunity to bridge the gap between humans and computers. Humans work with text, and computers work with objects. By learning to write parsers, you learn to bridge the gap between computers and the users of your language. You can create a new language for any niche, defining how your users interact with computers using text.

1.1 The Role of Parsers

English is a powerful language. With it, we can write plays and sonnets, grocery lists and business plans, love notes and contracts. A self-evident example is this book, which uses the English language to explain how to write parsers using the Java computer language. If computers could understand English, we would have little need for Java or any other programming language. Perhaps there is some potential to invent a human language that is less flexible and less ambiguous than English—for critical tasks such as launching a spacecraft—but people generally thrive using natural languages, applying the flexibility and even the ambiguity of language to good purpose. With computers, however, this does not work because they require precise commands to execute correctly.

Computers understand very little, and arguably nothing at all. They can add numbers and move strings of text but cannot in themselves understand the idea of, say, doing something 10 times. So on the one hand we have English, which is enormously expressive, and on the other hand we have computers, which understand almost nothing. This is why programming languages emerge. A programming language such as Java is a compromise between the expressive eloquence of English and the primitive receptive abilities of a computer. Most of the words in Java are English words, and these words typically retain their English meaning. For example, `while` in Java has essentially the same meaning as the word *while* in an English sentence. Other words (`public`, for example) have meaning that is specific to a programming concept but is still related to the same word in English. Java is as English-like as it can be, but Java focuses on its task of enabling us to command computers.

It is reasonable to ask what the ideal programming language is, and indeed this question leads to progress and new languages such as Java. You might agree that Java is a better language because it is *object-oriented*. People tend to mentally model the world in terms of objects, and Java's object orientation makes it a ready receptacle for these thoughts. It simplifies the connections between, say, a real furnace and a `Furnace` object, and that in turn simplifies the control of a real furnace from a Java program. Object-oriented languages ease the programmer's task of interacting with objects in the real world. In addition to its object orientation, Java has many other features that make it the right choice of a computer language for many applications.

Java is an excellent choice of language when the problem at hand requires giving computers precise commands. However, if you want to describe what a Web page should look like, HTML (Hypertext Markup Language) and XML (Extensible Markup Language) are more appropriate choices. XML is different from Java—a different compromise between human understanding and computer understanding.

The ideal compromise between English and computer languages depends on the context and purpose of what you are doing with the computer. This is why every programmer can benefit from learning how to create new languages. The point of learning to write parsers is that you can craft a language that fits the context you are working in. You can write a search language that is easier to use than SQL (Structured Query Language) and more specific to the data in your database. You can write a language that lets you command a robot, or one that lets you move an order through its workflow. You can create a privilege language for logically modeling which users should have access to which transactions in a system. Whatever your application is, parsers let you concoct an English-like interface to it.

Parsers help computers, which work with objects, to cooperate with people, who read and write text. In practice, particularly in Java-based parsers, this implies that parsers translate text into objects. For example, a parser can translate a textual command for a robot into a command object. Another parser might translate a textual description of a product into an object that represents the product. A query parser translates textual queries into commands that a query engine understands. Parsers, then, translate between text and objects, letting you trade text for objects and objects for text, in a way that exactly suits the domain you are working in.

As a language designer, you will craft a compromise between a language that is easy for humans to use and a language that computers can understand. It is well worth learning to write parsers because you will have many chances in your career to orchestrate how humans and computers interact using text.

1.2 What Is a Language?

For the purposes of this book, a *language* is a set of strings. For example,

```
{"Hello, World."}
```

is a very little language. Another little example is the following:

```
{"", "a", "aa", "aaa", ...}
```

This language is the set of strings of zero or more *a*s. The description of this set uses "..." to mean that the initial pattern continues. The strings that make up a language are the *elements* of that language. A *parser* is an object that recognizes the elements of a language. Most of the parsers in this book also build an object as the result of recognizing a language element.

Interesting languages usually contain strings that follow a certain pattern and are related in some way. For example, the following well-known languages are the subject of many books:

- Structured Query Language (SQL)

- Hypertext Markup Language (HTML)

- Extensible Markup Language (XML)

You can think of these languages as specifying patterns of admissible text. In terms of *sets*, SQL is the language that contains all valid SQL strings. Similarly, Java as a language is the set of strings that are valid Java classes and interfaces. Every string either defines or does not define a valid Java class.

Java is different from these three languages in that it is a *programming* language—a language that is geared toward execution on a computer. In addition to Java, popular examples include Basic, C, C++, and Smalltalk.

Famous languages tend to be large, difficult to implement, and subject to standardization and control. These features of famous languages can obscure how effective little languages can be. Unlike famous languages, little languages tend to be small, easy to implement, and subject to your own control.

1.3 The Organization of This Book

This book explains how to write parsers for new computer languages that you create. Each chapter focuses on background, techniques, or applications. Chapters on background give you the tools to build parsers. Chapters on techniques show you how to apply the tools. Chapters on applications explain how to create a specific parser for a particular type of language. Figure 1.1 shows the role of each chapter.

The structure of the book is fairly linear, with each chapter dependent only on preceding chapters. For example, Chapter 5, "Parsing Data Languages," depends primarily on background and techniques from Chapters 2 and 3. You can skip the middle chapters of the book—on tokenizing, mechanics, and new types—if you want to get right to the chapters on advanced languages.

	Chapter	Background	Techniques	Applications	
1	Introduction	░			
2	The Elements of a Parser	░			
3	Building a Parser		░		
4	Testing a Parser		░		
5	Parsing Data Languages			░	
6	Transforming a Grammar		░		
7	Parsing Arithmetic			░	
8	Parsing Regular Expressions			░	
9	Advanced Tokenizing		░		
10	Matching Mechanics	░			
11	Extending the Parser Toolkit		░		
12	Engines	░			
13	Logic Programming	░			
14	Parsing a Logic Language			░	
15	Parsing a Query Language			░	
16	Parsing an Imperative Language			░	
17	Directions			░	
A	UML Twice Distilled	░			

Figure 1.1 Each chapter in this book focuses on either background that supports later chapters, techniques that apply across parsers, or applications of parsers to a specific language type.

Chapter 2, "The Elements of a Parser," explains what a parser is, introduces the building blocks of applied parsers, and shows how to compose new parsers from existing ones.

Chapter 3, "Building a Parser," explains the steps in designing and coding a working parser.

Chapter 4, "Testing a Parser," explains how to test the features of a new language and how to use random testing to detect ambiguity and other potential problems.

Chapter 5, "Parsing Data Languages," shows how to create a parser to read elements of a data language. A *data language* is a set of strings that describe objects following a local convention. This chapter also explains that, given the opportunity, you should consider migrating data-oriented languages to XML.

Chapter 6, "Transforming a Grammar," explains how to ensure the correct behavior of operators in a language and how to avoid looping in a parser, which can follow from loops in a grammar.

Chapter 7, "Parsing Arithmetic," develops an arithmetic parser. Arithmetic usually appears as part of a larger language, and the ideas in this chapter reappear in the chapters on query, logic, and imperative languages. To focus on the correct interpretation of arithmetic, this chapter develops an independent parser.

Chapter 8, "Parsing Regular Expressions," develops a *regular expression* parser. A regular expression is a string that uses symbols to describe a pattern of characters. For example, "~.txt" might represent all file names that end with .txt. This chapter explains how to read a string such as "~.txt" and create a parser that will recognize all the strings the given pattern describes.

Chapter 9, "Advanced Tokenizing," describes the tokenizers that come with Java and the customizable tokenizer used in this book. *Tokenizing* a string means breaking the string into logical nuggets, something that lets you define a parser in terms of the nuggets instead of individual characters. The default operation of the tokenizer used in this book is sufficient for many languages, so customizing a tokenizer is an advanced topic.

Chapter 10, "Matching Mechanics," explains how the fundamental types of parsers in this book match text.

Chapter 11, "Extending the Parser Toolkit," explains how to extend a parser toolkit, introducing new types of terminals or completely new parser types.

Chapter 12, "Engines," introduces a logic engine used in later chapters to build a logic language and a query language.

Chapter 13, "Logic Programming," explains how to program in logic, which means programming with facts and rules.

Chapter 14, "Parsing a Logic Language," explains how to construct a parser for a logic language. Chapter 13 explains logic programming, giving examples in the Logikus programming language; Chapter 14 explains how to construct a Logikus parser.

Chapter 15, "Parsing a Query Language," describes how to construct a parser for a query language. A query language parser translates textual queries into calls to an engine. The engine proves the query against a source of rules and data and returns successful proofs as the result of the query.

Chapter 16, "Parsing an Imperative Language," shows how to create a parser for an imperative language. An imperative language parser translates a textual script into a composition of commands that direct a sequence of actions.

Chapter 17, "Directions," points out areas for further reading and programming.

Appendix A, "UML Twice Distilled," explains the features of the Unified Modeling Language that this book applies.

1.4 Summary

Parsers strike a compromise between people and computers. The language recognized by a parser may be a simple data language, or it may be a programming language such as a query, logic, and imperative language. This book shows how to create parsers for all these languages so that you can fit just the right language into whatever niche you are programming for.

CHAPTER 2
The Elements of a Parser

Parsers are compositions of other parsers, built from instances of a few fundamental parser classes. Learning to create parsers begins with learning to create new compositions of existing parsers.

2.1 What Is a Parser?

A parser is an object that recognizes the elements of a language and translates each element into a meaningful result. A language is a set of strings, and we usually have some way of describing a language as containing all the strings that match a pattern. A fundamental ability of a parser is the ability to declare whether or not a given string belongs to a language. Consider the following language:

```
{"hot coffee",
 "steaming coffee",
 "hot hot hot coffee",
 "hot hot steaming hot coffee",
 ...}
```

This language contains all strings that begin with some sequence of "hot" and "steaming" and end with "coffee". A parser for this language is an object that can recognize whether or not a given string is an element of this language. For example, this parser will be able to determine that the following is a member of the language:

```
"hot hot hot steaming hot steaming hot coffee"
```

whereas the following is not:

```
"lukewarm coffee"
```

Every parser defines a language—the language that is the set of all strings that the parser recognizes. Notice that such sets are usually infinite. In practice, you never create a set that contains all the members of a language. Rather, you construct parsers to match patterns of text.

To create a new language you create a new parser object, and this means that you need a `Parser` class. This class does not operate alone; it collaborates with two other classes.

2.2 Parser Collaborations

As a parser recognizes a string, it usually performs a corresponding function, translating the string into a meaningful result. This work forms the *semantics*, or meaning, that the parser brings to a language.

The methods that perform a parser's work must appear as methods of a class. This book places such methods in subclasses of an `Assembler` class. To allow a parser to build a meaningful result, a `Parser` object collaborates with `Assembler` objects that know which work to perform as a parser recognizes parts of a string.

The results of a parser's work must, logically, produce or modify objects. This book associates *work areas* with the text to recognize `Assembly` subclasses. A `Parser` object uses `Assembly` objects to record the progress of `Assembler` objects.

Figure 2.1 shows the three main classes that are used to make practical parsers. These classes complement the `Parser` class hierarchy with `Assembly` and `Assembler` hierarchies. The following summarizes the roles of these three classes.

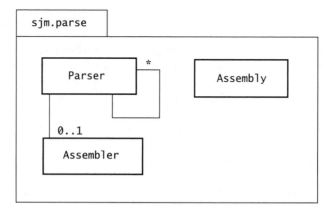

Figure 2.1 The three main classes that collaborate to create a working parser are Parser, Assembly, and Assembler.

- A parser is an object that recognizes a language.

- An assembler helps a parser build a result.

- An assembly provides a parser with a work area.

Objects of these three classes collaborate to recognize an element of a language and to perform work based on the recognition.

This diagram is consistent with the Unified Modeling Language [Booch], as are most of the diagrams in this book. Appendix A explains the features of the Unified Modeling Language that this book applies.

2.3 Assemblies

In practice, we demand more of parsers than simply saying whether a string is a valid member of a language. As a parser recognizes a string, it is useful for the parser to react to the contents of the string and build something. The parser also needs to keep an index of how much of the string it has recognized. An `Assembly` object wraps a string with an index and with work areas for a parser, providing a stack and a target object to work on. For example, a parser that recognizes a data language for coffee might set the target to be a basic `Coffee` object. This parser could work on the target as it recognizes an input string, informing the `Coffee` object of the coffee attributes the string indicates.

If a parser needs to build something based on the content of the string it is recognizing, you can think of the string as a set of instructions. As the parser makes progress recognizing the string, the assembly's index moves forward and the assembly's target begins to take shape. Figure 2.2 shows a partially recognized assembly.

The figure indicates that a parser is working to recognize this string:

```
"place carrier_18 on die_bonder_3"
```

String	"place carrier_18 on die_bonder_3"
index	2
Stack	"carrier_18"
Target	a PlaceCommand object

Figure 2.2 An assembly example. An assembly wraps a string and provides a work area for a parser and its assemblers.

An internal index records the fact that the parser has already recognized two words. On seeing the word "`place`", the parser set the assembly's target to be a `PlaceCommand` object. Now the parser has seen "`carrier_18`" and presumably is about to inform the `PlaceCommand` object which carrier to place.

2.3.1 The Assembly Class Interfaces

An assembly records the progress of a parser's recognition of an input string. Because the recognition may proceed along different paths, a parser may create multiple copies of an assembly as it tries to determine which is the right path. There are other approaches to modeling the nondeterminism inherent in parsing text, but the parsers in this book consistently use copying. To support this copying and to provide an enumeration interface, the `Assembly` class in `sjm.parse` implements the interfaces `PubliclyCloneable` and `Enumeration`. Figure 2.3 shows a partial class diagram for `Assembly`.

`PubliclyCloneable` is an interface in `sjm.utensil`. This interface declares that its implementers must implement a public version of the `clone()` method. The `clone()` method on `java.lang.Object` is protected, meaning that unrelated objects cannot use the `clone()` method. Because `Assembly` implements `PubliclyCloneable`, any object can request a clone of an assembly object.

For an assembly to make a clone of itself, it must in turn clone its target, so a target object must itself implement the `PubliclyCloneable` interface. In fact, the only

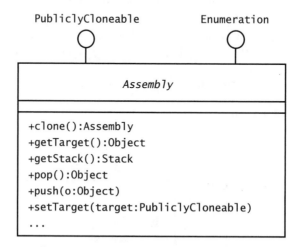

Figure 2.3   The `Assembly` class. This class implements interfaces that declare that assemblies are cloneable and offer the `Enumeration` methods `hasMoreElements()` and `nextElement()`.

requirement for a target object is that it implement this interface, and so `Assembly` declares its target to be of this type. Chapter 3, "Building a Parser," describes how to make a target cloneable (see Section 3.3.8).

Implementing `Enumeration` means that `Assembly` must implement the two methods `hasMoreElements()` and `nextElement()`.

The `Assembly` class itself does not implement these methods, leaving their implementation to subclasses. The two types of assemblies are assemblies of tokens and assemblies of characters.

2.3.2 Token and Character Assemblies

We have said that an assembly is a wrapper around a string. In practice, there are two choices for how to regard the composition of a string. A normal Java `String` object is a string of characters. For example,

```
"hello, world"
```

contains 12 characters, including the blank and the comma. For many parsers, it is far more convenient to treat such a string as a string of *tokens*, where a token can be a word, a number, or a punctuation mark. For example, the string "hello, world" can be seen as a string of three tokens:

```
"hello"
','
"world"
```

To allow parsing text as strings of tokens, `Assembly` has two subclasses: `CharacterAssembly` and `TokenAssembly`. Figure 2.4 shows these subclasses and the packages they lie in.

Package `sjm.parse.chars` contains classes that support character-based recognition. Package `sjm.parse.tokens` contains classes that support token-based recognition. Essentially, a `CharacterAssembly` object manipulates an array of characters, and a `TokenAssembly` object manipulates an array of tokens.

The methods `consumed()` and `remainder()` show the amount of input consumed and the amount that remains. The `defaultDelimiter()` method allows the `Assembly` subclasses to decide how to separate their elements. The `TokenAssembly` class places a slash between each token, whereas the `CharacterAssembly` places nothing (an empty string) between characters when showing elements consumed or remaining. The remaining methods of `Assembly` let a calling class request the next element (a character or token) or peek at the next element without removing it.

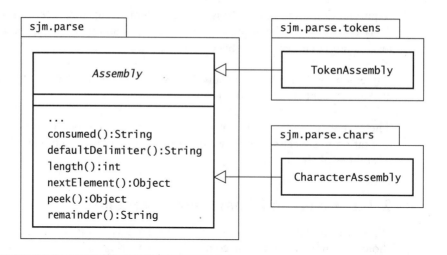

Figure 2.4 The `Assembly` hierarchy. Token and character assemblies implement the `Assembly` methods related to progress in recognizing input.

2.3.3 Tokenizing

Tokenizing a string means breaking the string into logical chunks, primarily words, numbers, and punctuation. This dissection of text is sometimes called *lexical analysis*. Chapter 9, "Advanced Tokenizing," covers tokenization in depth. The point of tokenization is that it can make the task of recognition much easier. It can be much simpler and much more appropriate to describe text as a series of tokens than as a series of characters. For example, consider the string

```
int i = 3;
```

A human reader, especially a Java programmer, will read this as a line of Java. The string contains a data type, a variable name, an equal sign, a number, and a semicolon. It would be accurate, but strange, to describe this string as an "i" followed by an "n" followed by a "t" followed by a blank, another "i", and so on. This string is a pattern of tokens and not a pattern of characters. On the other hand, consider the string

```
"Ja.*"
```

In the right context, this string might describe all words beginning with the letters "J" and "a". Here, the string is best understood and most easily recognized as a "J" followed by an "a" followed by a dot and an asterisk.

The tokenizer used in this book stores tokens in a `Token` class, which is in `sjm.parse.tokens`. Figure 2.5 shows the `Token` class.

```
                    ┌──────────────────────────┐
                    │          Token           │
                    ├──────────────────────────┤
                    │ #sval:String             │
                    │ #nval:double             │
                    ├──────────────────────────┤
                    │ +Token(c:char)           │
                    │ +Token(sval:String)      │
                    │ +Token(nval:double)      │
                    │ +nval():double           │
                    │ +sval():String           │
                    └──────────────────────────┘
```

Figure 2.5 The Token class. Typically, a Token is a receptacle for the results of reading a small amount of text, such as a word or a number.

You will most likely encounter tokens in practice when you need to retrieve a token that a terminal has stacked. If a token contains a string, you can retrieve its string value using the sval() method. If a token contains a number, you can retrieve the number using the nval() method. You can also construct tokens from a string or number, or from a single character that the Token constructor converts into a string.

2.3.4 Default and Custom Tokenization

It is imprecise to say that tokenizing breaks a string into "words, numbers, and punctuation." We can find examples that challenge exactly what is and is not a separate token. For example, is an underscore part of a word, or is it a punctuation mark? Does the string ">=" contain one token or two?

To begin writing parsers you need to know what to expect from the class TokenAssembly. When you construct a TokenAssembly from a string, TokenAssembly breaks the string into tokens, relying primarily on the services of another class, Tokenizer.

Class Tokenizer provides a good set of default rules for how to divide text into tokens. For example, a default Tokenizer object properly tokenizes this string:

```
"Let's 'rock and roll'!"
```

The Tokenizer object treats the apostrophe in "Let's" as part of the word, but it treats the single quotation marks around "rock and roll" as single quotes. Here is code that shows this:

```
package sjm.examples.introduction;

import sjm.parse.tokens.*;
import sjm.utensil.*;
```

```
/**
 * Show that apostrophes can be parts of words and can
 * contain quoted strings.
 */
public class ShowApostrophe {

public static void main(String[] args) {
    String s = "Let's 'rock and roll'!";
    TokenAssembly a = new TokenAssembly(s);
    while (a.hasMoreElements()) {
        System.out.println(a.nextElement());
    }
}
}
```

Running this class prints the following:

```
Let's
'rock and roll'
!
```

You may find that the default tokenization does not fit the purposes of your language. For example, you may need to allow blanks to appear inside words. For this and other types of customization, consult Chapter 9, "Advanced Tokenizing."

2.3.5 Assembly Appearance

The preceding example shows the effect of printing one element at a time from an assembly. If you print an entire assembly, it shows its stack, all its elements, and the position of its index. For example:

```
package sjm.examples.introduction;

import sjm.parse.tokens.*;

/**
 * Show how an assembly prints itself.
 */
public class ShowAssemblyAppearance {

public static void main(String[] args) {

    String s1 = "Congress admitted Colorado in 1876.";
    System.out.println(new TokenAssembly(s1));

    String s2 = "admitted(colorado, 1876)";
    System.out.println(new TokenAssembly(s2));
}
}
```

Running this class prints the two `TokenAssembly` objects:

```
[]^Congress/admitted/Colorado/in/1876.0
[]^admitted/(/colorado/,/1876.0/)
```

Both assemblies print their stacks, which are empty and appear as a pair of brackets. These stacks can gain contents only when a parser parses the assembly. Both assemblies show all their elements, separated by slashes. The caret symbolizes the amount of progress a parser has made in recognizing the assembly. Because this example has no parser, both indexes are at the beginning. Note that assemblies include no description of their target when they print. When you want a target to print, you retrieve the target from the assembly and print the target.

2.3.6 Assembly Summary

The `Assembly` classes wrap a string and provide a work area for a parser to record progress in recognizing the string and building a corresponding object. The assembly may tokenize the string, and that simplifies the parser's job of recognition.

2.4 The Parser Hierarchy

A parser is an object that recognizes strings. The examples in this book always wrap a string to be recognized in an `Assembly` object, as an assembly of either characters or tokens. Figure 2.6 shows the public interface of `Parser` objects that the examples use.

The `Parser` class in `sjm.parse` recognizes assemblies and returns assemblies. Often, you want to see whether a parser can recognize an entire string. If the parser can recognize the assembly you provide, its `completeMatch()` method returns a new assembly with its index at the end. If the parser does not recognize an assembly, it returns `null`. If you want a parser only to match as much of a string as it can, `bestMatch()`

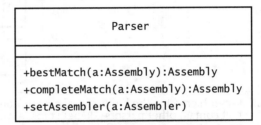

Figure 2.6 Parser class. A parser is an object that can recognize a string (wrapped in an Assembly object) and assemble a result.

returns an assembly with its index moved as far forward as possible through the supplied assembly. The `Parser` class also has methods for matching collections (`Vectors`) of assemblies and for associating assemblers with the parser.

2.4.1 The Composition of a Parser

The parsers in this book follow the *composite* pattern [Gamma et al.]. This means that some classes in the `Parser` hierarchy define aggregations of other parsers. Other classes in the hierarchy are *terminals*, which are parsers that can match an assembly without the aid of other parsers. They get their name from the fact that they terminate the recursion inherent in the idea that parsers are compositions of parsers. Because there are many types of terminals, there are many ways a parser can look for characters or tokens to appear in an assembly. This also means that there are many terminal classes.

Three types of *nonterminals*—parsers that are compositions of other parsers—are sufficient to build an infinite variety of parsers. Figure 2.7 shows the top of the hierarchy of parser classes. The three types of composition are repetition, sequence, and alternation. Many of the examples that lie ahead show how to use these compositions. In brief,

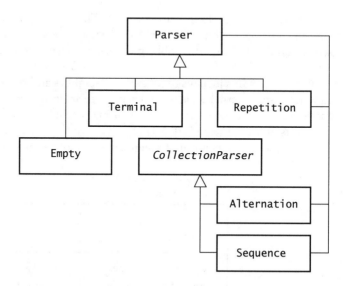

Figure 2.7 Parser hierarchy. The hierarchy of parsers contains three concrete classes that contain other parsers—`Repetition`, `Alternation`, and `Sequence`—and two that do not: `Terminal` and `Empty`.

- A *repetition* matches its underlying parser repeatedly against an assembly.

- A *sequence* is a collection of parsers, all of which must in turn match against an assembly for the sequence parser to successfully match.

- An *alternation* is a collection of parsers, any one of which can successfully match against an assembly.

It is also helpful, if not strictly necessary, to have an empty parser:

- An *empty* parser reports a successful match without consuming any elements from the assembly.

As Figure 2.7 shows, repetitions, alternations, and sequences are compositions of other parsers. The overall composition of a parser can be arbitrarily deep. For example, a parser for a programming language might itself be a sequence of declaration statements followed by executable statements. The parser for executable statements is typically an alternation of different types of statements. Each of these alternatives might be a sequence, and so on.

The composite nature of parsers implies that you must create simple parsers before you make complex ones. The simplest parsers are terminals, which match string assemblies without using other parsers.

2.5 Terminal Parsers

The examples in this book wrap strings either as assemblies of characters or assemblies of tokens. Each terminal must be geared toward one of these two types of assemblies. Each time a terminal asks an assembly for its `nextElement()`, the terminal must anticipate receiving either a character or a token; the terminal decides whether the character or token it receives is a match. Figure 2.8 shows the hierarchy of terminals that work with tokens. The subclasses of `Terminal` in Figure 2.8 are members of the package `sjm.parse.tokens`.

2.5.1 Using Terminals

For an example of how to use a terminal, consider the following program:

```
package sjm.examples.introduction;

import sjm.parse.*;
import sjm.parse.tokens.*;
```

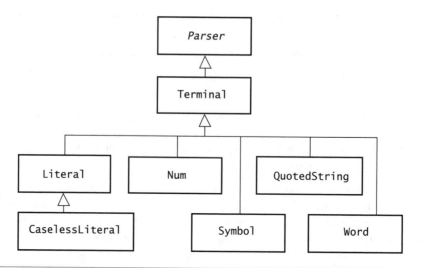

Figure 2.8 Token terminals. The subclasses of `Terminal` shown here expect an assembly's elements to be complete tokens.

```
/**
 * Show how to recognize terminals in a string.
 */
public class ShowTerminal {

public static void main(String[] args) {
    String s = "steaming hot coffee";
    Assembly a = new TokenAssembly(s);
    Parser p = new Word();
    while (true) {
        a = p.bestMatch(a);
        if (a == null) {
            break;
        }
        System.out.println(a);
    }
}
}
```

The parser p is a single `Word` object. The assembly a is a `TokenAssembly` from the string `"steaming hot coffee"`. The code asks the parser to return the parser's best match against this assembly. Because the parser matches any word, its best match will be a new assembly with the same string and an index moved forward by one word. The first line the program prints is

```
[steaming]steaming^hot/coffee
```

This output demonstrates how an assembly represents itself as a string. The assembly first shows the contents of its stack, [steaming]. The default behavior of all Terminal objects is to push whatever they recognize onto the assembly's stack. You can prevent this pushing by sending a Terminal object a discard() message.

After the stack, the assembly shows its tokens, separated by slashes, and shows the location of the index.

The while loop of the program asks the parser to return its best match against the revised assembly. In this pass, the program prints

```
[steaming, hot]steaming/hot^coffee
```

Now the stack contains two words, and the index has moved past two words. In the next pass, the program prints

```
[steaming, hot, coffee]steaming/hot/coffee^
```

Now the stack has all three words, and the index is at the end. In the next pass, the while loop will again ask the parser for its best match. Because the index of the assembly is at the end, there is no match; the bestMatch() method returns null, and the logic breaks out of the loop.

2.5.2 Word Terminals

In the preceding example, the parser p recognizes the set of all words. To be more specific, the language that p recognizes is the set of all strings that class Tokenizer in package sjm.parse.tokens recognizes as words.

2.5.3 Num Terminals

As a language designer, you can decide what constitutes a number. The default value of Tokenizer will find that the string

```
"12 12.34 .1234"
```

contains the numbers 12.0, 12.34, and 0.1234. The default tokenizer will not recognize exponential notation or anything beyond digits, a decimal point, and more digits. Here is a program that shows the default tokenization of numbers:

```
package sjm.examples.introduction;

import sjm.parse.tokens.*;
import sjm.utensil.*;
```

```
/**
 * Show what counts as a number.
 */
public class ShowNums {

public static void main(String[] args) {
    String s = "12 12.34 .1234 1234e-2";
    TokenAssembly a = new TokenAssembly(s);
    while (a.hasMoreElements()) {
        System.out.println(a.nextElement());
    }
}
}
```

Running this class prints the following:

```
12.0
12.34
0.1234
1234.0
e-2
```

Note that by default the tokenizer does not comprehend the exponential notation of the last number. Chapter 9, "Advanced Tokenizing," explains how to change the tokenization of a string to allow for exponential notation. In your own languages, you can use the default number recognition in Tokenizer and simply disallow exponential notation. Alternatively, you can customize a Tokenizer object to allow exponential, imaginary, and other types of notation for numbers.

2.5.4 Literals

A *literal* is a specific string. Consider the following declaration:

```
"int iq = 177;"
```

In this declaration, the word "int" must be a specific, literal value, whereas the variable name that follows it can be any word. To create a Literal parser, specify in a constructor the string the parser needs to match, as in

```
Literal intType = new Literal("int");
```

2.5.5 Caseless Literals

Sometimes you want to let the people using your language enter specific values without worrying about capitalization. For example, in a coffee markup language, you might establish a roast parameter that looks for strings such as

```
<roast>French</roast>
```

In building the parser to recognize this parameter, you might include a literal value for the roast parameter using the following object:

```
new Literal("roast")
```

It would be more flexible to allow your language user to type "Roast" or "ROAST" in addition to the all-lowercase "roast". To achieve this, use a *caseless* literal in place of the normal literal using an object such as:

```
new CaselessLiteral("roast")
```

2.5.6 Symbols

A *symbol* is generally a character that stands alone as its own token. For example, semicolons, equal signs, and parentheses are all characters that a typical tokenizer treats as symbols. In particular, both StreamTokenizer in java.io and Tokenizer in sjm.parse.tokens treat such characters as symbol tokens. The default instance of Tokenizer treats the following characters as symbols:

```
! # $ % & ( ) * + , : ; < = > ? @ ` [ \ ] ^ _ { | } ~
```

In addition, the default value of Tokenizer treats the following multicharacter sequences as symbols:

```
!=    <=    >=    :-
```

These symbols commonly represent "not equal," "less than or equal," "greater than or equal," and "if." The "if" symbol is common in logic languages (see Chapter 13, "Logic Programming"). The Tokenizer class gives you complete control over which characters and multicharacter sequences a Tokenizer object returns as symbols.

2.5.7 Quoted Strings

You may want to allow users of your language to enter quoted strings in some contexts—for example, when you want to allow a string value to contain a blank. The following program accepts a secret identity as a quoted string:

```
package sjm.examples.introduction;

import sjm.parse.*;
import sjm.parse.tokens.*;
```

```
/**
 * Show how to recognize a quoted string.
 */
public class ShowQuotedString {

public static void main(String[] args) {
    Parser p = new QuotedString();
    String id = "\"Clark Kent\"";
    System.out.println(p.bestMatch(new TokenAssembly(id)));
}
}
```

This program creates and applies a parser that recognizes a quoted string. Running this program prints

```
["Clark Kent"]"Clark Kent"^
```

The output shows that the parser matches the entire string, moving the ^ index past the token and stacking the token. Note that "Clark Kent" is a single token even though it contains a blank. Also note that the token contains the quote symbols themselves.

2.6 Composite Parsers

Every parser is either a terminal or a composite. A terminal is a parser that recognizes all or part of a string without using other parsers. For example, a terminal might check that the next word in a string is "hello". A composite parser is a parser that accomplishes its task by using other parsers. The three fundamental ways to compose parsers are repetition, sequence, and alternation.

2.6.1 Repetition

Like a tree that is composed of other trees and leaves, a composite typically contains several subcomponents. A repetition contains only one component: another parser that the repetition applies repeatedly against an assembly to recognize. Figure 2.9 shows this structure.

The repetition can match its underlying parser zero times, one time, two times, or n times, where n can be arbitrarily large. When a repetition matches an assembly, many versions of the assembly are possible, with the resulting assemblies' indexes at different positions.

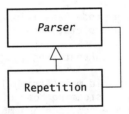

Figure 2.9 The Repetition class. Composites usually contain one or more sub-parsers, but a Repetition object contains only one.

For example, consider the phrase "steaming hot coffee". If you match words from the beginning of this phrase, you can match zero, one, two, or three words. You could mark these relative states of progress as follows:

```
"^steaming hot coffee"
"steaming^ hot coffee"
"steaming hot^ coffee"
"steaming hot coffee^"
```

The power of the idea of repetition is that it allows you to describe a variable number of language elements. The challenge this creates for parsers is that a repetition does not know the right number of times to match. It may appear that the right answer is for a repetition to match as many times as possible. However, it turns out that this approach is not always sufficient. For example, you could define a language as a repetition of words, followed by the specific word "coffee". In this case, the "right" number of words for a repetition object to match is two, stopping before the word "coffee".

To avoid the problem of deciding how many times to match, a simple approach is to return a set of all possible matches. This is the approach taken by class Repetition in package sjm.parse. In fact, each of the composite parsers in the code for this book takes this approach. The subclasses of Parser implement match(), which accepts a Vector of Assembly objects and returns a Vector of Assembly objects. To comply with Java 1.1.6 code, the sample code uses Vector instead of Set.

To see match() and Repetition in action, consider the following program:

```
package sjm.examples.introduction;

import java.util.*;
import sjm.parse.*;
import sjm.parse.tokens.*;
```

```
/**
 * Show that a <code>Repetition</code> object creates
 * multiple interpretations.
 */
public class ShowRepetition {

public static void main(String[] args) {
    String s = "steaming hot coffee";
    Assembly a = new TokenAssembly(s);
    Parser p = new Repetition(new Word());

    Vector v = new Vector();
    v.addElement(a);

    System.out.println(p.match(v));
}
}
```

This prints the following (with some added whitespace):

```
[
[]^steaming/hot/coffee,
[steaming]steaming^hot/coffee,
[steaming, hot]steaming/hot^coffee,
[steaming, hot, coffee]steaming/hot/coffee^
]
```

Note that this sample program uses match() instead of bestMatch(). The match()
method accepts a Vector of assemblies and returns a Vector of assemblies. This
reflects the underlying mechanics of the parsers in sjm.parse. Chapter 10, "Matching Mechanics," describes in detail how matching works.

To show the results of a Repetition object, the example prints the results of the
underlying match() method. When the code constructs a new Repetition object, it
passes in the parser to repeat. Because a Repetition always repeats a single parser,
the only constructor for this class requires its caller to supply the parser to repeat.
The parser p creates a set (or Vector) of possible matches against the input. The output shows the outermost pair of brackets that the Vector object prints. Inside the
vector are four assemblies, with four states of possible matching, including zero, one,
two, or three word matches.

2.6.2 Alternation and Sequence

An alternation is a composite of other parsers, any of which may match a provided
assembly. A sequence is a composite of other parsers, each of which must match in
turn. Figure 2.10 shows the structure of these classes.

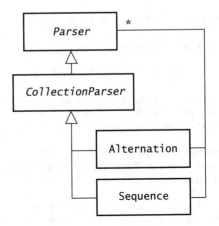

Figure 2.10   The `Alternation` and `Sequence` classes. `Alternation` objects and
`Sequence` objects are compositions of other parsers.

2.6.3 Composing a Parser

Creating a new parser is a matter of composing it from an existing selection of terminal and composite parsers. A small example that uses each of the composite parsers is as follows. Consider this string:

```
"hot hot steaming hot coffee"
```

Let us say that this string is a member of a language that, in general, contains strings with any combination of `"hot"` and `"steaming"` adjectives, followed by `"coffee"`. In other words, this language contains all sentences that are

- A sequence of *adjectives* followed by the literal `"coffee"`

where adjectives are

- A repetition of an adjective

and an adjective is:

- An alternation, a choice between `"hot"` and `"steaming"`

Having described this language fairly precisely, we can create a parser object directly from the language description, as the following program shows.

```
package sjm.examples.introduction;

import sjm.parse.*;
import sjm.parse.tokens.*;
```

```
/**
 * Show how to create a composite parser.
 */
public class ShowComposite {

public static void main(String[] args) {

    Alternation adjective = new Alternation();
    adjective.add(new Literal("steaming"));
    adjective.add(new Literal("hot"));

    Sequence good = new Sequence();
    good.add(new Repetition(adjective));
    good.add(new Literal("coffee"));

    String s = "hot hot steaming hot coffee";
    Assembly a = new TokenAssembly(s);
    System.out.println(good.bestMatch(a));

}
}
```

Running this class prints the following:

```
[hot, hot, steaming, hot, coffee]
hot/hot/steaming/hot/coffee^
```

The result of sending bestMatch() to good is an assembly with all five words placed on its stack and with its index at the end of its tokens.

Figure 2.11 shows an object diagram of good.

In Figure 2.11, the box that contains good:Sequence means that good is an object of type Sequence. The underline means that good is an object, and the colon separates the object from its type. Some of the objects, such as :Repetition, are nameless in the diagram, as they are in the sample program. The literals in the diagram indicate their literal values, although this does not imply that the variable literal is publicly accessible.

The leaf nodes of this object diagram are all literals, which are terminals. A parser's composition always terminates with terminals, hence the name "terminal."

2.6.4 The Empty Parser

Sometimes it is convenient to have a parser that returns successfully, having matched nothing at all. For example, you might want to match a list of equipment, recognizing strings such as

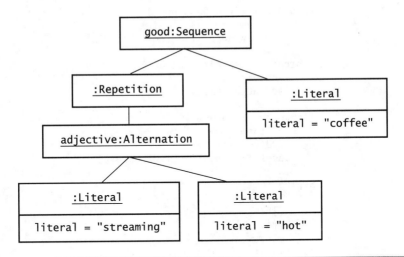

Figure 2.11 Good coffee. This object diagram shows the composition of a good parser, which recognizes a description of a good cup of coffee.

```
"[die_bonder_2, oven_7, wire_bonder_3, mold_1]"
"[]"
"[mold_1]"
```

The contents of the list may be empty, or it may contain a single name or a series of names separated by commas. To match such strings, you could say that the content of a list is either empty or an actual list. An actual list is a name followed by a repetition of (comma, word) sequences. Here is an example that uses Empty to help match these lists:

```
package sjm.examples.introduction;

import sjm.parse.*;
import sjm.parse.tokens.*;

/**
 * Show how to put the <code>Empty</code> class to good use.
 */
public class ShowEmpty {

public static void main(String args[]) {

    Parser empty, commaTerm, actualList, contents, list;
    empty = new Empty();
    commaTerm = new Sequence()
        .add(new Symbol(',').discard())
        .add(new Word());
```

```
        actualList = new Sequence()
            .add(new Word())
            .add(new Repetition(commaTerm));

        contents = new Alternation()
            .add(empty)
            .add(actualList);

        list = new Sequence()
            .add(new Symbol('[').discard())
            .add(contents)
            .add(new Symbol(']').discard());

        String test[] = new String[]{
            "[die_bonder_2, oven_7, wire_bonder_3, mold_1]",
            "[]",
            "[mold_1]"};

        for (int i = 0; i < test.length; i++) {
            TokenAssembly a = new TokenAssembly(test[i]);
            System.out.println(
                list.completeMatch(a).getStack());
        }
    }
}
```

This prints the following:

```
[die_bonder_2, oven_7, wire_bonder_3, mold_1]
[]
[mold_1]
```

The brackets in the output are part of the way a Stack object represents itself; they are not the brackets from the input. The output shows that the list parser recognizes lists with many elements, zero elements, or one element.

2.6.5 Parser Summary

In general, a parser is an object that recognizes a string. The code in this book wraps the string to be recognized in either a CharacterAssembly object or a TokenAssembly object. This approach simplifies the parser's job by giving the parser a place to work as it begins to recognize the contents of the string. In the next section we cover assemblers, which are objects that work on an assembly as the parser recognizes it.

You can create simple parsers by creating instances of subclasses of Terminal. You can create more-complex parsers by composing new parsers as sequences, alternations, or repetitions of other parsers. This method scales up, so you can create advanced parsers, building them from other terminal and composite parsers.

2.7 Assemblers

To this point, this book has emphasized *recognizing* the strings that make up a language. In practice, you usually want to react to this recognition by doing something. What you do gives meaning, or semantics, to your parser. What you might want to do is unbounded. A common task is the creation of an object that a string describes. For example, consider a file that contains the following textual description of types of coffees:

```
Brimful, Regular, Kenya, 6.95
Caress (Smackin), French, Sumatra, 7.95
Fragrant Delicto, Regular/French, Peru, 9.95
Havalavajava, Regular, Hawaii, 11.95
Launch Mi, French, Kenya, 6.95
Roman Spur (Revit), Italian, Guatemala, 7.95
Simplicity House, Regular/French, Columbia, 5.95
```

You can use a parser to verify that each line of this file is an element of a coffee description language. In addition to this verification, in practice you often want to produce objects from such textual data. In this case, you would want your coffee parser to create a collection of coffee objects so that the meaning of the input is a corresponding set of objects. Assemblers make this meaning possible.

2.7.1 Parsers Use Assemblers

Any `Parser` object can have an associated assembler. When a parser is a composite, it can have its own assembler, and any of its subparsers can have their own assemblers, all the way down to the terminals. Figure 2.12 shows the relationship of parsers and assemblers.

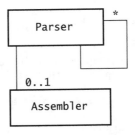

Figure 2.12 The Parser/Assembler relation. A parser can have an assembler, which it uses to work on an assembly after the parser matches against the assembly.

```
                        Assembler

      workOn(a:Assembly)
      elementsAbove(
            a:Assembly,fence:Object):Vector
```

Figure 2.13 The Assembler class. The Assembler class is abstract, requiring subclasses to implement the workOn() method.

Figure 2.13 shows the Assembler class. After a parser matches successfully against an assembly, it calls its assembler's workOn() method.

2.7.2 Assemblers Work On Assemblies

When an assembler's workOn() method is called, the assembler knows that its parser has just completed a match. For example, a parser that recognizes the preceding coffee text will include a parser to match only the country portion of a coffee description as part of building a target Coffee object. The terminal that matches "Sumatra" in the middle of

```
    Caress (Smackin), French, Sumatra, 7.95
```

will place "Sumatra" on the assembly's stack, something that terminals do by default. After this terminal matches, it will ask its assembler to go to work. Its assembler might look like this:

```
    package sjm.examples.coffee;

    import sjm.parse.*;
    import sjm.parse.tokens.*;

    /**
     * This assembler pops a string and sets the target
     * coffee's country to this string.
     */
    public class CountryAssembler extends Assembler {

    public void workOn(Assembly a) {
        Token t = (Token) a.pop();
        Coffee c = (Coffee) a.getTarget();
        c.setCountry(t.sval().trim());
    }
    }
```

This class assumes that a parser will call this class's workOn() method in the appropriate context. This includes the assumption that the top of the assembly's stack is, in fact, a token containing the name of a country. The assembler also assumes that the assembly's target object is a Coffee object. In practice, these assumptions are safe, because the parser that calls this assembler knows with certainty that it has just matched a country name as part of an overall task of recognizing a type of coffee.

2.7.3 Elements Above

The Assembler class includes the static method elementsAbove(), which lets you design a parser that stacks a *fence* and later retrieves all the elements above the fence. A fence is any kind of marker object. For example, suppose a list parser is matching this list:

```
"{Washington Adams Jefferson}"
```

The list parser might allow the opening curly brace to go on an assembly's stack while discarding the closing curly brace. This lets the opening brace token act as a fence. After matching the elements in the list, the parser can retrieve them with an assembler that removes all the elements on the stack above the '{' token. The parser's assembler can use the elementsAbove() method, passing it the assembly and the opening brace as the fence to look for. For example:

```
package sjm.examples.introduction;

import sjm.parse.*;
import sjm.parse.tokens.*;

/**
 * Show how to use <code>Assembler.elementsAbove()</code>.
 */
public class ShowElementsAbove {

public static void main(String args[]) {

    Parser list = new Sequence()
        .add(new Symbol('{'))
        .add(new Repetition(new Word()))
        .add(new Symbol('}').discard());

    list.setAssembler(new Assembler() {
        public void workOn(Assembly a) {
            Token fence = new Token('{');
            System.out.println(elementsAbove(a, fence));
        }
    });
```

```
        list.bestMatch(
            new TokenAssembly("{ Washington Adams Jefferson }"));
    }
}
```

This class's `main()` method creates a list parser that implements this pattern:

```
list = '{' Word* '}';
```

In the code, the `list` parser allows the opening brace to go onto an assembly's stack, and discards the closing brace. The `main()` method gives `list` an assembler by using an anonymous subclass of `Assembler` that retrieves the elements that match after the opening brace.

Note that the opening brace terminal stacks a *token* and not a brace character or a string. Thus, the fence the assembler looks for is a `'{'` token. In this example the assembler retrieves the elements above the opening brace and prints them. Running this class prints the vector

```
[Jefferson, Adams, Washington]
```

The Logikus parser in Chapter 14, "Parsing a Logic Language," uses the `elementsAbove()` method to collect the elements of a Logikus list. The Sling parser in Chapter 16, "Parsing an Imperative Language," uses `elementsAbove()` to collect the statements in the body of a `for` loop.

2.8 Summary

A parser is an object that recognizes the elements of a language and builds meaningful target objects based on the text it recognizes. To achieve this combination of recognition and building, this book uses a collaboration of three hierarchies of classes: `Parser`, `Assembler`, and `Assembly`. An assembly contains both the text to be recognized and work areas that house the results of work completed in building a result. Assemblers plug in to parsers and work on assemblies as the parsers recognize text.

The `Assembly` hierarchy has two subclasses: one that provides individual characters as its elements and a second one that provides tokens.

The `Parser` hierarchy has four main subclasses: `Terminal`, `Sequence`, `Alternation`, and `Repetition`. The `Terminal` class itself is at the top of a wide variety of subclasses. You need a `Terminal` subclass for each group of characters or tokens you want to recognize.

You can compose new parsers as sequences, alternations, and repetitions of other parsers, creating an infinite variety of parsers from these few building blocks.

CHAPTER 3

Building a Parser

T his chapter explains the steps in designing and coding a working parser. The core design of a parser is the same for all the parsers in this book: recognize a language and build a result.

3.1 Design Overview

Usually the first step in designing a parser is to think of some sample strings that you want your parser to recognize. To parse this set of strings, you will create a new language. A language is always a set of strings, and your language will become a set that includes your sample strings.

You can begin to design your parser by writing the rules, or *grammar*, of your language. (Section 3.4, "Grammars: A Shorthand for Parsers," explains how to write your grammar.) Your parser will recognize strings that follow the rules of your grammar. Once you have a grammar, you can write the Java code for your parser as a direct translation of the grammar rules.

The other main aspect of a parser's design is the design of your assemblers. Assemblers let you create a new object when your parser recognizes an input string. After you have designed your assemblers and your rules, you bring them together. You plug assemblers in to subparsers to assemble parts of a target object as your parser recognizes text.

It is a good idea to work incrementally and iteratively. When you work incrementally, you get part of your language to work before the entire language works. Working iteratively means that you can expect to cycle through the steps of designing, coding, and testing many times on each increment you create.

Build your language gradually, expanding your parser and adding new features as you go. You will see your language grow, and you will become skillful in expanding the features of your language.

3.2 Deciding to Tokenize

An early design decision is whether you want to treat your language as a pattern of characters or as a pattern of tokens. Most commonly, you will *not* want to use a tokenizer for languages that let a user specify patterns of characters to match against. Chapter 8, "Parsing Regular Expressions," gives an example of parsing without using a tokenizer.

Tokens are composed of characters, so every language that is a pattern of tokens is also a pattern of characters. Theoretically, then, tokenizers are never necessary. However, it is usually practical to tokenize text and to specify a grammar for a language in terms of token terminals. Consider a robot control language that allows this command:

```
move robot 7.1 meters from base
```

If you do not plan to tokenize, your parser must recognize every character, including the whitespace between words. You also must ensure that you properly gather characters into words, and you must build the number value yourself. All of this is work that a tokenizer will happily perform for you. Chapter 9, "Advanced Tokenizing," discusses how to customize a tokenizer. When you are learning to design new languages, you may want to limit your languages to those that can benefit from the default behavior of class Tokenizer in package sjm.parse.tokens.

3.3 Designing Assemblers

One way to get a grip on the design of your parser is to think about how you will build the result you want from the text you recognize. So one way to get started with the design of a new parser is to start designing your assemblers.

3.3.1 The Collaboration of Parsers, Assemblers, and Assemblies

An assembly provides both a stack and a *target* object for the parser's assemblers to work on. The target object is like a sculpture, taking form as the parser recognizes the input text. Figure 3.1 shows the Parser, Assembler, and Assembly classes, which collaborate to sculpt text into a result.

3.3.2 Using an Assembly's Stack

Assembly objects contain two work areas: a stack and a target. By default, subclasses of Terminal, such as Word and Num, place on an assembly's stack the object they recognize from the assembly object's text. (You can prevent this by sending the

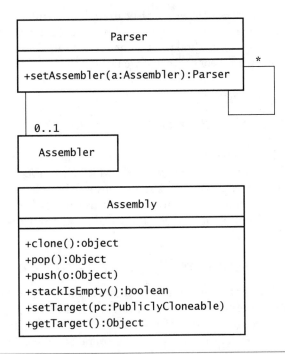

Figure 3.1 The Parser, Assembler, and Assembly classes. Each parser in a parser composite tries to match against the assembly, and each may use an assembler to work on the assembly after a successful match.

Terminal object a discard() message.) The following code shows a repetition of a Num parser that recognizes and stacks a series of numbers.

```
package sjm.examples.design;

import sjm.parse.*;
import sjm.parse.tokens.*;

/**
 * Show how to use an assembly's stack.
 */
public class ShowStack {

public static void main(String args[]) {

    Parser p = new Repetition(new Num());
    Assembly a = p.completeMatch(
        new TokenAssembly("2 4 6 8"));
    System.out.println(a);
}
}
```

This code creates a `TokenAssembly` around the string "2 4 6 8" and passes it to the parser p. The result of sending `completeMatch()` to p is a *new* `TokenAssembly`. The `completeMatch()` method returns the result as an abstract `Assembly` object, which we could cast to a `TokenAssembly` if we needed to.

Running this class prints

```
[2.0, 4.0, 6.0, 8.0]2.0/4.0/6.0/8.0^
```

When the assembly a prints itself, it first shows its stack, which is [2.0, 4.0, 6.0, 8.0]. This demonstrates the nature of `Num`, which treats every number as a `double` and places on the assembly's stack the tokens it finds. The output assembly also shows its tokenized input text, separating the tokens with slashes. Finally, the output assembly shows the location of its index at the end of the tokens.

3.3.3 Assemblers Plug In to Parser Composites

When a parser recognizes text, it knows nothing about the big picture in which it executes. For example, consider the `Num` parser in `sjm.parse.tokens`. A `Num` object might be recognizing one of a series of numbers in a string such as "1.2 2.3 3.4", or it might be recognizing the price of a pound of coffee. The `Num` parser simply puts its number on the assembly's stack, leaving any further work to other assemblers. Typically, `Num` parsers and other terminals are not stand-alone parsers but rather are part of a composite. After a terminal places an object on an assembly's stack, another parser higher in the composite can find this object and do other work on the assembly.

3.3.4 A Language to Plug In To: Minimath

To see how assemblers plug in to a parser composite, consider a minimal arithmetic parser that recognizes only the "-" operator. That is, you want to recognize a language that contains numbers, all differences of two numbers, differences of three numbers, and so on. For example, the language contains the following:

```
{"0.0",
 "1.1 - 2.2",
 "1.1 - 2.2 - 3.3",
 "1.1 - 2.2 - 3.3 - 4.4", ...}
```

Let's call this language Minimath. You can describe the contents of Minimath with the following rules:

```
expression = Num minusNum*;
minusNum   = '-' Num;
```

These rules are shorthand for describing a language. They are also shorthand for describing the composition of a parser. Section 3.4 explains the rules for this shorthand in detail. You can abbreviate these rules to

```
e = Num m*;
m = '-' Num;
```

The first rule means that e is a number followed by zero or more occurrences of m. For example, "25 - 16 - 9" is the number "25" followed by "- 16" and "- 9". The first rule uses the capitalized word Num to mean a terminal. In fact, you will use the class Num in sjm.parse.tokens when you build the e parser. The e rule uses the non-capitalized word m to refer to another rule, and it uses an asterisk ("*") to indicate repetition of m. The m rule indicates a pattern that has a minus sign ("-") followed by a number.

These rules describe the patterns of strings that make up the Minimath language, and they give you a formula for composing a parser to match Minimath. For example, the parser e recognizes a string such as "25 - 16 - 9" as an element of the Minimath language. If all you want is to recognize elements of Minimath and not compute their value, you can build the e parser as follows:

```
package sjm.examples.minimath;

import sjm.parse.*;
import sjm.parse.tokens.*;

/**
 * Show how to build a parser to recognize elements
 * of the language "Minimath".
 */
public class MinimathRecognize {

public static void main(String args[]) {
    Sequence e = new Sequence();

    e.add(new Num());

    Sequence m = new Sequence();
    m.add(new Symbol('-'));
    m.add(new Num());

    e.add(new Repetition(m));

    System.out.println(
        e.completeMatch(
            new TokenAssembly("25 - 16 - 9")));
}
}
```

This code prints the following:

```
[25.0, -, 16.0, -, 9.0]25.0/-/16.0/-/9.0^
```

This shows that the parser e recognizes the text "25 - 16 - 9". Of course, the point of having a Minimath parser is not only to recognize text but also to build the value that the text represents.

3.3.5 Calculating a Minimath Result

You want the parser e to calculate a difference and leave it as a Double object on an assembly's stack. To accomplish this, you need two assemblers: one to handle numbers as the Num subparser finds them, and a second one to handle subtraction.

When a Num parser recognizes a number, it places an sjm.parse.tokens.Token object on the assembly's stack. To calculate an arithmetic sum, your Num parser needs an assembler to replace this Token object with a Double value that corresponds to the token's value. You can describe the design of the assembler you need as, "Pop the token at the top of the assembly's stack and push a corresponding number." In this example, you can reuse an assembler from sjm.examples.arithmetic. The code for NumAssembler is as follows:

```
package sjm.examples.arithmetic;

import sjm.parse.*;
import sjm.parse.tokens.*;

public class NumAssembler extends Assembler {
/**
 * Replace the top token in the stack with the token's
 * Double value.
 */
public void workOn(Assembly a) {
    Token t = (Token) a.pop();
    a.push(new Double(t.nval()));
}
}
```

This method assumes that the top of the input assembly's stack is a Token object. In practice, this assumption is safe as long as the assembler plugs in to a parser that stacks a token. Assemblers are small, non-reusable classes that plug behavior in to a particular parser.

The other assembler that a Minimath parser needs is one to handle subtraction. You can design the assembler without addressing which subparser it belongs to. Let us assume that, at some point, a Minimath composite parser places two numbers on the stack of the assembly it is matching. At that point, you can describe the design of the needed assembler as, "Pop the top two numbers and push their difference." Again, you can reuse an assembler from `sjm.examples.arithmetic`. The code for `MinusAssembler` is as follows:

```
package sjm.examples.arithmetic;

import sjm.parse.*;

public class MinusAssembler extends Assembler {
/**
 * Pop two numbers from the stack and push the result of
 * subtracting the top number from the one below it.
 */
public void workOn(Assembly a) {
    Double d1 = (Double) a.pop();
    Double d2 = (Double) a.pop();
    Double d3 =
        new Double(d2.doubleValue() - d1.doubleValue());
    a.push(d3);
}
}
```

The only remaining design question is where this assembler belongs. Note from the rules that an expression e is a number followed by one or more occurrences of m. An effective strategy is to associate a `NumAssembler` with each `Num` parser, and a `MinusAssembler` with the m parser. The code looks like this:

```
package sjm.examples.minimath;

import sjm.parse.*;
import sjm.parse.tokens.*;
import sjm.examples.arithmetic.*;

/**
 * ...
 * This class shows, in a minimal example, where assemblers
 * plug in to a parser composite.
 */
public class MinimathCompute {

public static void main(String args[]) {
    Sequence e = new Sequence();

    Num n = new Num();
    n.setAssembler(new NumAssembler());

    e.add(n);

    Sequence m = new Sequence();
    m.add(new Symbol('-').discard());
```

```
        m.add(n);
        m.setAssembler(new MinusAssembler());

        e.add(new Repetition(m));

        TokenAssembly t = new TokenAssembly("25 - 16 - 9");
        Assembly out = e.completeMatch(t);
        System.out.println(out.pop());
    }
}
```

The `main()` method creates a composite parser e for Minimath and plugs in assemblers to assemble a result for an arithmetic string. The code discards the minus signs because they serve their purpose in guiding the parser and need not appear on the stack. The method asks the parser for a complete match against a tokenized string and prints the top of the stack of the resulting assembly. Running this class prints the conventional answer:

```
0.0
```

3.3.6 The Minimath Parser as an Object

Figure 3.2 shows an object diagram for the parser e. The parser e is a sequence of two subparsers: a Num and a Repetition. Each time the Num parser in e recognizes a number token, it uses a `NumAssembler` object to replace the number token on the stack with a corresponding `Double`. Two of the subparsers—n and m—use assemblers to work on the assembly they match against. There is only one n subparser, although this object appears twice in the diagram.

3.3.7 Building a Target

In addition to being unusually small, Minimath is unusual in that you can build a parser for it that uses only the assembly's stack while creating a useful result. Usually, you want a parser to build some kind of domain object. The `Assembly` class maintains a `target` attribute and provides methods for manipulating it, as Figure 3.1 shows. These methods let you build any kind of object from input text, with one restriction: The target of an `Assembly` object must be publicly cloneable (a topic addressed in the following section).

Consider designing a program that calculates the average length of words in a string. Let us take the approach of first creating a `RunningAverage` class that accepts word lengths and keeps track of the total number of words and their total length. With such a class available, you can create an `Assembler` class that works by updating a target `RunningAverage` object. Specifically, you can create an `AverageAssembler` class that

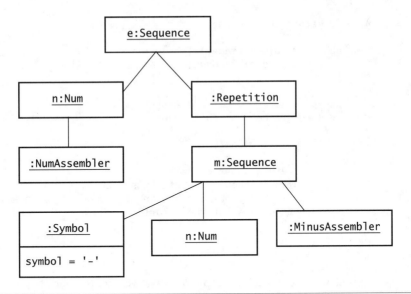

Figure 3.2 Minimath. This object diagram shows the structure of a parser composite that matches Minimath expressions such as "3 - 2 - 1".

pops a word from the stack of an `Assembly` object and updates a target `RunningAverage` object with the length of the popped string. Here is `RunningAverage.java`:

```java
package sjm.examples.design;

/**
 * Objects of this class maintain a running average. Each
 * number that is added with the <code>add</code> method
 * increases the count by 1, and the total by the amount
 * added.
 */
public class RunningAverage
    implements sjm.utensil.PubliclyCloneable {

    protected double count = 0;
    protected double total = 0;

/**
 * Add a value to the running average, increasing the count
 * by 1 and the total by the given value.
 */
public void add(double d) {
    count++;
    total += d;
}
```

```
/**
 * Return the average so far.
 */
public double average() {
    return total / count;
}

/**
 * Return a copy of this object.
 */
public Object clone() {
    try {
        return super.clone();
    } catch (CloneNotSupportedException e) {
        // this shouldn't happen, since we are Cloneable
        throw new InternalError();
    }
}
}
```

This class makes it easy to keep a running average. In your design, you can use a RunningAverage object as the target of an assembly. You can write an AverageAssembler class that expects this target. Here is the code for AverageAssembler.java:

```
package sjm.examples.design;

import sjm.parse.*;
import sjm.parse.tokens.*;
import sjm.engine.*;

public class AverageAssembler extends Assembler {

/**
 * Increases a running average, by the length of the string
 * on the stack.
 */
public void workOn(Assembly a) {
    Token t = (Token) a.pop();
    String s = t.sval();
    RunningAverage avg = (RunningAverage) a.getTarget();
    avg.add(s.length());
}
}
```

The AverageAssembler class updates a RunningAverage target object by the length of whatever string is on the input assembly's stack. Now you have the pieces you need to create a program that calculates the average length of words in a string. You will use a RunningAverage object as the target object of an assembly. You will use a Word object to recognize words, and you will plug an AverageAssembler object in to it. Then you can use a Repetition of the Word object to match a string of words. Figure 3.3 shows the objects you need.

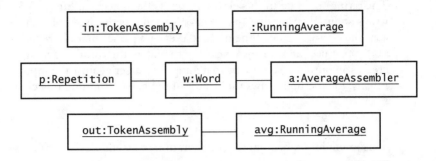

Figure 3.3 Object diagram for calculating a running average. An input assembly and an output assembly both have RunningAverage objects as their targets. The parser p is a repetition of a Word object that uses an AverageAssembler object to update a running average.

The parser p in Figure 3.3 matches an input assembly and creates an output assembly. The output has an updated clone of the RunningAverage object that reflects the average length of words in an input string. Here is a program that shows the objects in action:

```
package sjm.examples.design;

import sjm.parse.*;
import sjm.parse.tokens.*;

/**
 * Show how to use an assembler. The example shows how to
 * calculate the average length of words in a string.
 */
public class ShowAssembler {

public static void main(String args[]) {

    // As Polonius says, in "Hamlet"...
    String quote = "Brevity is the soul of wit";

    Assembly in = new TokenAssembly(quote);
    in.setTarget(new RunningAverage());
    Word w = new Word();
    w.setAssembler(new AverageAssembler());
    Parser p = new Repetition(w);

    Assembly out = p.completeMatch(in);

    RunningAverage avg = (RunningAverage) out.getTarget();
    System.out.println(
        "Average word length: " + avg.average());
    }
}
```

The `main()` method in this class constructs the objects in Figure 3.3. This method wraps an input string in a `TokenAssembly` and sets the assembly's target to be a `RunningAverage` object. The method creates a parser that is a repetition of a `Word` object that uses an `AverageAssembler` to update the running average. The method creates an output assembly by matching the parser against the input assembly. Finally, the method shows the results of the parse. Running this class prints:

```
Average word length: 3.5
```

This example shows a typical collaboration of assemblies, assemblers, targets, and parsers:

- An input target plugs in to an input assembly.

- A parser establishes an assembler to work on the target. (In a composite parser, each subparser can have its own assembler.)

- The parser matches the input assembly, creating an output assembly.

- The output assembly contains an updated target.

This approach relies on the ability to clone an assembly as the parser pursues a match. Because the target is a part of the assembly, targets must also be cloneable.

3.3.8 Making a Target Cloneable

Assembly objects know almost nothing about the targets that they hold, but one message that an assembly sends to its target is `clone()`. This springs from the way that the parsers in `sjm.parse` model the nondeterminism inherent in recognizing most languages. These parsers use a backtracking mechanism, and this means that they must clone an assembly and its target each time they consume a token.

When you design your parser to create a target object from input text, your target class must have a public `clone()` method. To enforce this, the package `sjm.utensil` includes the interface `PubliclyCloneable`, whose code is as follows:

```
package sjm.utensil;

/**
 * Defines a type of object that anybody can clone.
 */
public interface PubliclyCloneable extends Cloneable {

public Object clone();
}
```

Providing a public clone method without implementing `PubliclyCloneable` is insufficient. The `Assembly.setTarget()` method must know that the object it receives is an instance of a class that implements a public `clone()`. It insists on this by receiving its input as datatype `PubliclyCloneable`.

To clone an object means to make a copy of the object. To make a class cloneable by any object, write a `clone()` method and declare that the class implements `PubliclyCloneable`. A typical cloneable class method looks like this:

```
package sjm.examples.cloning;

import sjm.utensil.*;

/**
 * This class shows a typical clone() method.
 */
public class Course implements PubliclyCloneable {
    protected Professor professor;
    protected Textbook textbook;

// gets and sets...

/**
 * Return a copy of this object.
 */
public Object clone() {
    try {
        Course copy = (Course) super.clone();
        copy.setProfessor((Professor) professor.clone());
        copy.setTextbook((Textbook) textbook.clone());
        return copy;
    } catch (CloneNotSupportedException e) {
        // this shouldn't happen, since we are Cloneable
        throw new InternalError();
    }
}
}
```

The sample method calls `super.clone()`, referring to the method `clone()` of class `Object`. This method creates a new object of the same class as the object that receives the `clone()` message; then it initializes each of the new object's fields by assigning them the same values as the corresponding fields in the copied object. This is a *shallow* copy as opposed to a *deep* copy, which would also make copies of each of an object's fields. You might think of `Object.clone()` as `Object.newObjectSameFields()`. In your `clone()` method, you must create a clone of each attribute in your class that is not a primitive type or a string. (Strings are immutable, so there is no need to clone them.)

The `Object.clone()` method throws `CloneNotSupportedException`, which you must handle. Surround your call to `super.clone()` in a `try/catch` block that throws `InternalError`. The `InternalError` exception is arguably the wrong exception to throw, because this error indicates a problem in the virtual machine. However, `Vector` and other important classes in Java throw an `InternalError` in this situation, and this book follows that precedent.

With an understanding of assemblers, assemblies, and parsers, you can begin to create meaningful new languages. Before you begin to code, however, it will prove helpful to have a way to work with parsers at a design level.

3.4 Grammars: A Shorthand for Parsers

A *grammar* is a collection of related parser definitions in which the definitions follow a standard shorthand. A goal of the design phase in software construction is to illustrate in compact form the important features that will appear in Java code. Consider again the code that builds a parser to recognize a description of a good cup of coffee:

```java
package sjm.examples.introduction;

import sjm.parse.*;
import sjm.parse.tokens.*;

/**
 * Show how to create a composite parser.
 */
public class ShowComposite {

public static void main(String[] args) {

    Alternation adjective = new Alternation();
    adjective.add(new Literal("steaming"));
    adjective.add(new Literal("hot"));

    Sequence good = new Sequence();
    good.add(new Repetition(adjective));
    good.add(new Literal("coffee"));

    String s = "hot hot steaming hot coffee";
    Assembly a = new TokenAssembly(s);
    System.out.println(good.bestMatch(a));
}
}
```

You can more simply describe the good parser with the following shorthand, or grammar:

```
good      = adjective* "coffee";
adjective = "steaming" | "hot";
```

This shorthand relies on a few conventions, including showing literal values in quotes, showing alternation with a bar, and showing repetition with an asterisk. The point of using a grammar is that it is far more manageable than its corresponding Java code.

3.4.1 Standard Grammar Shorthand

This book observes the following conventions for writing a grammar, which is a compact definition of a parser.

1. Show the definition of a parser by giving its name, an equal sign, a subparser expression, and a semicolon. For example, the rule

   ```
   adjective = "steaming" | "hot";
   ```

   defines the makeup of an `adjective`.

2. Reference other subparsers as words that begin with a lowercase letter. For example, the rule

   ```
   good = adjective* "coffee";
   ```

   defines a good parser by referring to the `adjective` subparser.

3. Show a specific string to match by writing it in quotes. For example, the rule

   ```
   adjective = "steaming" | "hot";
   ```

   uses quotes to show that `"steaming"` and `"hot"` are specific strings to match.

4. Show a specific single character to match by writing it in single quotes, such as `'-'` in the Minimath rule:

   ```
   m = '-' Num;
   ```

   Note that a tokenizer will return many, but perhaps not all, arithmetic operators, Boolean operators, and punctuation marks as separate symbol tokens, rather than as parts of words. Section 9.6, "Tokenizer Lookup Tables," describes which characters the `Tokenizer` class treats (by default) as individual symbols.

5. Show repetition by using an asterisk ("*"). Consider the good grammar:

   ```
   good      = adjective* "coffee";
   adjective = "steaming" | "hot";
   ```

   The rule for good uses an asterisk to describe a string that begins with 0 or more `adjectives` and ends with `"coffee"`.

6. Imply sequence by writing subparsers next to each other. For example, the good grammar implies that good is a sequence of a-repetition-of-adjectives followed by the word "coffee".

7. Show alternation by using a vertical bar. For example, the adjective rule declares that both "steaming" and "hot" are suitable adjectives.

8. Indicate precedence by using parentheses. For example, if you wanted to show the good grammar on one line, you could write

```
good = ("hot" | "steaming")* "coffee";
```

9. Show terminals as words that begin with a capital letter, such as Num, as in

```
phrase = '(' expression ')' | Num;
```

Section 2.5, "Terminal Parsers," shows the terminals available in sjm.parse.tokens. Chapter 11, "Extending the Parser Toolkit," describes how to add new types of terminals.

10. Parameterize subparsers if it makes your grammar a better design. (This is an optional element of grammar design. It works only if you will code your subparsers as methods of a class. See Section 3.6, "Translating a Grammar to Code.") For example, consider a grammar for a small set of markup tags:

```
tag      = nameTag | roastTag | priceTag;
nameTag  = '<' "name" '>';
roastTag = '<' "roast" '>';
priceTag = '<' "price" '>';
```

To avoid repeating the pattern of writing angle braces around a literal value, you can use a parameterized rule:

```
tag       = braces("name") | braces("roast") |
            braces("price");
braces(p) = '<' p '>';
```

The parameter to braces is a parser, specifically a CaselessLiteral for "name", "roast", or "price".

3.4.2 Top-Down Grammar Design

When you design a parser for a language, you can use either a top-down or a bottom-up approach to design. A bottom-up approach includes designing small parts of your parser that you know you will need. If you understand the goal of your parser, you may be able to design your assemblers, which can help guide the decomposition of the language you intend to recognize. When you reach the point of designing the grammar itself, you will most likely find that a top-down approach to grammar writing is natural and intuitive.

A top-down design approach begins by breaking the design problem into components. When you are using a top-down approach to write a parser, you state the design problem as, "Can I decompose this design into parts?" You can also state the design challenge as, "Can I represent the parser I want as a composition?" As it happens, parsers are always either terminals or composites of other parsers. The fact that parsers are composites makes the top-down design approach natural. Here is an effective algorithm for designing a new parser:

1. Define the parser you want as a composite of subparsers.

2. Repeat step 1 until every subparser is defined or is a terminal.

This algorithm creates a grammar that will often be sufficient for direct translation to Java code. Otherwise, you must transform the grammar before implementing it, a topic described in Section 3.6, "Translating a Grammar to Code." Before looking at grammar transformation, it is useful to walk through an example of applying the design algorithm to a small example.

3.5 Example: Designing a Grammar for a Track Robot

Figure 3.4 shows a miniature factory for which we want to design a command language. The heart of the factory is a track robot, a machine that can move forward and backward along a track. The robot can pick up material from conveyor belts and place

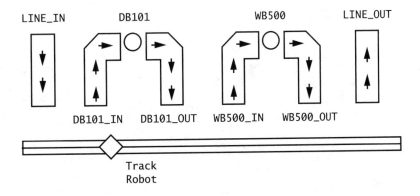

Figure 3.4 A track robot. In this miniature automated factory, a simple robot runs along a track, picking and placing material on machines.

the material on other conveyors. The robot transports material in metal containers called "carriers." The basic flow of the factory has the robot pick and place carriers so that they go through two processing machines and arrive at an output conveyor. Carriers have bar code labels that the robot is able to scan, letting the robot ascertain the identity of a carrier and arrive at a machine's output.

Humans tend to see the factory in Figure 3.4 as consisting of a track robot, two input and output conveyors, and two processing machines. The robot does not see the machines—it sees only conveyors—so our command language for the robot will be conveyor-centric. Here are some example commands for the robot:

```
pick carrier from LINE_IN
place carrier at DB101_IN
pick carrier from DB101_OUT
place carrier at WB500_IN
pick carrier from WB500_OUT
place carrier at LINE_OUT
scan DB101_OUT
```

3.5.1 A Track Robot Grammar

You want a command parser that will recognize the language that will drive the robot. Initially, your grammar is

```
command
```

You need to define the command parser in terms of other parsers, and you know that you want to recognize three commands. So you can give the first rule of the grammar as

```
command = pickCommand | placeCommand | scanCommand;
```

You need to refine this grammar, expanding every parser on the right side of a definition until every subparser is defined or is a terminal. Consider the subparser pickCommand. You know that the robot is willing to pick up carriers; you only have to tell it the location. For a definition that matches your sample strings, you can augment the grammar:

```
command     = pickCommand | placeCommand | scanCommand;
pickCommand = "pick" "carrier" "from" location;
```

You could make the words "carrier" and "from" optional, but let's keep the language simple for now. With simplicity in mind, let's also assume that each word in quotes in the grammar will be a CaselessLiteral so that users can type "pick", "Pick", or "PICK".

Judging by the sample command strings, a location is always a single word:

```
command     = pickCommand | placeCommand | scanCommand;
pickCommand = "pick" "carrier" "from" location;
location    = Word;
```

You can complete the grammar design by defining the remaining subparsers—
placeCommand and scanCommand:

```
command      = pickCommand | placeCommand | scanCommand;
pickCommand  = "pick" "carrier" "from" location;
placeCommand = "place" "carrier" "at" location;
scanCommand  = "scan" location;
location     = Word;
```

3.5.2 Checking for Left Recursion and Cycles

The grammar for the track robot language is complete, but only because it contains
no left recursion and no cyclic dependencies. Left recursion exists if a parser's definition begins with itself. Cyclic dependencies exist if a parser's definition ultimately
depends on itself. The grammar doesn't have these features so you can skip some
steps described in Chapter 6, "Transforming a Grammar."

3.6 Translating a Grammar to Code

You can write the code of a parser directly from its grammar. You apply each principle of grammar translation in turn until the grammar becomes a set of Java statements that define a parser. The following principles apply:

- Treat quoted strings as CaselessLiteral objects.

- Create Sequence objects for sequences.

- Create Alternation objects for alternations.

- Translate Terminal references to objects.

- Create a subparser for each rule.

- Declare each subparser, or arrange subparsers as methods.

- Add a start() method.

3.6.1 Translate Quoted Strings

Treat each quoted word, such as "pick", as a CaselessLiteral. For example, translate

```
pickCommand  = "pick" "carrier" "from" location;
```

to

```
pickCommand = new CaselessLiteral("pick")
              new CaselessLiteral("carrier")
              new CaselessLiteral("from")
              location;
```

This translation immediately begins to look like Java code, although it is not yet compilable. When all translations are complete, the result will be compilable code.

3.6.2 Translate Sequences

When you write a grammar, you imply sequences simply by showing two subparsers next to each other. For example,

```
placeCommand = "place" "carrier" "at" location;
```

implies

```
placeCommand  = new Sequence();
placeCommand.add(new CaselessLiteral("place"));
placeCommand.add(new CaselessLiteral("carrier"));
placeCommand.add(new CaselessLiteral("at"));
placeCommand.add(location);
```

Note that this is still not valid Java code, although you are approaching that goal. Specifically, you have not yet declared the type of placeCommand, nor have you established a strategy for referring to other subparsers. These translations follow shortly.

3.6.3 Translate Alternations

A vertical bar in a subparser definition means that the subparsers on either side of the bar may produce a successful match. When a series of vertical bars appears, you can create a single Alternation object. For example, translate

```
command = pickCommand | placeCommand | scanCommand;
```

to

```
command = new Alternation();
command.add(pickCommand);
command.add(placeCommand);
command.add(scanCommand);
```

This code looks almost like compilable Java, but you still have to translate references to subparsers.

3.6.4 Translate Terminals

Many of the terminals in the track robot language are literals, such as "place" and "carrier". The only other terminal is Word in the location definition. To translate the grammar to Java code, replace each such terminal with a new terminal object of the specified type:

```
location = new Word();
```

3.6.5 Create a Subparser for Each Rule

The translation steps given so far leave each subparser as a word that begins with a lowercase letter, such as pickCommand. There are two strategies for translating subparser definitions into Java code. You can declare each subparser as an appropriate kind of parser, or you can arrange the subparsers as a class's methods.

3.6.6 Option 1: Declare Each Subparser

For a small language, you can make each subparser a separate variable. The track robot command language is a little too large for this approach. To illustrate, here is RobotMonolithic.java:

```
package sjm.examples.robot;

import sjm.parse.*;
import sjm.parse.tokens.*;

/**
 * Show how to create a parser and use it in a single
 * method.
 */
public class RobotMonolithic {

public static void main(String[] args) {
    Alternation command = new Alternation();
    Sequence pickCommand = new Sequence();
    Sequence placeCommand = new Sequence();
    Sequence scanCommand = new Sequence();
    Word location = new Word();
```

```
command.add(pickCommand);
command.add(placeCommand);
command.add(scanCommand);

pickCommand.add(new CaselessLiteral("pick"));
pickCommand.add(new CaselessLiteral("carrier"));
pickCommand.add(new CaselessLiteral("from"));
pickCommand.add(location);

placeCommand.add(new CaselessLiteral("place"));
placeCommand.add(new CaselessLiteral("carrier"));
placeCommand.add(new CaselessLiteral("at"));
placeCommand.add(location);

scanCommand.add(new CaselessLiteral("scan"));
scanCommand.add(location);

String s = "pick carrier from DB101_IN";

System.out.println(
    command.bestMatch(new TokenAssembly(s)));
    }
}
```

All the subparser declarations appear at the top of the code. The assignment statements build the `command` object into a parser for the track robot command language. Running this class prints the following:

```
[pick, carrier, from, DB101_IN]
pick/carrier/from/DB101_IN^
```

The output shows that the `command` parser can completely parse at least one sample element of the language.

3.6.7 Option 2: Arrange Subparsers as Methods

For readability, you can create a method for each subparser of a grammar. For example, you can lift out the preceding code that creates the `command` object and place it in a method called `command()`. You can reapply this strategy, creating a method for each subparser. Because all the subparsers except `command` are useful only in constructing the `command` subparser, it is a good idea to make them protected and not public. Subparsers such as `location` are not intended for public use but might be overridden in a subclass.

Refactoring the `RobotMonolithic` class to apply the strategy of making subparsers methods results in the following:

```java
package sjm.examples.robot;

import sjm.parse.*;
import sjm.parse.tokens.*;

/**
 * Provide an example of a class that affords a parser for
 * the "robot" command language. This class is a refactored
 * version of the <code>RobotMonolithic</code> class, with
 * one method for each subparser in the robot language.
 */
public class RobotRefactored {

public Parser command() {
    Alternation a = new Alternation();
    a.add(pickCommand());
    a.add(placeCommand());
    a.add(scanCommand());
    return a;
}

protected Parser pickCommand() {
    Sequence s = new Sequence();
    s.add(new CaselessLiteral("pick"));
    s.add(new CaselessLiteral("carrier"));
    s.add(new CaselessLiteral("from"));
    s.add(location());
    return s;
}

protected Parser placeCommand() {
    Sequence s = new Sequence();
    s.add(new CaselessLiteral("place"));
    s.add(new CaselessLiteral("carrier"));
    s.add(new CaselessLiteral("at"));
    s.add(location());
    return s;
}

protected Parser scanCommand() {
    Sequence s = new Sequence();
    s.add(new CaselessLiteral("scan"));
    s.add(location());
    return s;
}

protected Parser location() {
    return new Word();
}
}
```

Here's a class that uses the refactored parser class:

```
package sjm.examples.robot;

import sjm.parse.*;
import sjm.parse.tokens.*;

/**
 * Show how to use a parser class that arranges its
 * subparsers as methods.
 */
public class ShowRobotRefactored {

public static void main(String[] args) {
    Parser p = new RobotRefactored().command();
    String s = "place carrier at WB500_IN";
    System.out.println(p.bestMatch(new TokenAssembly(s)));
}
}
```

Running this class prints the following:

```
[place, carrier, at, WB500_IN]
place/carrier/at/WB500_IN^
```

The class RobotRefactored is a refactoring of RobotMonolithic, with the subparsers arranged as a coordinated set of methods. This approach can lead to an infinite loop if rules in your grammar refer to each other in a cycle. Fortunately, you can eliminate such loops by using lazy initialization; Section 6.5 explains how. Many grammars, including the track robot grammar, are small and acyclic, so we defer this topic for now.

In the refactoring, I changed the variable names. This is an esthetic choice. You can decide whether you think it is easier to read and understand this:

```
protected Parser scanCommand() {
    Sequence s = new Sequence();
    s.add(new CaselessLiteral("scan"));
    s.add(location());
    return s;
}
```

or this:

```
protected Parser scanCommand() {
    Sequence scanCommand = new Sequence();
    scanCommand.add(new CaselessLiteral("scan"));
    scanCommand.add(location());
    return scanCommand;
}
```

3.6.8 Add a Start Method

A user of your class needs to be able to tell which subparser is the "primary" parser, the one that matches a useful language. To tell your prospective user which parser to use, introduce a start() method that returns the primary parser. For example, you could add the following method to RobotRefactored to make it easy for a user of the class to find the primary parser:

```
/**
 * Returns a parser that will recognize a command for a
 * track robot, and build a corresponding command object.
 */
public static Parser start() {
    return new RobotParser().command();
}
```

Making this method static allows a user to simply call start() as a class method.

3.7 Completing a Parser

The class RobotRefactored is the result of a translation from the track robot command language grammar into code. It is complete in that it provides a parser that recognizes the desired language. This parser is not complete, however, in the sense of doing anything useful. To go beyond recognition of a language to taking some useful action based on the recognition, a parser must control the pushing of terminals onto an assembly's stack, and it must plug assemblers in to the appropriate subparsers.

3.7.1 Control Pushing

By default, all terminals push whatever they recognize onto an assembly's stack. For most terminals, this is a useful and often necessary function. For example, when a parser recognizes a Word or a Num, the parser usually needs to do something with whatever Word or Num it recognizes. On the other hand, when a parser recognizes a Literal or CaselessLiteral, such as "carrier", the parser normally does not need to do any work with the literal it sees. For example, consider the subparser for pickCommand:

```
pickCommand = "pick" "carrier" "from" location;
```

In this subparser, the words "pick", "carrier", and "from" serve to identify a particular type of command. The pickCommand subparser successfully matches only text that begins with these three words. There is no reason to stack these words; you know what they are, and you know you must be recognizing a pickCommand if the match succeeds. Typically, you will want to ask all the Literal parsers in your parser to discard the terminal they see. To ask a Literal not to push itself, send it a discard() message. Making this change in RobotRefactored.pickCommand() results in the following:

```
protected Parser pickCommand() {
    Sequence s = new Sequence();
    s.add(new CaselessLiteral("pick").discard());
    s.add(new CaselessLiteral("carrier").discard());
    s.add(new CaselessLiteral("from").discard());
    s.add(location());
    return s;
}
```

Keeping the literals from pushing means that after a pickCommand() matches an assembly's text, the assembly's stack will contain only the value of the location for the command. You will see shortly how to plug in assemblers to work on the assembly's stack and target.

3.7.2 Design the Target

Having developed the code to recognize a robot command language, the next step is to arrange for the parser to actually build a command object from input command text. In this example, the target of parsing text is an object from a hierarchy of commands. Figure 3.5 shows the targets for the robot language, namely the three subclasses of RobotCommand.

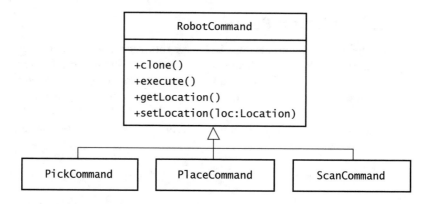

Figure 3.5 A command hierarchy. You can run a little factory with commands for picking, placing, and scanning carriers.

Here is the code for RobotCommand:

```java
package sjm.examples.robot;

/**
 * A <code>RobotCommand</code> encapsulates the work that
 * lies behind a high-level command such as "pick carrier from
 * input1". In this package, the commands are just sample
 * targets of a parser; their <code>execute()</code> methods
 * are not implemented.
 */
public class RobotCommand
    implements sjm.utensil.PubliclyCloneable {

    protected String location;

/**
 * Return a copy of this object. If the location attribute
 * becomes something more complicated than a String, then
 * this method will become insufficient if location is not
 * immutable.
 */
public Object clone() {
    try {
        return super.clone();
    } catch (CloneNotSupportedException e) {
        // this shouldn't happen, since we are Cloneable
        throw new InternalError();
    }
}

/**
 * If we were really driving a factory, this is where we
 * would turn high-level commands into the protocols that
 * various machines would understand. For example, a pick
 * command might send messages to both a conveyor and
 * a track robot.
 */
public void execute() {
}

/**
 * Return the location that this command is for.
 */
public String getLocation() {
    return location;
}

/**
 * Set the location for this command.
 */
public void setLocation(String location) {
```

```
        this.location = location;
    }
}
```

The purpose of a `RobotCommand` object is to operate real equipment when the command's `execute()` method runs. In a real factory system you would have to write the code that makes this execution happen. Each subclass of `RobotCommand` would override `execute()` appropriately. In this example you are aiming only to translate text into the right kind of command object, so the subclasses are empty. For example, the code for `PickCommand` is

```java
package sjm.examples.robot;

/**
 * Just for demonstration.
 */
public class PickCommand extends RobotCommand {

/**
 * Return a textual description of this object.
 */
public String toString() {
    return "pick " + location;
}
}
```

3.7.3 Plug In Assemblers

The assemblers for your parser set an assembly's target and inform the target of its associated location. Each subclass of the command needs a corresponding assembler to set the appropriate target. For example, you will need a `PickAssembler` class:

```java
package sjm.examples.robot;

import sjm.parse.*;
import sjm.parse.tokens.Token;

/**
 * Sets an assembly's target to be a <code>PickCommand
 * </code> object and notes its location.
 */
public class PickAssembler extends Assembler {

public void workOn(Assembly a) {
    PickCommand pc = new PickCommand();
    Token t = (Token) a.pop();
    pc.setLocation(t.sval());
    a.setTarget(pc);
}
}
```

The approach taken here assumes the parser will parse a single command and construct a corresponding RobotCommand object. Which subclass of RobotCommand to instantiate and to set as the target of the parse depends on the input text. The PickAssembler object plugs in to the pickCommand subparser, which will successfully match a "pick" command. The assembler's workOn() method executes after an (entire) pickCommand subparser matches. At this time, a pick location will be on the stack. When the workOn() method executes, it creates a PickCommand object and sets this object as the target of the parse. The assembler pops the location object and uses it to establish the location of the PickCommand object.

You can now convert the code for RobotRefactored into RobotParser, plugging in the assemblers and adding some comments. The result is as follows:

```
package sjm.examples.robot;

import sjm.parse.*;
import sjm.parse.tokens.*;

/**
 * This class's start() method provides a parser that
 * will recognize a command for a track robot and build a
 * corresponding command object.
 * <p>
 * The grammar for the language that this class recognizes
 * is:
 *
 * <blockquote><pre>
 *     command      = pickCommand | placeCommand |
 *                    scanCommand;
 *     pickCommand  = "pick" "carrier" "from" location;
 *     placeCommand = "place" "carrier" "at" location;
 *     scanCommand  = "scan" location;
 *     location     = Word;
 * </pre></blockquote>
 */
public class RobotParser {

/**
 * Returns a parser that will recognize a command for a
 * track robot and build a corresponding command
 */
public static Parser start() {
    return new RobotParser().command();
}

/**
 * Returns a parser that will recognize a command for a
 * track robot and build a corresponding command object.
 *
 * (This method returns the same value as
```

```
 * <code>start()</code>).
 */
public Parser command() {
    Alternation a = new Alternation();
    a.add(pickCommand());
    a.add(placeCommand());
    a.add(scanCommand());
    return a;
}

/*
 * Returns a parser that will recognize the grammar:
 *
 *     pickCommand = "pick" "carrier" "from" location;
 */
protected Parser pickCommand() {
    Sequence s = new Sequence();
    s.add(new CaselessLiteral("pick"));
    s.add(new CaselessLiteral("carrier"));
    s.add(new CaselessLiteral("from"));
    s.add(location());
    s.setAssembler(new PickAssembler());
    return s;
}

/*
 * Returns a parser that will recognize the grammar:
 *
 *     placeCommand = "place" "carrier" "at" location;
 */
protected Parser placeCommand() {
    Sequence s = new Sequence();
    s.add(new CaselessLiteral("place"));
    s.add(new CaselessLiteral("carrier"));
    s.add(new CaselessLiteral("at"));
    s.add(location());
    s.setAssembler(new PlaceAssembler());
    return s;
}

/*
 * Returns a parser that will recognize the grammar:
 *
 *     scanCommand = "scan" location;
 */
protected Parser scanCommand() {
    Sequence s = new Sequence();
    s.add(new CaselessLiteral("scan"));
    s.add(location());
    s.setAssembler(new ScanAssembler());
    return s;
}
```

```
/*
 * Returns a parser that will recognize the grammar:
 *
 *      location = Word;
 */
protected Parser location() {
    return new Word();
}
}
```

You can use the `RobotParser.start()` parser as follows:

```
package sjm.examples.robot;

import sjm.parse.*;
import sjm.parse.tokens.*;

/**
 * Show how to use the <code>RobotParser</code> class.
 */
public class ShowRobotParser {

public static void main(String[] args) {
    Parser p = RobotParser.start();

    String[] tests = new String[]{
        "pick carrier from LINE_IN",
        "place carrier at DB101_IN",
        "pick carrier from DB101_OUT",
        "place carrier at WB500_IN",
        "pick carrier from WB500_OUT",
        "place carrier at LINE_OUT",
        "scan DB101_OUT"};

    for (int i = 0; i < tests.length; i++) {
        TokenAssembly ta = new TokenAssembly(tests[i]);
        Assembly out = p.bestMatch(ta);
        System.out.println(out.getTarget());
    }
}
}
```

Running this class prints the results of parsing a few sample commands:

```
pick LINE_IN
place DB101_IN
pick DB101_OUT
place WB500_IN
pick WB500_OUT
place LINE_OUT
scan DB101_OUT
```

These are the results of the `toString()` methods of the commands built by the `RobotParser.start()` parser. If the command target objects were wired into a factory with functional `execute()` methods, you could use these commands to control the factory.

3.8 Summary

Building a new parser starts with envisioning the language you want to recognize. Write a few sample sentences of the language that you want, and write a grammar that comprehends these examples. A grammar shows the pattern of strings in your language and serves as a design document. Next, translate your grammar to code and verify that your parser recognizes the sample strings of your language. Once you get a parser working that recognizes your examples, you can add more grammar rules. You can work iteratively to build the complete language you want to recognize. At some point, you must start creating the auxiliary classes that let your parser do more than just recognize an input string. These supporting classes are assemblers and potentially a target. After a subparser recognizes text, the subparser's assembler can work on the assembly that contains the text. This work may be limited to the assembly's stack, or it may include changes to the assembly's target. You have complete control over how you define a target class except that your class must implement `PubliclyCloneable`.

Work iteratively, creating your parser as a composition of subparsers and plugging in assemblers that build a target. In a short time you can learn to create powerful new languages from these few steps.

CHAPTER 4
Testing a Parser

B efore you empower your users with a new language, you should test your parser to ensure that it meets its requirements. There are two steps worth taking: feature testing and random testing.

4.1 Feature Testing

In *feature* testing, you create tests that verify that your parser produces the correct translation of text. For example, you should be able to test that an arithmetic parser evaluates "7 - 3 - 1" as 3. It is important to automate your tests, because during development a test that has previously passed can suddenly fail. For example, a new error in a tokenizer can cause a formerly effective arithmetic parser to fail.

You can write your own testing tools or use an existing framework. Several testing frameworks are available, including JUnit, which was used in writing the code for this book. JUnit, developed by Kent Beck and Erich Gamma, is freely available on the Internet.

Testing frameworks typically offer a standard way to define and execute test methods and to make assertions about these methods' results. The framework then automatically checks such assertions as often as you run your tests.

For example, to build an automated test for an arithmetic parser, you can create a subclass of a `junit.framework.TestCase`. The `TestCase` class provides a variety of assertion methods that you can call. Your subclass might include a method that makes the call

```
assertEquals(ArithmeticParser.value("7 - 3 - 1"), 3, 0);
```

The `assertEquals()` method will throw an exception if the values of the first two parameters are not equal, or at least within the specified tolerance. In this example the tolerance is 0, so the two parameters must be exactly equal.

If you include assertion calls in a method whose name begins with the word `test`, the JUnit framework will comprehend that it should execute the method when conducting a test. Here is a complete testing class designed to test the `ArithmeticParser` class using JUnit:

```
package testing;

import junit.framework.*;
import sjm.examples.arithmetic.*;

/**
 * Test <code>sjm.examples.arithmetic.ArithmeticParser
 * </code>.
 */

public class ArithmeticParserTest extends TestCase {

public ArithmeticParserTest(String name) {
    super(name);
}

public void testAssociativity()
    throws ArithmeticExpressionException {

    // subtraction
    assertEquals(
        ArithmeticParser.value("7 - 3 - 1"), 3, 0);

    // exponentiation
    assertEquals(
        ArithmeticParser.value("2 ^ 1 ^ 4"), 2, 0.01);
}

public void testExpressionException() {
    try {
        ArithmeticParser.value(" 7 / ");
        fail("should throw ArithmeticExpressionException");
    } catch (ArithmeticExpressionException e) {
    }
}

public void testInteger()
    throws ArithmeticExpressionException {

    assertEquals(ArithmeticParser.value("42"), 42, 0);
}

public void testParentheses()
    throws ArithmeticExpressionException {

    assertEquals(
```

```
                        ArithmeticParser.value(" ((3 * 7) + (11 * 3)) / 3"),
                        18,
                        0);
        }

        public void testPrecedence()
            throws ArithmeticExpressionException {

            assertEquals(
                ArithmeticParser.value("7 - 3 * 2 + 6"), 7, 0);

            assertEquals(
                ArithmeticParser.value("2^1^4"), 2, 0);

            assertEquals(
                ArithmeticParser.value("2^3^2"), 512, 0);

            assertEquals(
                ArithmeticParser.value("1000+2*2^3^2/2"), 1512, 0);

            assertEquals(
                ArithmeticParser.value("3*2^2*3"), 36, 0);
        }
    }
```

The JUnit framework includes a `TestRunner` class that executes all the test methods in a test class. For example, you can run `TestRunner` and pass it the class name `testing.ArithmeticParserTest` as a command line parameter. The framework detects which methods in `ArithmeticParserTest` begin with `test` and executes these methods. As `TestRunner` executes, a progress bar shows your tests executing and a message area points out tests that fail.

Many developers find that once they begin using an automated testing framework, the security and empowerment they obtain makes them question how they ever lived without it.

4.2 Random Testing

In addition to testing whether your language supports the features you intend, it is a good idea to conduct random tests by running random language elements through your parser. Figure 4.1 shows the abstract class `ParserTester`, from package `sjm.parse`. This class accepts a parser in its constructor and tests the parser in response to a `test()` message.

The `ParserTester` class is abstract because its `assembly()` method is abstract. Subclasses implement this method to treat the string as a sequence of either tokens or

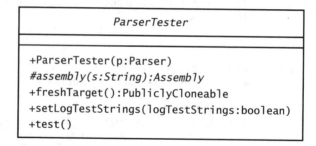

Figure 4.1 The ParserTester class. This class tests the parser that it accepts in its constructor.

characters. The setLogTestStrings() method determines whether the tester object prints out each random test string. The test() method applies a parser against many test inputs. This method creates a new assembly for each test string and sets that assembly's target to the value of freshTarget(). The ParserTester class implements this method to return null. Subclasses can override this to insert a new target object for each test assembly.

Figure 4.2 shows the two primary subclasses of ParserTester. These classes implement the assembly() method, which determines whether to create a CharacterAssembly or a TokenAssembly from a given string.

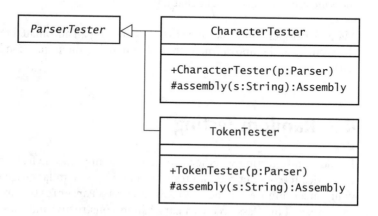

Figure 4.2 Concrete subclasses of ParserTester. Class CharacterTester from sjm.parse.chars and class TokenTester from sjm.parse.tokens determine how to create an assembly from a random string.

In response to a `test()` message, the tester classes generate a large number of random language elements and ask the parser to test them. For example, here is a program that tests an arithmetic parser:

```
package sjm.examples.tests;

import sjm.parse.*;
import sjm.parse.tokens.*;
import sjm.examples.arithmetic.*;

/**
 * Test the <code>ArithmeticParser</code> class.
 */
public class ShowArithmeticTest {

public static void main(String[] args) {
    new TokenTester(ArithmeticParser.start()).test();
}
}
```

Running this class prints a series of random tests, such as the following:

```
Testing depth 2...
    Testing string 66.1 / 81.0 + 63.1 ^ 50.1 ^ 61.1 ^ 45.0
                    ^ 4.3 ^ 96.3

    Testing string ( 90.1 ^ 9.5 ^ 89.6 ^ 84.2 ^ 33.9 ^ 87.9
                    ^ 28.5 ^ 43.5 ) ^ 98.4 / 92.3 + 85.8 ^
                    45.8 ^ 82.1

    Testing string ( 7.5 ) ^ 15.0 / 62.2 * 22.9 ^ 39.9 * 57.7
                    ^ 15.4 + 16.1 ^ 17.4

    Testing string 55.8 ^ 87.5 ^ 89.0 ^ 93.3 / 70.4 / 53.6 /
                    20.8 + 12.4

    Testing string 75.5 ^ 53.1 * 40.1 ^ 79.4 + 26.1 ^ 13.6 -
                    50.0 ^ 28.3 ^ 56.9 ^ 8.1

    ...
```

These tests will continue for some time, and for the given parser they will find no errors. The *depth* of the test relates to how many parser expansions the test allows before it tries to resolve the test by preferring expansions to terminals over nonterminals. The class shown will generate hundreds of test strings, confirming that the parser `ArithmeticParser.start()` can parse each result.

The tester classes rely on support from the `Parser` hierarchy for these random expansions. Each subclass of `Parser` must be able to provide a random element of the parser's language. For example, the class Word produces a random word, and the class Literal always returns its literal value. The classes Sequence, Alternation, and Repetition are subtler, and a detailed explanation of their design is outside the scope of this book. The code for these classes is available on the CD that comes with this book.

4.2.1 Ambiguity Testing

A grammar is *ambiguous* if a parser for the grammar allows more than one way to completely match an assembly. This is usually an error because a language user normally expects a single interpretation of a given string. Unfortunately, "there exists no general method for determining whether an arbitrary [grammar] is ambiguous or not" [Slonneger and Kurtz]. In practice, random testing provides an effective approach to discovering ambiguity in a grammar. The tester classes in the ParserTester hierarchy will find ambiguity in a parser, although this is not guaranteed to work because the tests are random.

A classic case of ambiguity is the *dangling else* problem. Consider an imperative language that includes statements such as this one:

```
if (overdueDays > 90)
    if (balance >= 1000)
        callCustomer();
else sendBill();
```

To a human reader, there may be some question as to whether the else clause belongs to the first or second if. Java associates the else with the nearest preceding if, although the indentation in this example implies otherwise. Although a person reading this code may incorrectly predict how Java will interpret the code, Java will find exactly one interpretation. It is also possible that a parser will find *two* ways to parse this code, giving one parse with the else associated with the first if and another parse with it associated with the second. Such a parser comes from an ambiguous grammar.

The following ambiguous grammar comprehends the preceding if statement:

```
statement    = "if" comparison statement optionalElse |
                 callCustomer | sendBill;
comparison   = '(' expression operator expression ');
expression   = Word | Num;
operator     = '<' | '>' | '=' | "<=" | ">=" | "!=";
optionalElse = "else" statement | Empty;
callCustomer = "callCustomer" '(' ')' ';';
sendBill     = "sendBill" '(' ')' ';';
```

You can generate a parser class from this grammar: the class `Dangle` in `sjm.examples.tests` contains this code. To parse an `if` statement, you can apply the parser object

```
Dangle.statement()
```

This parser sometimes finds more than one way to parse an input string. You can verify this by generating and parsing random elements of the language. Here is a program that tests the dangling `else` grammar:

```
package sjm.examples.tests;

import sjm.parse.*;
import sjm.parse.tokens.*;

/**
 * Test the statement parser from class <code>Dangle</code>
 */
public class ShowDangleTest {

public static void main(String[] args) {
    Parser p = new Dangle().statement();
    TokenTester tt = new TokenTester(p);
    tt.setLogTestStrings(false);
    tt.test();
}
}
```

This class creates a `TokenTester` object with the `Dangle.statement()` parser. The code asks the tester not to print the test strings and launches the test. A sample run of the program produces

```
Testing depth 2...
Problem found for string:
    if ( mnyawp > zzprr ) if ( 53.6 >= olzu ) sendBill ( ) ;
    else callCustomer ( ) ;
The parser found 2 ways to parse this string.
```

A random test of the parser will quickly determine that the grammar is ambiguous, but it will not show how the parses of a given input differ. The package `sjm.examples.pretty` includes a `PrettyParser` class that resets the assemblers in a parser composite to show the order in which a parser parses input text. This reformats, or *pretty prints* the input string into a *parse tree* that indicates the order of the parse.

For example, the following program prints the two parses that a dangling `else` grammar produces:

```
package sjm.examples.pretty;

import java.util.*;
import sjm.parse.*;
import sjm.parse.tokens.*;
import sjm.examples.tests.*;

/**
 * Show that the <code>Dangle.statement()</code> parser
 * is ambiguous.
 */
public class ShowDangle {

public static void main(String[] args) {
    String s;
    s  = "if (overdueDays > 90)     \n";
    s += "    if (balance >= 1000) \n";
    s += "          callCustomer();  \n";
    s += "else sendBill();";

    TokenAssembly ta = new TokenAssembly(s);

    PrettyParser p = new PrettyParser(Dangle.statement());

    Vector out = p.parseTrees(ta);

    Enumeration e = out.elements();
    while (e.hasMoreElements()) {
        System.out.println("The input parses as:");
        System.out.println("--------------------------");
        System.out.println(e.nextElement());
    }
}
}
```

The `main()` method creates a token assembly from a sample string and creates a `PrettyParser` object from the `Dangle.statement()` parser. The code asks the `PrettyParser` object to produce a collection of parse trees for the input token assembly. The program displays the following:

```
The input parses as:
--------------------------
    if
        (
            overdueDays
            >
            90.0
        )
            if
                (
                    balance
```

```
                              >=
                              1000.0
                    )
                              callCustomer
                              (
                              )
                              ;
                    else
                              sendBill
                              (
                              )
                              ;

The input parses as:
-------------------------
    if
        (
                    overdueDays
                    >
                    90.0
        )
                    if
                        (
                                    balance
                                    >=
                                    1000.0
                        )
                                    callCustomer
                                    (
                                    )
                                    ;
        else
                    sendBill
                    (
                    )
                    ;
```

The TokenTester class detects a problem with the dangling else grammar, and the PrettyParser class shows the different paths the grammar takes for a given input. Still, the problem remains that the grammar is ambiguous, and neither the TokenTester class nor the PrettyParser class shows how to remove this ambiguity. A simple solution is to require an if statement to conclude with the word endif. The book *Compilers* [Aho et al.] provides other cures for several forms of ambiguity, including curing the dangling else problem by rewriting the grammar as follows:

```
statement = matched | unmatched;
matched   = "if" expression "then" matched "else" matched
          | other;
unmatched = "if" expression "then" statement
          | "if" expression "then" matched "else" unmatched;
```

If you need to remove ambiguity from a grammar, you may be able to follow this pattern to solve the problem.

4.2.2 Terminal Ambiguity

In addition to the classic dangling else case and other cases when ambiguity is inherent in a grammar, a common case of ambiguity occurs when two terminal parsers recognize a given language element. Consider a grammar for queries about relative volumes:

```
query  = (Word | volume)* '?';
volume = "cups" | "gallon" | "liter";
```

The idea of this grammar is that we can interpret user queries such as this one:

```
"How many cups are in a gallon?"
```

To answer such questions you could discard meaningless words and use assemblers to manipulate recognizable units. You first need to address the ambiguity that occurs when you translate this grammar to code. Here is a parser class that implements the grammar:

```
package sjm.examples.tests;

import sjm.parse.*;
import sjm.parse.tokens.*;

/**
 * This class provides an ambiguous parser in its <code>
 * query</code> method, ....
 */
public class VolumeQuery {

/*
 * Return a parser that recognizes the grammar:
 *
 *     query = (Word | volume)* '?';
 */
public static Parser query() {
    Parser a = new Alternation()
        .add(new Word())
        .add(volume());
    Parser s = new Sequence()
        .add(new Repetition(a))
        .add(new Symbol('?'));
    return s;
}
```

```
/*
 * Return a parser that recognizes the grammar:
 *
 *     volume = "cups" | "gallon" | "liter";
 */
public static Parser volume() {
    Parser a = new Alternation()
        .add(new Literal("cups"))
        .add(new Literal("gallon"))
        .add(new Literal("liter"));
    return a;
    }
}
```

The problem with this class is that the volume words, such as "cups", qualify as both the literal values in the volume() parser and as Word values in the query() parser. You can see the ambiguity by sending the query parser to a tester:

```
package sjm.examples.tests;

import sjm.parse.*;
import sjm.parse.tokens.*;

/**
 * Test the query parser from class <code>VolumeQuery
 * </code>.
 */
public class ShowVolumeTest {

public static void main(String[] args) {
    Parser p = VolumeQuery.query();
    TokenTester tt = new TokenTester(p);
    tt.test();
    }
}
```

A sample run of this class prints the following:

```
Testing depth 2...
    Testing string glmtt qbz ?
    Testing string wqrab gallon eeoaqr ?
Problem found for string:
    wqrab gallon eeoaqr ?
The parser found 2 ways to parse this string.
```

A random test of this parser cannot go far. When it uses the volume rule it produces an element that qualifies both as a volume and as a meaningless word. To remove the ambiguity from this parser, you can create a new terminal type to distinguish reserved words from nonreserved words. Chapter 11, "Extending the Parser Toolkit," explains how to implement such a solution.

4.3 Special Tokenizers and Targets

If your parser needs a special tokenizer or target, you can create a new subclass of
ParserTester and override the assembly() and freshTarget() methods. For example, the SlingParser class in Chapter 16, "Parsing an Imperative Language," uses a
special tokenizer that recognizes reserved words. This parser class also requires an
assembly to have as its target a SlingTarget object. To provide for these special target
and tokenization needs, the class SlingTester in sjm.examples.sling overrides the
freshTarget() and assembly() methods of its superclasses. Here is SlingTester.java:

```
package sjm.examples.sling;

import sjm.parse.*;
import sjm.parse.tokens.*;
import sjm.examples.sling.*;

/**
 * This class tests that class <code>SlingParser</code> can
 * parse random language elements.
 */
public class SlingTester extends TokenTester {

/**
 * Create a tester for the primary Sling parser.
 */
public SlingTester() {
    super(new SlingParser().statement());
}

/*
 * Return an assembly for a given string, using the Sling
 * tokenizer.
 */
protected Assembly assembly(String s) {
    Tokenizer t = new SlingParser().tokenizer();
    t.setString(s);
    return new TokenAssembly(t);
}

/*
 * The Sling parser expects a SlingTarget object as an
 * assembly's target. Normally, this target expects two
 * sliders to be available, but we send nulls here because
 * there is no GUI in use during random testing.
 */
protected sjm.utensil.PubliclyCloneable freshTarget() {
    return new SlingTarget(null, null);
}
```

```
/**
 * Run a test.
 */
public static void main(String[] args) {
    new SlingTester().test();
}
}
```

A sample run of this class prints the following (with some whitespace changes):

```
Testing depth 2...
    Testing string for (vrnjex, (pi), -t) {gnu = (t);}
    Testing string for (zllciub, s2, (s2)) {uuezrpu = (pi);}
    Testing string plot (3.3);
    Testing string plot ceil (-hrnpb);
    Testing string plot ceil (-random);
    Testing string for (umq, -s2, ((-t))) {
        for (iojf, schq, random) {hrbr = - t;}}
    Testing string plot ((s2));
    ...
```

Although an explanation of the Sling language lies ahead, you can probably imagine that these are not normal-looking Sling programs. One strength of random testing is that it produces valid language elements that you might not create in your feature testing. These elements include strings that perhaps no one would ever try but also include types of strings that your users might think of that you would not. Random testing is an important complement to feature testing of a parser.

4.4 Summary

Random testing and feature testing complement each other, testing all the language features you can think of and testing valid language elements you might never think of. For random testing, you can use the ParserTester hierarchy in the sjm packages. You may need to override these classes if your parser requires a special tokenizer or a target. For feature testing, you should acquire a testing framework such as JUnit and use it to verify that your parser (still) has all the functionality you intend.

CHAPTER 5

Parsing Data Languages

This chapter explores data languages, whose elements are textual representations of objects. Data languages are common and relatively simple, and they provide good examples of how to apply the techniques this book has covered to this point. This chapter focuses on a sample application that parses a file that describes types of coffee. Sections in this chapter show how to build the assemblers and the grammar for a coffee language and how to generate a parser from the grammar. This chapter also includes a brief introduction to XML, which provides an alternative and potentially simpler approach to defining and parsing a data language.

5.1 The Role of Data Languages

A data language has elements that specify, in human-readable form, data intended for a computer program. These languages appear when a need arises for users to be able to describe data in an input file. For example, users may need to type a record of orders taken while the system was down. In the example treated in this chapter, a marketing department passes a list of featured coffees to the group that writes a monthly brochure. This group has a computer application that reads the list and provides links to other information about the coffee types in the list. In examples such as these, existing code usually applies some variety of string matching to read such data, and this code can be complex.

The role of a data language parser is to simplify the reading of a legacy language. This chapter shows how to create such a parser. If you are creating a new language, you should consider using XML (Extensible Markup Language) rather than writing a parser. XML makes it easy to create new languages without writing parsers at all. In XML, you specify the pattern of a new language in a text file. Standard and freely available tools read the pattern of your language and validate input files against it. After explaining how to parse existing languages, this chapter gives a brief introduction to the use of XML as a language creation tool.

5.2 A Data Language Example

Consider a coffee company that creates a monthly brochure that promotes certain coffees. The marketing director types a list each month of coffees that she wants the brochure to mention, and she sends the list to a creative writer elsewhere in the department. This writer has a small, homegrown application that reads the file and provides a user interface with links to other information, specifically a data warehouse with demographics about the sales of each coffee in the file. This application has been plagued with defects, especially around the reading of the input file. Your job is to simplify the reading of this file. The marketing director has flatly refused to change how she enters the file and will not listen to anyone who uses acronyms, especially if the acronym begins with *X*. Thus, you cannot move this application to XML; you must simply clean up the reading of the current language. Here is this month's list of coffees to read:

```
Brimful, Regular, Kenya, 6.95
Caress (Smackin), French, Sumatra, 7.95
Fragrant Delicto, Regular/French, Peru, 9.95
Havalavajava, Regular, Hawaii, 11.95
Launch Mi, French, Kenya, 6.95
Roman Spur (Revit), Italian, Guatemala, 7.95
Simplicity House, Regular/French, Colombia, 5.95
```

With a little analysis, you determine that the file contains descriptions of types of coffee. Each line has the name, roast, country of origin, and price (per pound) for the coffees featured this month. If a type of coffee has a new name, the former name appears in parentheses after the new name. If the coffee is offered as a French roast in addition to its normal roast, the characters /French follow the normal roast.

In addition to the existing business rules, there is an existing `Coffee` class, shown in Figure 5.1.

The goal in this example is to create a new parser that recognizes the existing language and builds `Coffee` objects from their textual descriptions. The tasks are as follows:

- Write a grammar.
- Write assemblers to build a `Coffee` object.
- Generate the parser from the grammar, plugging in the assemblers.

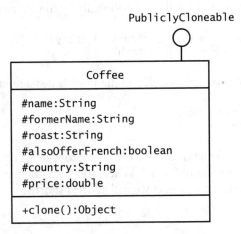

Figure 5.1 The Coffee class. A Coffee object has various attributes and is publicly cloneable because Coffee implements the PubliclyCloneable interface.

5.3 A Coffee Grammar

You can create a grammar for the coffee data language by applying the following algorithm:

1. Define the parser you want as a composite of subparsers.
2. Repeat step 1 until every subparser is defined or is a terminal.

The parser you want to define is

```
coffee
```

From the preceding language element, you can see that a coffee description is, at a high level, the following:

```
coffee = name ',' roast ',' country ',' price;
```

A coffee's name is a word followed optionally by a former name. The former name is a word in parentheses.

```
name       = Word (formerName | Empty);
formerName = '(' Word ')';
```

The roast is a word followed optionally by the characters /French:

```
roast   = Word (orFrench | Empty);
orFrench = '/' "french";
```

The country is just a word, and the price is just a number:

```
country = Word;
price   = Num;
```

You can translate this grammar directly to code using the rules in Section 3.6 "Translating a Grammar to Code." When you write the parser, you will want to plug in your assemblers, a subject we will address shortly.

5.4 A Tokenizing Problem

The coffee grammar accepts coffee names, roasts, and countries as Word terminals. This creates a problem if any of these "words" contains a blank. For example, a coffee name might be "Toasty Rita," from Costa Rica. By default, the class Tokenizer in sjm.parse.tokens treats a blank as the end of a word. When tokenizing the text

```
Toasty Rita, Italian, Costa Rica, 9.95
```

a default tokenizer would return Toasty as a Word, followed by Rita as a Word. After the first word, the grammar will be looking for a comma and not another word, and a parser generated from the grammar will fail to match the input text.

One solution is to ask the tokenizer to allow blanks to occur inside words. The following code snippet creates such a tokenizer:

```
Tokenizer t = new Tokenizer();
t.wordState().setWordChars(' ', ' ', true);
```

This code says that a blank is a legal part of a word. The CoffeeParser class that appears later in this chapter provides a tokenizer() method that returns a tokenizer that accepts blanks inside words. The ShowCoffee class, which also appears later in this chapter, uses this tokenizer when parsing an input file of coffee types. Chapter 9, "Advanced Tokenizing," covers tokenizing in detail.

5.5 Coffee Assemblers

The coffee grammar suggests the need for six assemblers, which define actions to take upon seeing a name, a former name, a roast, the /French qualifier, the country, and the price. Figure 5.2 shows the assemblers and other classes in the coffee package.

Figure 5.3 shows where the assemblers plug in to the subparsers of the CoffeeParser class.

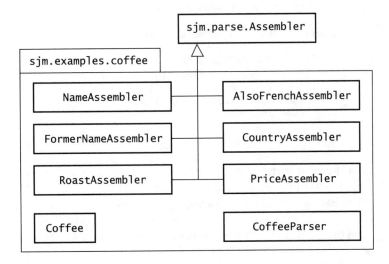

Figure 5.2 The coffee package. This package contains classes that collaborate to create a Coffee object from text.

Parser	Assembler
Word object in name()	NameAssembler()
Word object in formerName()	FormerNameAssembler()
Word object in roast()	RoastAssembler()
Literal sequence in orFrench()	AlsoFrenchAssembler()
Word object in country()	CountryAssembler()
Num object in price()	PriceAssembler()

Figure 5.3 Coffee assembler placement. This table shows the assembler that each coffee subparser employs.

5.5.1 Coffee Assembler Code

The `NameAssembler` class is typical of the assemblers that build a `Coffee` object. This assembler pops a coffee's name from an assembly's stack and sets the assembly's target to be a new `Coffee` object with this name.

```
package sjm.examples.coffee;

import sjm.parse.*;
import sjm.parse.tokens.*;

/**
 * This assembler pops a coffee's name...
 */
public class NameAssembler extends Assembler {

public void workOn(Assembly a) {
    Coffee c = new Coffee();
    Token t = (Token) a.pop();
    c.setName(t.sval().trim());
    a.setTarget(c);
}
}
```

For the most part, the coffee assemblers pop a token off the stack, extract the meaningful part of the token, and update the target `Coffee` object. The `NameAssembler` class has the special job of placing a new `Coffee` object as the assembly's target. One other point is that the assemblers that pop a string may have to trim blanks from the end of the string because the tokenizer allows blanks as characters inside a word.

Classes similar to `NameAssembler` assign the coffee's former name, roast, and country. An assembler for handling the `/French` qualifier does not pop anything; it just sets this attribute of the target coffee to be `true`. An assembler for the coffee's price is also similar, but it pops a token and not a number. This assembler takes care to set the coffee's price to the number value of the token, using the `nval()` method of `Token`.

With the assemblers in place, you can translate the grammar directly to code.

5.6 Translating the Coffee Grammar to Code

You can follow the rules of Section 3.6 "Translating a Grammar to Code," and code subparsers as methods on a parser class. Figure 5.4 shows `CoffeeParser`.

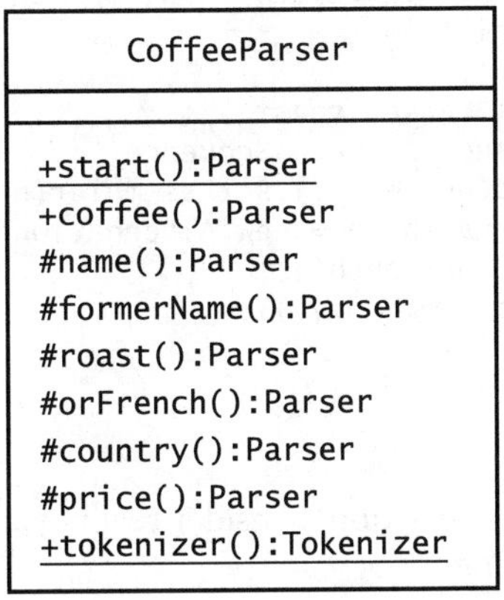

```
                    ┌─────────────────────────────────┐
                    │          CoffeeParser           │
                    ├─────────────────────────────────┤
                    ├─────────────────────────────────┤
                    │ +start():Parser                 │
                    │ +coffee():Parser                │
                    │ #name():Parser                  │
                    │ #formerName():Parser            │
                    │ #roast():Parser                 │
                    │ #orFrench():Parser              │
                    │ #country():Parser               │
                    │ #price():Parser                 │
                    │ +tokenizer():Tokenizer          │
                    └─────────────────────────────────┘
```

Figure 5.4 The CoffeeParser class. This class organizes its subparsers as individual methods.

Most of the methods of the CoffeeParser class return a parser that recognizes one aspect of the coffee grammar. For example, the price() method returns a parser for the rule

```
price = Num;
```

The code for CoffeeParser.price() plugs in the price assembler:

```
/*
 * Return a parser that will recognize the sequence:
 *
 *     price = Num;
 *
 * Use a PriceAssembler to update the target coffee object.
 */
protected Parser price() {
    return new Num().setAssembler(new PriceAssembler());
}
```

The methods for some of the other subparsers are longer. For example, here is the code for CoffeeParser.roast():

```
/*
 * Return a parser that will recognize the grammar:
 *
 *     roast = Word (orFrench | Empty);
 *
 * Use a RoastAssembler to update the target coffee object
```

```
 * with the recognized Word; orFrench also uses an
 * assembler.
 */
protected Parser roast() {
    Sequence s = new Sequence();
    s.add(new Word().setAssembler(new RoastAssembler()));
    Alternation a = new Alternation();
    a.add(orFrench());
    a.add(new Empty());
    s.add(a);
    return s;
}
```

To see the parser in action, consider reading a list of coffees from the file that contains the following:

```
Brimful, Regular, Kenya, 6.95
Caress (Smackin), French, Sumatra, 7.95
Fragrant Delicto, Regular/French, Peru, 9.95
Havalavajava, Regular, Hawaii, 11.95
Launch Mi, French, Kenya, 6.95
Roman Spur (Revit), Italian, Guatemala, 7.95
Simplicity House, Regular/French, Colombia, 5.95
```

The following code reads this file, creates a Coffee object for each line, and displays the object:

```
package sjm.examples.coffee;

import java.io.*;
import sjm.parse.*;
import sjm.parse.tokens.*;

/**
 * Show the recognition of a list of types of coffee,
 * reading from a file.
 */
public class ShowCoffee {

public static void main(String args[]) throws Exception {

    InputStream is =
        ClassLoader.getSystemResourceAsStream("coffee.txt");
    BufferedReader r =
        new BufferedReader(new InputStreamReader(is));

    Tokenizer t = CoffeeParser.tokenizer();
    Parser p = CoffeeParser.start();

    while (true) {
        String s = r.readLine();
```

```
                    if (s == null) {
                        break;
                    }
                    t.setString(s);
                    Assembly in = new TokenAssembly(t);
                    Assembly out = p.bestMatch(in);
                    System.out.println(out.getTarget());
                }
            }
        }
```

This file `coffee.txt` is on this book's CD. If you copy the file to any directory in your CLASSPATH, then `ClassLoader` will be able to find it. Run the program, and it will print the following:

```
Brimful, Regular, Kenya, 6.95
Caress(Smackin), French, Sumatra, 7.95
Fragrant Delicto, Regular/French, Peru, 9.95
Havalavajava, Regular, Hawaii, 11.95
Launch Mi, French, Kenya, 6.95
Roman Spur(Revit), Italian, Guatemala, 7.95
Simplicity House, Regular/French, Colombia, 5.95
```

This output differs from the input only with regard to some whitespace. The output shows, however, that you made the transition from text to objects and back to text.

Note that `ShowCoffee.main()` is careful to use the tokenizer that `CoffeeParser` provides. This tokenizer allows blanks to occur inside words after the first letter of the word. The `main()` routine gets a copy of this tokenizer and feeds it each line of the input file.

5.7 Data Language Parser Summary

You should find that you can write a data language parser in a few days, if not a few hours. To create the parser, write a grammar that describes the language you want to match. Write assemblers that will build your target object, and generate the parser from the grammar, plugging in your assemblers.

Although parsers for data languages are among the simplest practical parsers, there is an even simpler approach: Do not write a parser at all. XML makes this possible by standardizing a way to write grammars and elements for data-oriented languages.

5.8 Parsers with XML

XML is a project of the World Wide Web Consortium (W3C). XML is actually a metalanguage—a facility for creating new languages using *markup*.

5.8.1 A Brief History of XML

The idea of markup languages is to include datatype information along with data in a human-readable form. Markup originated in printed form, when editors literally marked up printed pages, indicating changes and printing information, such as whether a word should be in bold. Carrying over this idea to computers seems natural—just write something like <bold>this</bold> to tell the computer to write a word in bold.

Over time, developers found that they wanted to be able to set up templates so that two different documents would have the same look. A *template* is essentially a grammar— a definition of a set of strings, namely all strings whose contents match the template. Thus, each new template defines a new language, and a facility for creating new templates is a metalanguage. This is a strong argument that a markup language should be a "metamarkup" language, a facility for creating new templates. This line of thinking, in part, led to the creation of SGML, the Standard Generalized Markup Language.

SGML is an unusually powerful language that includes the ability to define new document templates and many other facilities. This power comes at the price of complexity—so much complexity that some developers feel that people with little computer expertise will never learn SGML. This line of thinking leads us back to simpler languages, such as HTML (Hypertext Markup Language). HTML is not a metalanguage for creating new templates; rather it is a language for describing a Web page, and it is much simpler than SGML.

If you wanted to restore some of the power of SGML, including at least the ability to define new templates (and thus new languages), you might invent something like XML. Many people see XML as striking the right compromise between power and simplicity. XML makes it comparatively easy to create new markup languages and to create documents that are elements of those languages. You can get an XML parser for free and start creating your own languages within a few hours.

5.8.2 The Evolution of XML

XML standardizes the definition of new languages enough that parsers for XML itself need only be written once. This has led to the free availability of XML parsers. Instead of writing your own parser, you can use a free, existing parser to read a data file into Java.

At the time of this writing, XML is evolving rapidly, so this book is limited in its ability to advise you where to get XML tools and even which ones to get. For example, during the writing of this book, IBM donated its popular (and free) XML parser to Apache. Another important recent change is the movement toward stricter definitions of grammars. Initially, grammars appeared in XML *document type definition* files. Now there is work to allow XML developers to specify grammars in XML *schemas*, which allow a tighter mapping to Java and other languages. It is predictable that other, unpredictable advances will have occurred by the time you read this. It is also predictable that XML will still be evolving, so good advice is to keep watching XML.

5.8.3 An XML Example

You can parse the marketing department's coffee input file by converting it to XML. Imagine that the old director leaves and the new director demands to know why the information technology group is behind the times and not using XML. To catch up, you can create an XML version of the coffee input file and use an XML parser to read the file. In a markup format, the example of coffees to feature in a given month's brochure might look like this:

```
<?xml version="1.0"?>

<brochureCoffees>
<coffee>
    <name>Brimful</name>
    <roast>Regular</roast>
    <price>6.95</price>
    <country>Kenya</country>
</coffee>

<coffee>
    <name>Caress</name>
    <formerName>Smackin</formerName>
    <roast>French</roast>
    <price>7.95</price>
    <country>Sumatra</country>
</coffee>

<coffee>
    <name>Fragrant Delicto</name>
    <roast>Regular</roast>
    <orFrench/>
    <price>9.95</price>
    <country>Peru</country>
</coffee>

<coffee>
    <name>Havalavajava</name>
```

```
        <roast>Regular</roast>
        <price>11.95</price>
        <country>Hawaii</country>
    </coffee>

    <coffee>
        <name>Launch Mi</name>
        <roast>French</roast>
        <price>6.95</price>
        <country>Kenya</country>
    </coffee>

    <coffee>
        <name>Roman Spur</name>
        <formerName>Revit</formerName>
        <roast>Italian</roast>
        <price>7.95</price>
        <country>Guatemala</country>
    </coffee>

    <coffee>
        <name>Simplicity House</name>
        <roast>Regular</roast>
        <orFrench/>
        <price>5.95</price>
        <country>Colombia</country>
    </coffee>
    </brochureCoffees>
```

We can use a SAX parser to read in the markup version of the coffee file. SAX is the Simple Application Programming Interface for XML. SAX provides some callback features that let us build coffee objects as the parser sees them. An alternative to using SAX is to use a parser that builds a document object model (DOM) and then walk over the document building Java objects. Walking over documents can be tricky, however, and in general this book promotes building objects during recognition rather than building some kind of tree and walking over it.

Our strategy is to create a hierarchy of Helper classes, similar to assemblers. In this example, the helpers take data that the parser sees and apply it to the creation of coffee objects. A SAX parser makes two basic callbacks: when the parser sees an element, such as <roast>, and when it sees data, such as Italian. When the parser tells you that it has seen a new element, you set a Helper object to be the right kind of helper for the element. Then, when the parser sees the data for the element, you pass the data to the helper, which knows how to apply the data to a Coffee object. Figure 5.5 shows the classes in sjm.examples.coffee that help a SAX parser to build a list of coffees.

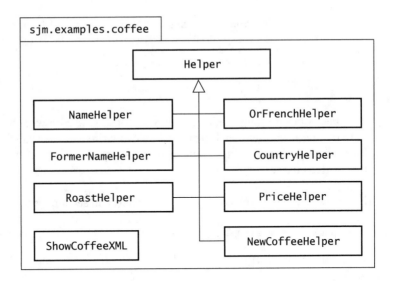

Figure 5.5 Support for SAX. This diagram shows classes in the coffee package that help a SAX parser to build a list of coffees.

5.9 Helpers

The *helpers* that build a `Coffee` object are similar to their assembler counterparts. The `Helper` class is the top of a hierarchy of classes that help to build an object based on recognizing elements of an XML markup file. An application (such as `ShowCoffeeXML`) that uses a SAX parser can pass control to helpers upon receiving SAX events. The idea is that the application will register itself with the SAX parser to receive recognition events. Then the application uses `Helper` objects to help build a target object.

```
package sjm.examples.coffee;

/**
 * This class is the top of a hierarchy of classes that help
 * to build a coffee object, based on recognizing elements
 * of an XML markup file....
 */
public class Helper {

/**
 * An application that uses a SAX parser should call this
 * method upon receiving a <code>characters</code> event.
 */
public void characters(String s, Object target) {
}
```

```
/**
 * An application that uses a SAX parser should call this
 * method upon receiving a <code>startElement</code> event.
 */
public void startElement(Object target) {
}
}
```

This class does nothing in either of its methods, which allows subclasses to override only the methods they need to apply. You can write a `Helper` subclass and register it for each kind of interesting event, such as finding a new coffee description or finding that coffee's name.

For example, here is the code to register when you see a new coffee description:

```
package sjm.examples.coffee;

import java.util.*;

/**
 * This helper adds a new coffee object to the end of
 * a vector of coffees.
 */
public class NewCoffeeHelper extends Helper {
/**
 * Add a new coffee object to the end of a vector of coffees.
 */
public void startElement(Object target) {
    Vector v = (Vector) target;
    v.addElement(new Coffee());
}
}
```

Other helpers set the attributes of a target `Coffee` object. For example, this helper sets the coffee's name.

```
package sjm.examples.coffee;

import java.util.*;

/**
 * This helper sets a target coffee object's <code>name
 * </code> attribute.
 */
public class NameHelper extends Helper {

/**
 * Sets a target coffee object's <code>name</code>
 * attribute to the given string. The target coffee is
 * the last coffee in a Vector of coffees.
 */
```

```
public void characters(String s, Object target) {
    Coffee c = (Coffee) ((Vector) target).lastElement();
    c.setName(s);
}
}
```

Subclasses similar to NameHelper set a coffee's former name, roast, country, price, and alsoOfferFrench attribute.

5.9.1 ShowCoffeeXML

This class uses a SAX parser from the Apache organization, which received some of its XML code from IBM. The class registers itself as the handler of SAX events, but then it delegates these events to appropriate Helper objects. The class uses a hashtable to look up which helper to use, depending on which element the SAX parser sees.

```
package sjm.examples.coffee;

import java.util.*;
import org.xml.sax.*;
import org.xml.sax.helpers.DefaultHandler;
import org.apache.xerces.parsers.SAXParser;

/**
 * Show the recognition of a list of types of coffee,
 * reading from an XML file....
 */
public class ShowCoffeeXML extends DefaultHandler {
    protected Hashtable helpers;
    protected Helper helper;
    protected Vector coffees = new Vector();

/*
 * Returns the lookup table that tells which helper to
 * use for which element.
 */
protected Hashtable helpers() {
    if (helpers == null) {
        helpers = new Hashtable();
        helpers.put("coffee", new NewCoffeeHelper());
        helpers.put("name", new NameHelper());
        helpers.put("formerName", new FormerNameHelper());
        helpers.put("roast", new RoastHelper());
        helpers.put("orFrench", new OrFrenchHelper());
        helpers.put("country", new CountryHelper());
        helpers.put("price", new PriceHelper());
    }
    return helpers;
}
```

```java
/**
 * Receive notification of the start of an element.
 *
 * <p>If the <code>helpers</code> hashtable has a key
 * for the given element name, then inform the helper that
 * this element has appeared.</p>
 */
public void startElement(
    String uri, String local, String raw, Attributes atts) {

    helper = (Helper) helpers().get(raw);
    if (helper != null) {
        helper.startElement(coffees);
    }
}


/**
 * Receive notification of character data inside an element.
 * If there is a helper ready to go, ask the helper to
 * process these characters.
 */
public void characters(char ch[], int start, int len) {
    if (helper != null) {
        helper.characters(
            new String(ch, start, len), coffees);
    }
}


/**
 * Receive notification of the end of an element, which
 * means that no helper should be active.
 */
public void endElement(
    String uri, String localName, String rawName) {

    helper = null;
}


/**
 * Show how to recognize coffees in an XML file.
 */
public static void main(String argv[]) throws Exception {
    SAXParser parser = new SAXParser();
    ShowCoffeeXML x = new ShowCoffeeXML();
    parser.setContentHandler(x);
    parser.setErrorHandler(x);
    parser.parse("coffee.xml");

    Enumeration e = x.coffees.elements();
    while (e.hasMoreElements()) {
        Coffee c = (Coffee) e.nextElement();
        System.out.println(c);
    }
}
}
```

The ShowCoffeeXML extends DefaultHandler, a class in org.xml.sax.helpers that implements the ContentHandler and ErrorHandler interfaces from org.xml.sax. By subclassing DefaultHandler, ShowCoffeeXML makes itself an acceptable argument to the SAX parser's setContentHandler() and setErrorHandler() methods. The main() method creates an instance of the ShowCoffeeXML class and registers this object to receive parsing events.

When the parser sees a new element, it calls the ShowCoffeeXML object's startElement() method and indicates which element it saw. For example, when the parser encounters a <roast> tag, it calls startElement() and includes the parameter roast. This method, as ShowCoffeeXML implements it, establishes a RoastHelper object as the helper to handle the forthcoming data. When the parser sees the data between tags, it calls the characters() method. This method passes the data to the established helper object, which uses the data to help build a target coffee object.

Running this class prints the following:

```
Brimful, Regular, Kenya, 6.95
Caress(Smackin), French, Sumatra, 7.95
Fragrant Delicto, Regular/French, Peru, 9.95
Havalavajava, Regular, Hawaii, 11.95
Launch Mi, French, Kenya, 6.95
Roman Spur(Revit), Italian, Guatemala, 7.95
Simplicity House, Regular/French, Colombia, 5.95
```

This is exactly the same result as before, but note that you did not write a parser. Rather, you used an existing parser, augmented with helper classes.

5.10 Summary

The acceptance of XML as a standard is on the rise. If you offer to pass data to another division or another company, the receiving information technology group can hardly say no to a request to encode the data in XML. On the other hand, the integration of XML and Java is still primitive at the time of this writing. The two main approaches—SAX and DOM—both have drawbacks.

If you read coffee data into DOM, for example, a coffee is a node that has roast as a node that has french as a node. All these nodes have equal status as nodes in the tree. But in Java, there are fundamental differences between these types of information. A coffee is an *object* with roast as an *attribute* and french as this attribute's *value*. The proper translation from nodes to objects, attributes, and values is the developer's responsibility. Assembling objects from DOM trees is extra work for developers, fraught with opportunities for introducing defects. By the time you read this, the

DOM approach may have yielded to schema-oriented approaches that tighten the connection between XML and Java.

The SAX approach to XML lets you plug behavior in to the parser's recognition process. However, the *S* in SAX stands for *Simple*, and the programming interface to SAX parsers is limited. You can receive notification of the two basic events—recognizing an element or recognizing text—but you cannot, for example, tie a specific behavior to recognizing a `<roast>` parameter.

By comparison, writing your own parser gives you more control but also more of a maintenance burden. Once you build a parser and your business comes to rely on it, someone will have to keep it running even as business conditions change. If you create a new language, you may also find that other departments or businesses cannot read in your data. You can assume that any information technology department can handle XML, but you cannot assume that any information technology department can write a parser.

There are, nonetheless, several reasons for creating a parser for a data language. First, if the language already exists, as in the coffee marketing example, and you cannot change it, you must write some kind of parser from scratch. Another constraint is that XML is clearly limited to markup languages. If you do not want markup tags in your language, XML is not the answer. A final motivation for writing your own parser is that climbing the learning curve for creating data languages will prepare you for building more-advanced parsers. Developing expertise at creating new languages from sequence, alternation, repetition, and terminal objects is a gateway to a world of languages that lie beyond markup.

CHAPTER 6

Transforming a Grammar

This chapter explains how to ensure the correct behavior of operators in a language. You'll also learn how to avoid looping in a parser, which can follow from loops in a grammar.

6.1 The Role of Grammar Transformation

Many simple languages, including most data languages, avoid the subtleties of grammar design by not introducing operators. Operators such as "+" and "-" bring up the question of whether

        11 + 5 * 2

should equal 32 or 21. Different languages, notably Smalltalk and Java, have different answers to this question, depending on the *precedence* of operators. Another question that arithmetic encounters is whether

        25 - 16 - 9

equals 0 or 18. Here the answer depends on the *associativity* of the "-" operator, which determines whether the rightmost or leftmost operator applies first. The grammar for your language determines the associativity and precedence of operators in your language.

In addition to establishing operator precedence and associativity, a grammar can contain *loops*. There is nothing wrong with a grammar that has loops, but translating such a grammar to code can result in code that contains infinite loops. In particular, a grammar rule that refers to itself with its leftmost element will cause a loop when you translate the grammar to code. In addition, if a grammar contains cyclic definitions, implementing the grammar as a parser class can cause looping in the code.

This chapter shows how to transform a grammar to attain the following objectives:

1. Ensure correct associativity.

2. Eliminate left recursion.

3. Ensure correct precedence.

4. Eliminate parser class loops.

6.2 Ensuring Correct Associativity

A convention that arises especially in arithmetic relates to associativity. Conventionally, multiplication, division, addition, and subtraction "associate" to the left. A parser must evaluate the leftmost operation first for operations of the same precedence. For example,

```
System.out.println(25 - 16 - 9);
```

prints 0. If Java calculated the rightmost subtraction first, the answer would instead be 18.

Exponentiation, on the other hand, conventionally associates *to the right*. Associating to the right means that a parser must evaluate the rightmost exponentiation first. Thus, 5^3^2 is equal to 5^9, or 1953125. If exponentiation associated to the left, like subtraction, then 5^3^2 would equal 125^2, or 15625. Java sidesteps the particular point of power precedence by not offering an exponentiation operator. However, in Java the assignment operator "=" and all assignment-with-operation operators, such as "*=", associate to the right, as does the conditional operator "?=". *Java in a Nutshell* [Flanagan] discusses all of Java's operators.

Chapter 3, "Building a Parser," uses the reduced arithmetic language Minimath to show where assemblers plug in to a parser. This little language also serves to show associativity problems that can arise in a grammar. Minimath contains arithmetic expressions that contain only the minus operator. For example, Minimath contains

```
{"0.0",
 "1.2 - 2.3",
 "100 - 90 - 80 - 70",
 "47 - 43 - 41", ...}
```

The following grammar describes this language.

```
// Grammar G1

e = Num '-' e | Num; // suffers from incorrect associativity!
```

Let's call this grammar G1. G1 describes all the elements of Minimath, but G1 is problematic because of associativity. For example, consider how this grammar will portray the string "25 - 16 - 9". Conventionally, this string is equal to "(25 - 16) - 9". This convention means that subtraction associates to the left; in other words, the leftmost subtraction should happen first. However, G1 matches this string as "Num - e", or "25 - e". This guides a parser for G1 to calculate the value of e and subtract it from 25, and that gives an incorrect result. Here is an implementation of G1:

```java
package sjm.examples.minimath;

import sjm.parse.*;
import sjm.parse.tokens.*;
import sjm.examples.arithmetic.*;

/**
 * This class uses a problematic grammar for Minimath. For
 * a better grammar, see class <code>MinimathCompute</code>.
 * Here, the grammar is:
 *
 * <blockquote><pre>
 *     e = Num '-' e | Num;
 * </pre></blockquote>
 *
 * Writing a parser directly from this grammar will show
 * that the associativity is wrong. For example, this
 * grammar will lead to a parser that calculates the value
 * of 25 - 16 - 9 as 18.
 */
public class MiniWrongAssociativity {

/**
 * Demonstrates incorrect associativity.
 */
public static void main(String args[]) {
    Alternation e = new Alternation();
    Num n = new Num();
    n.setAssembler(new NumAssembler());

    Sequence s = new Sequence();
    s.add(n);
    s.add(new Symbol('-').discard());
    s.add(e);
    s.setAssembler(new MinusAssembler());

    e.add(s);
    e.add(n);

    Assembly out = e.completeMatch(
        new TokenAssembly("25 - 16 - 9"));

    System.out.println(out.pop() + " // arguably wrong!");
}
}
```

This class uses assemblers from `sjm.examples.arithmetic` to show the results that the grammar leads to. This class prints

```
18.0 // arguably wrong!
```

To get conventional associativity, you really want this grammar:

```
// Grammar G2

e = e '-' Num | Num; // suffers from left recursion!
```

This grammar has a new problem, namely left recursion, that the next section addresses. It turns out that you can transform a grammar to avoid left recursion. It is important to fix associativity first because transformation to avoid left recursion does not alter the grammar's associativity.

Getting the desirable associativity depends on whether an operator should associate to the right or the left. If a rule needs right association for an operator, then you should write the grammar so that it will first match the rightmost operator in a sequence of like operators. For example, exponentiation should associate to the right; "2 ∧ 1 ∧ 4" should equal "2 ∧ 1". To achieve this effect, write the grammar as follows:

```
// Grammar G3
e = Num '∧' e | Num;
```

This grammar matches "2 ∧ 1 ∧ 4" as "2 ∧ e", which is correct. The conventional value of this string is 2∧e, where e is the value of 1∧4.

In short, you can use G2 as a template for achieving left associativity in a rule, and G3 as a template for achieving right associativity. Once the associativity of your language is correct, you need to check it for left recursion.

6.3 Eliminating Left Recursion

Grammar G2 in the preceding section describes the Minimath language, but it translates to code that will not work. Once again, the grammar is

```
// Grammar G2

e = e '-' Num | Num; // suffers from left recursion!
```

The problem with G2 is that e depends directly on e. When e tries to parse text, it starts by trying its first alternative. Thus, trying e means trying e, which means trying e.... This loops indefinitely.

It does not help to reverse the alternation, writing

```
// Grammar G2b

e = Num | e '-' Num; // suffers too!
```

Here, when e tries its second alternative, it will try to match e, which has two alternatives. When e matches its second alternative, it will try to match e again. This cycling continues until the Java virtual machine runs out of stack space. In other words, it loops indefinitely. For example, compiling and running the following class will hang or crash, depending on your compiler and virtual machine implementation:

```java
package sjm.examples.minimath;

import sjm.parse.*;
import sjm.parse.tokens.*;

/**
 * This class uses a problematic grammar for Minimath. For
 * a better grammar, see class <code>MinimathCompute</code>.
 * Here, the grammar is:
 *
 * <blockquote><pre>
 *     e = Num | e '-' Num;
 * </pre></blockquote>
 *
 * Writing a parser directly from this grammar will show
 * that left recursion will hang a parser.
 */
public class MiniLeftRecursion {

public static void main(String args[]) {
    Alternation e = new Alternation();
    Num n = new Num();

    Sequence s = new Sequence();
    s.add(e);
    s.add(new Symbol('-').discard());
    s.add(n);

    e.add(n);
    e.add(s);

    // now hang (or crash)
    e.completeMatch(new TokenAssembly("25 - 16 - 9"));
}
}
```

It may be tempting to "fix" the grammar by switching the parsers around the minus sign, giving

```
e = Num - e | Num; // suffers from incorrect associativity!
```

This grammar for Minimath is insufficient because it subtracts numbers in the wrong order. You must eliminate left recursion without discarding the proper associativity of a grammar.

To solve the problem of left recursion, it helps to think of the grammar as *generating* the language rather than recognizing it. For example, given an e in grammar G2, you can generate e - Num. If you use the symbol "=>" to mean "generates," you can apply G2 to write

    e => e - Num => e - Num - Num => e - Num - Num - Num - Num

This series of generations applies the e - Num side of the alternation in grammar G2. You can ultimately apply the other side, namely that e = Num, to get

    e => … => e - Num - Num - Num - Num
         => Num - Num - Num - Num - Num

By looking at the way e generates language elements, it becomes apparent that you could write the grammar as

    e = Num ('-' Num)*;

Equivalently, you can write this as

    e = Num m*;
    m = '-' Num;

This arrives at the first grammar we used for Minimath. This grammar avoids left recursion, and it associates the subtraction in the right order. The class MinimathCompute uses a translation of this grammar, augmenting it with assemblers to generate a correct Minimath result:

```
package sjm.examples.minimath;

import sjm.parse.*;
import sjm.parse.tokens.*;
import sjm.examples.arithmetic.*;
/**
 * This class provides a parser that recognizes minimal
 * arithmetic expressions, specifically allowing only the
 * '-' operator. The rules of the Minimath language are:
 *
 * <blockquote><pre>
 *     e = Num m*;
 *     m = '-' Num;
 * </pre></blockquote>
 *
```

```
 *  ...
 */

public class MinimathCompute {

public static void main(String args[]) {
    Sequence e = new Sequence();

    Num n = new Num();
    n.setAssembler(new NumAssembler());

    e.add(n);

    Sequence m = new Sequence();
    m.add(new Symbol('-').discard());
    m.add(n);
    m.setAssembler(new MinusAssembler());

    e.add(new Repetition(m));

    TokenAssembly t = new TokenAssembly("25 - 16 - 9");
    Assembly out = e.completeMatch(t);
    System.out.println(out.pop());
    }
}
```

Running this class prints the conventional value of 25 - 16 - 9:

```
0.0
```

6.3.1 An Algorithm

You can always eliminate left recursion without changing associativity when you have a grammar of this form:

```
e = e f | g; // Grammar with left recursion
```

Such a grammar suffers from left recursion, but clearly its meaning is, "Substitute e f for e as many times as you like; then substitute g for e." For example:

```
e => e f => e f f => e f f f => e f f f f => g f f f f
```

You can achieve this same pattern with this grammar:

```
e = g f*; // Equivalent grammar without left recursion
```

If your grammar suffers from left recursion, use these steps to transform it to an equivalent grammar that does not have left recursion. This algorithm works with most left-recursive grammars encountered in practice. If, however, your grammar suffers from *indirect* left recursion, you need a more advanced algorithm. See *Compilers* [Aho et al.] for an algorithm that works with any grammar.

6.4 Ensuring Proper Precedence

Proper precedence means that some operators in a language should evaluate before others. In regular expression languages, for example, sequence usually has a higher precedence than alternation. In arithmetic, convention gives multiplication and division a higher precedence than addition and subtraction. In Java,

```
System.out.println(11 + 5 * 2);
```

prints "21". Java recognizes that multiplication has higher precedence, so it computes 5 times 2 before adding this product to 11. The idea that multiplication should proceed before addition is a convention and not a law of the universe. The designers of the Smalltalk programming language gave up traditional arithmetic precedence in order to preserve a simple and consistent messaging model. Smalltalk ignores arithmetic operator precedence, so

```
11 + 5 * 2
```

is equal to 32 and not 21. As a language designer, you make the rules for your language, but you may confuse the users of your language if you ignore convention. To ensure that your parser will recognize some operators before others, you can declare this precedence in your grammar.

For example, consider an arithmetic subset that allows only the "+" operator and the "*" operator. Let us call this language Midimath. The challenge is to design a grammar that forces multiplication to come first. You can begin writing a grammar for this language by writing something like this:

```
expression = term '+' term | term;
```

The idea is that you can declare that there is some subparser "term" that recognizes, in particular, any text that contains an "*" sign. That is, you are declaring that you will recognize addition only after any multiplications are done. For example, expression can see "1 * 2 + 3 * 4" only as "term + term". By declaring in the grammar that expression cannot comprehend an "*", you are declaring that addition must go last.

One problem with this definition of expression is that the definition does not allow multiple plus signs. To fix that, you write the definition as

```
expression = expression '+' term | term;
```

This definition allows an unbounded number of plus signs and ensures that addition will associate to the left, but it introduces left recursion. You can repair that using the principles of the preceding section, resulting in:

```
expression = term ('+' term)*;
```

Now you need to provide a definition of term. A parser for term will match any mathematical expression that contains only numbers and the "*" operator. An initial definition for term is

```
term = term '*' Num | Num;
```

This definition matches the correct sublanguage and sets the associativity of "*" to the left, but it introduces left recursion. You can transform this definition into

```
term = Num ('*' Num)*;
```

So a complete grammar for Midimath is as follows:

```
expression = term ('+' term)*;
term       = Num ('*' Num)*;
```

This grammar is close to a complete language for arithmetic, which is explored in Chapter 7 "Parsing Arithmetic." Before developing a complete arithmetic parser, however, you must be able to handle grammar cycles.

6.5 Eliminating Parser Class Loops

You can write the code for the Midimath parser by creating a method for each grammar definition. This approach helps organize the code, but it introduces the prospect of looping during the construction of the parsers. Translating a grammar to a parser class creates a definition loop if the grammar contains a cycle. For example, you might extend Midimath to allow parentheses:

```
expression = term ('+' term)*;
term       = factor ('*' factor)*;
factor     = '(' expression ')' | Num;
```

This grammar allows an expression such as "(7 + 13) * 5" to use parentheses to control precedence. Using this grammar to build a parser creates a cycle: Building `expression` requires building `term`, which requires building `factor`, which requires building `expression`. The way to avoid this looping is to create a variable for at least one subparser that is involved in each cycle of the grammar. In this example, you can declare `expression` as an instance variable and then *lazy-initialize* it. This means the code leaves the instance variable null until its first use, as follows:

```
public Parser expression() {
    if (expression == null) {
        expression = new Sequence();

        Sequence plusTerm = new Sequence();
        plusTerm.add(new Symbol('+').discard());
        plusTerm.add(term());
        plusTerm.setAssembler(new PlusAssembler());

        expression.add(term());
        expression.add(new Repetition(plusTerm));
    }
    return expression;
}
```

It is still the case that `expression()` calls `term()`, which calls `factor()`, which calls `expression()`. However, the first time `expression()` runs, the instance variable `expression` is null. The code in `expression()` immediately changes this, giving `expression` the value of an empty Sequence. When the method refers to `term()`, it results in a call to `factor()` and a call back to `expression()`. On this call, the instance variable `expression` is no longer empty; rather, it is a partially constructed Sequence. So `expression()` returns with no problem, `term()` and `factor()` return, and the first call to `expression()` returns.

If a grammar has more than one cycle, each cycle must have at least one subparser that breaks the looping of the definitions. One way to ensure that your parser class does not encounter loops as it builds its subparsers is to create an instance variable for each subparser and lazy-initialize each of these variables, as in `expression()` earlier. On the other hand, you may want to create a minimal number of variables and just test that your class does not loop. The difference in these approaches is primarily esthetic.

6.6 Summary

A grammar establishes the pattern of strings that make up a language. You can think of a grammar running forward, generating strings, or running backward, recognizing strings. Equivalent grammars may recognize the same strings in different orders.

This means that you can use a grammar to specify the order in which to recognize operators, and that in turn lets you control precedence and associativity.

Once you have a grammar that recognizes the strings of your language in the right order, you must consider potential infinite loops when you implement the grammar with a parser. You can remove left recursion in the grammar by transforming it to an equivalent grammar that recognizes the same strings in the same order, but without using left recursion. After removing left recursion, you must manage the presence of cycles in the grammar, initializing variables to avoid cyclic definitions in a parser's code.

CHAPTER 7

Parsing Arithmetic

This chapter explains how to build an arithmetic parser. Arithmetic parsers usually appear as part of larger parsers for richer languages. In particular, query languages, logic languages, and imperative languages frequently contain arithmetic features. By learning to write an arithmetic parser, you can add arithmetic to your own languages. This chapter explains the principles behind proper and conventional parsing of arithmetic.

7.1 Building an Arithmetic Parser

Some of the rules of arithmetic are so familiar that it is hard to imagine an alternative, and others are subtle enough that you may not have thought about them. However, the subtle rules of arithmetic are important, and your user may know them and rely on them.

7.1.1 Conventional Symbols

The most obvious convention for arithmetic is the meaning of the symbols for addition, subtraction, multiplication, and division. Addition and subtraction almost always appear as "+" and "-". Multiplication varies a little more but most often appears as "*". One alternative for division is the symbol "÷", although this is giving way to the more popular "/", which appears on most keyboards. Symbols for exponentiation include "**", "↑", and "^". As a language developer, you have the choice of using whatever symbols you want to represent arithmetic operations. The remainder of this chapter uses the symbols "+", "-", "*", "/", and "^".

7.1.2 Conventional Precedence

Regardless of which operators you include in a language for arithmetic, parentheses always take the highest precedence. After parentheses, exponentiation, or "powers," have the highest precedence, followed by multiplication and division, and then addition and subtraction. For example, a parser must evaluate

```
(5 + 4) * 3 ^ 2 - 81
```

as 0.

7.1.3 Conventional Associativity

Multiplication and division have the same precedence, so a question arises about the order in which to apply the operators if they occur in succession. The conventional answer is to apply the operators left to right. For example,

```
35 / 7 * 3 / 15
```

should equal 1, the result of dividing 35 by 7, multiplying by 3, and dividing by 15. Applying operators in this order means that they "associate" to the left. Similarly, addition and subtraction have the same precedence as each other, and they also associate to the left. Exponentiation, on the other hand, associates to the right.

A grammar can recognize proper precedence and associativity and adopt a conventional set of symbols. If it does, an arithmetic parser follows almost directly from its grammar. The tasks for building the parser are as follows:

- Write a grammar.
- Write assemblers to build an arithmetic result.
- Generate the parser from the grammar, plugging in the assemblers.

7.2 An Arithmetic Grammar

To observe four levels of precedence, an arithmetic grammar needs to have four subparsers. Each of these subparsers handles operators of a common precedence, delegating interpretation of other operators to other subparsers. You can use the words expression, term, factor, and phrase to denote the four subparsers.

To begin, you can define expression as observing the lowest level of precedence.

```
expression = expression '+' term |
             expression '-' term |
             term;
```

This rule suffers from left recursion, but it properly recognizes all pluses and minuses to the left of a term before adding or subtracting the term. To remove the left recursion, it helps to abbreviate the rule

```
e = e '+' t | e '-' t | t;
```

and look at what an e might generate. For example:

```
e => e '+' t

   => e '-' t '+' t
   => e '+' t '-' t '+' t
   ...
   => e ('+' t | '-' t)*
   => t ('+' t | '-' t)*
```

As a pattern, e generates another e followed by 0 or more ('+' t) or ('-' t) sequences, until you generate a plain t, using the third alternate choice for e. You can describe this same pattern, avoiding left recursion, as

```
e = t ('+' t | '-' t)*;
```

Or, unabbreviated:

```
expression = term ('+' term | '-' term)*;
```

Using the same logic, you can define term to recognize multiplication and division as follows:

```
term = factor ('*' factor | '/' factor)*;
```

To recognize exponents, associating them to the right, you can define factor as

```
factor = phrase '^' factor | phrase;
```

Notice that this definition requires exponentiation of phrase to occur only after recognition of the factor to the right of the exponent sign. Thus, if a factor contains another exponent sign, the definition calls for a parser to recognize it first, and exponentiation associates to the right. There is no left recursion to remove in this rule, so it is fine as written.

The last rule the grammar needs is for phrase, which defines the highest level of precedence:

```
phrase = '(' expression ')' | Num;
```

Putting the rules together, the grammar is

```
expression = term ('+' term | '-' term)*;
term       = factor ('*' factor | '/' factor)*;
factor     = phrase '^' factor | phrase;
phrase     = '(' expression ')' | Num;
```

This grammar recognizes properly formed arithmetic expressions. The next step in designing an arithmetic parser is to determine how to use assemblers to evaluate expressions as the parser recognizes them.

7.3 Arithmetic Assemblers

An arithmetic parser has no need of a target because you can accumulate a result of recognizing an assembly by working on the assembly's stack. The key design idea, then, is to produce the right number on an assembly's stack.

First, when the parser sees a number with Num, the Num terminal places a token on the stack. The arithmetic parser must replace this token with its Double value, and to perform this task it needs an assembler. The parser also needs an assembler for each of the five operators. For example, after seeing ('+' term), the parser must perform an addition. To see where assemblers plug in to subparsers, it helps to write each operator on a separate line, as follows:

```
expression    = term (plusTerm | minusTerm)*;
term          = factor (timesFactor | divideFactor)*;
plusTerm      = '+' term;
minusTerm     = '-' term;
factor        = phrase expFactor | phrase;
timesFactor   = '*' factor;
divideFactor  = '/' factor;
expFactor     = '^' factor;
phrase        = '(' expression ')' | Num;
```

The plusTerm parser must pop two terms and push their sum. The minusTerm parser must pop two terms and push their difference. Similarly, timesFactor, divideFactor, and expFactor must pop two terms and push their product, quotient, or exponentiation, respectively. Figure 7.1 shows the assembler classes that ArithmeticParser uses as it builds a value.

Figure 7.2 shows where the assemblers plug in to the subparsers of the ArithmeticParser class.

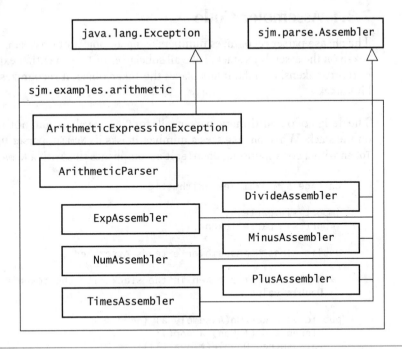

Figure 7.1 The arithmetic package. This package contains classes that collaborate to create an arithmetic value from text.

Parser	Assembler
plusTerm()	PlusAssembler()
minusTerm()	MinusAssembler()
timesFactor()	TimesAssembler()
divideFactor()	DivideAssembler()
expFactor()	ExpAssembler()
Num object in phrase()	NumAssembler()

Figure 7.2 Arithmetic parser assembler placement. This table shows the assembler that each arithmetic subparser employs.

7.3.1 Assembler Code

The phrase parser recognizes numbers using an object of class Num, which places a Token on the assembly's stack. Like all subclasses of Terminal that expect an assembly to return tokens, by default Num places the Token object it recognizes onto the assembly's stack.

The design of our arithmetic parser calls for Double values, and not Tokens, to appear on the stack. When phrase sees a number, it asks its Num subparser to replace the Token with a corresponding Double. It accomplishes this with a NumAssembler:

```
package sjm.examples.arithmetic;

import sjm.parse.*;
import sjm.parse.tokens.*;

public class NumAssembler extends Assembler {
/**
 * Replace the top token in the stack with the token's
 * Double value.
 */
public void workOn(Assembly a) {
    Token t = (Token) a.pop();
    a.push(new Double(t.nval()));
}
}
```

The remaining assemblers plug in after seeing an operator and a term or factor. These assemblers can assume that there are two numbers on the stack. For example, from the grammar rules the parser knows that the first time it recognizes a plusTerm, a term has immediately preceded it. Both the value of the preceding term and the value of the term in plusTerm will be on the stack. The job of PlusAssembler is to replace these values with their sum. Here is the code for PlusAssembler:

```
package sjm.examples.arithmetic;

import sjm.parse.*;

public class PlusAssembler extends Assembler {
/**
 * Pop two numbers from the stack and push their sum.
 */
public void workOn(Assembly a) {
    Double d1 = (Double) a.pop();
    Double d2 = (Double) a.pop();
    Double d3 =
        new Double(d2.doubleValue() + d1.doubleValue());
    a.push(d3);
}
}
```

The implementations of workOn() in classes MinusAssembler, TimesAssembler, DivideAssembler, and ExpAssembler differ only in which operator they apply to the two numbers on the stack.

7.4 An Arithmetic Grammar Parser

You can create an arithmetic parser by translating the arithmetic grammar into a parser class and plugging in the assemblers. Section 3.6, "Translating a Grammar to Code," gives a set of rules for creating a parser from a grammar. The only remaining problem is to prevent looping in the subparser definitions.

Section 6.5, "Eliminating Parser Class Loops," explains how to address loops in a grammar. The arithmetic grammar has two cycles.

```
expression    = term (plusTerm | minusTerm)*;
term          = factor (timesFactor | divideFactor)*;
plusTerm      = '+' term;
minusTerm     = '-' term;
factor        = phrase expFactor | phrase;
timesFactor   = '*' factor;
divideFactor  = '/' factor;
expFactor     = '^' factor;
phrase        = '(' expression ')' | Num;
```

One cycle is in factor. This definition depends on expFactor, which depends on factor. The other cycle in the grammar begins with expression. The expression rule depends on term, which depends on factor, which depends on phrase, which depends on expression. To avoid loops in the code, use instance variables to hold the expression and factor parsers. Figure 7.3 shows the ArithmeticParser class.

To use this class, you can apply the parser ArithmeticParser.start() to match a token assembly. Alternatively, you can use this class's value() method, which takes a String and returns a double value. The following class shows this approach:

```
package sjm.examples.arithmetic;

/**
 * Show how to use the <code>ArithmeticParser</code> class.
 */

public class ShowArithmeticParser {
/*
 * Help out the main() method.
 */
```

```
        ArithmeticParser
─────────────────────────────────
#expression:Sequence
#factor:Sequence
─────────────────────────────────
+start():Parser
+expression():Parser
#term():Parser
#plusTerm():Parser
#minusTerm():Parser
#factor():Parser
#timesFactor():Parser
#divideFactor():Parser
#expFactor():Parser
+value(s:String):double
```

Figure 7.3 The `ArithmeticParser` class. This class holds a collection of methods that can be composed into a parser for arithmetic.

```java
private static void eval(String s, double d)
    throws ArithmeticExpressionException {

    System.out.println(
        "Given: "    + s +
        " Expected: " + d +
        "\tFound: "   + ArithmeticParser.value(s));
}

/**
 * Show a few examples of arithmetic.
 */
public static void main(String args[])
    throws ArithmeticExpressionException {

    eval("9^2 - 81      ",   0); // exponentiation
    eval("7 - 3 - 1     ",   3); // minus associativity
    eval("2 ^ 1 ^ 4     ",   2); // exp associativity
    eval("100 - 25*3    ",  25); // precedence
    eval("100 - 5^2*3   ",  25); // precedence
    eval("(100 - 5^2) * 3", 225); // parentheses
}
}
```

Running this class prints the following:

```
Given: 9^2 - 81      Expected: 0.0    Found: 0.0
Given: 7 - 3 - 1     Expected: 3.0    Found: 3.0
Given: 2 ^ 1 ^ 4     Expected: 2.0    Found: 2.0
Given: 100 - 25*3    Expected: 25.0   Found: 25.0
Given: 100 - 5^2*3   Expected: 25.0   Found: 25.0
Given: (100 - 5^2) * 3 Expected: 225.0 Found: 225.0
```

The display shows various expected results that demonstrate associativity, precedence, and the use of parentheses.

7.5 Summary

You may never need a parser that recognizes only arithmetic, but you will likely create parsers that include arithmetic features. Each of the larger languages that lie ahead in this book uses some form of arithmetic. There is potential for reusing the parser objects that the ArithmeticParser class offers, but larger languages usually need assemblers that are unique to the purpose the language serves.

CHAPTER 8

Parsing Regular Expressions

This chapter shows how to build a regular expression parser. A regular expression lets a user describe a pattern of text.

8.1 The Role of Regular Expressions

Regular expressions appear frequently in support of user interfaces. For example, a user might want to see all the files that end with ".txt" or all the books whose titles include "Java" and "Parsers". When you allow a user to specify such a pattern, you are using regular expressions to let the user create a new little language. You might decide, for example, to allow your user to use a tilde to mean zero or more characters. If your user types "~.txt", he or she is defining the language of all strings that end with ".txt".

The tools you provide your user for matching are a metalanguage, a language for defining new languages. Typically, developers provide users with symbols such as "~" and "|" to indicate which patterns of text the user is interested in. These symbols are the terminals in the metalanguage the developer provides. The user specifies a new language (a new set of strings) by typing text that uses the metalanguage symbols.

Because the user who specifies a pattern is specifying a new language, your code must take the user's text and parse it. This is the parser you write in advance of prompting your user. Your parser will take the user's input and create a new parser to recognize the language your user specifies. For example, you might write a parser to recognize patterns of book titles. When your user enters the string "Java | Parsers", your parser will recognize the two words and the vertical bar. Your parser then must build a *new* parser to recognize the language (or set of strings) that the user is specifying. You take the user's input, build a new parser, and then apply this to the books in your database to see which titles lie within this new, fleeting, little language.

The result of matching a parser against an input string is an object that is based on the parser's recognition of the string. For example, a parser for a coffee markup language will return a new `Coffee` object that reflects the description the parser recognizes in a markup string. In the case of a metalanguage, the object your parser returns is a new parser.

8.2 Building a Regular Expression Parser

Metalanguages that allow a user to specify character patterns, using symbols such as "|" and "~", are typically called *regular expressions*. There is no standard for which symbols belong in this type of metalanguage, although the language Perl is probably the most ambitious matcher of regular expressions. In the expression language you provide to your user, you have complete freedom in the symbols you provide and the meaning you assign to those symbols.

This section shows how to create a basic regular expression recognizer. This metalanguage will allow "|" to mean alternation, "*" to mean repetition, and simple juxtaposition (or "nextness") to mean sequence. Individual characters such as a and b simply stand for themselves. For example, a* means zero or more a characters.

You can certainly extend this metalanguage. For example, you might want to allow 9 to mean any digit, so that "(999)999-9999" would match most U.S. phone numbers. How you craft your metalanguage depends on what patterns you want to provide your user.

To build a simple regular expression parser, you need only three types of terminal: `Letter`, `Digit`, and `SpecificChar`. The `Letter` class matches any single letter; `Digit` matches any character from 0 to 9. `SpecificChar` matches a specified character. Figure 8.1 shows these classes, along with `Char`, which is not needed in this section. The subclasses of `Terminal` in Figure 8.1 are members of the package `sjm.parse.chars`.

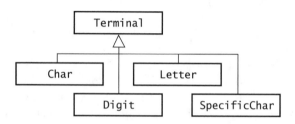

Figure 8.1 Character terminals. Shown here are subclasses of `Terminal` that work with `CharacterAssembly` objects.

The aim of a regular expression parser is to create a new parser. For example, given a*, your parser first recognizes the a and creates a parser that recognizes only the language {a}. Then your parser recognizes the "*" and creates a `Repetition` parser, passing it the a parser. This parser matches {"", "a", "aa", ...}. As another example, given the string "(a|b)*Z", you want to create a parser that will match any string that starts with as and bs and ends with Z.

The tasks for building a regular expression parser are as follows:

- Write a grammar.

- Write the assemblers that will build a parser from a user's input.

- Generate the parser from the grammar, plugging in the assemblers.

8.3 A Regular Expression Grammar

A modestly ambitious regular expression language allows the user to express sequences, alternations, and repetitions of characters. The following grammar is based on rules given in *Introduction to Automata Theory, Languages and Computation* [Hopcroft and Ullman]. The rules recognize conventional operator precedence, and they avoid the problem of left recursion.

```
expression    = term ('|' term)*;
term          = factor factor*;
factor        = phrase | (phrase '*');
phrase        = letterOrDigit | '(' expression ')';
letterOrDigit = Letter | Digit;
```

Note that there is a major difference between the meaning of a vertical bar by itself and a vertical bar in single quotes. There is also a major difference between an asterisk and an asterisk in single quotes. A character in single quotes means that the quoted character must appear in text that the grammar is matching. Without these quotes, a vertical bar means alternation, and an asterisk means repetition.

The function of the `term` rule would be more apparent if you required an ampersand, say, to mean sequence. Then, instead of typing the expression "ja|Ja|JA" the user would have to type "j&a|J&a|J&A". The grammar rule would appear as:

```
term = factor ('&' factor)*;
```

The given grammar follows the convention of using juxtaposition to indicate sequence. A sequence of letters such as "ja" implies a sequence to match, and no operator is necessary.

8.4 Regular Expression Assemblers

You need assemblers for each of the operators a user can specify, and an assembler to handle characters such as a and b. Figure 8.2 shows these assemblers as part of the regular package.

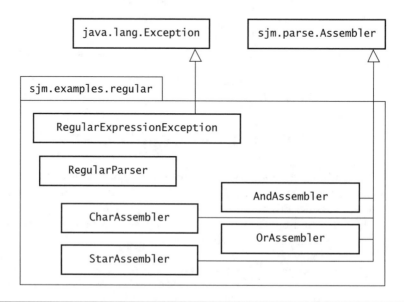

Figure 8.2 The regular expression package. This package contains classes that collaborate to create a new regular expression parser from text.

Parser	Assembler
orTerm	OrAssembler()
nextFactor	AndAssembler()
phraseStar	StarAssembler()
letterOrDigit	CharAssembler()

Figure 8.3 Regular expression assembler placement. This table shows the assembler employed by each subparser for the regular expression grammar.

You must plug in the operator assemblers where each operator appears in the grammar. To see where the assemblers belong, it helps to rewrite the grammar from this:

```
expression    = term ('|' term)*;
term          = factor factor*;
factor        = phrase | (phrase '*');
phrase        = letterOrDigit | '(' expression ')';
letterOrDigit = Letter | Digit;
```

to this:

```
expression    = term orTerm*;
term          = factor nextFactor*;
orTerm        = '|' term;
factor        = phrase | phraseStar;
nextFactor    = factor;
phrase        = letterOrDigit | '(' expression ')';
phraseStar    = phrase '*';
letterOrDigit = Letter | Digit;
```

This version of the grammar lets you specify the placement of the assemblers, as Figure 8.3 shows.

A key design principle of the regular expression parser is that each of its subparsers leaves a parser on the stack. For example, after orTerm matches, there will be two parsers on the stack: one for each of the two terms seen. The OrAssembler object pops these two parsers and pushes a new parser that is an Alternation of the parsers that were on the stack. Similarly, AndAssembly pushes a Sequence of two popped parsers, and StarAssembly pushes a repetition of one popped parser.

8.4.1 Assembler Code

Your user will supply strings such as "(a|b)*", which contain letters and the punctuation of your metalanguage. Each letter in such a string becomes a specific character that your parser will look for when it matches against a string such as "aabbaab". The Letter and Digit parsers simply stack whatever they see; that is, these terminal parsers stack Character objects. A CharAssembler object converts each such character into a SpecificChar parser. Here is the code for CharAssembler:

```
package sjm.examples.regular;

import sjm.parse.*;
import sjm.parse.chars.*;
```

```
/**
 * Pop a <code>Character</code> from the stack and push a
 * <code>SpecificChar</code> parser in its place.
 */
public class CharAssembler extends Assembler {

public void workOn(Assembly a) {
    a.push(new SpecificChar((Character) a.pop()));
}
}
```

This class expects the stack to have a Character at its top. Your parser fulfills the expectation: Whenever it sees a letter character, it stacks the character and uses CharAssembler to convert the character into a SpecificChar parser. For example, when your parser sees an a, it stacks it and then converts it into a parser that matches the character a.

When your parser sees an "*", it wants to form a repetition of whatever is at the top of the stack. The StarAssembler class performs that work.

```
package sjm.examples.regular;

import sjm.parse.*;

/**
 * Pop a parser from the stack and push a new <code>
 * Repetition</code> of it.
 */
public class StarAssembler extends Assembler {

public void workOn(Assembly a) {
    a.push(new Repetition((Parser) a.pop()));
}
}
```

When your parser sees two "factors" in sequence, it creates a Sequence of them. For example, your parser might be parsing the regular expression "(a|b)c". Your parser must place the results of parsing "(a|b)" on the stack and the results of parsing "c" on the stack first. After parsing both of these factors, your parser asks an AndAssembler to create a new sequence.

```
package sjm.examples.regular;

import sjm.parse.*;

/**
 * Pop two parsers from the stack and push a new <code>
 * Sequence</code> of them.
 */
```

```
public class AndAssembler extends Assembler {

public void workOn(Assembly a) {
    Object top = a.pop();
    Sequence s = new Sequence();
    s.add((Parser) a.pop());
    s.add((Parser) top);
    a.push(s);
}
}
```

Like AndAssembler, the OrAssembler class expects two parsers to be at the top of an assembly's stack. This class pops them, composes an Alternation of them, and pushes back the Alternation. Here is the code:

```
package sjm.examples.regular;

import sjm.parse.*;

/**
 * Pop two parsers from the stack and push a new <code>
 * Alternation</code> of them.
 */
public class OrAssembler extends Assembler {

public void workOn(Assembly a) {
    Object top = a.pop();
    Alternation alt = new Alternation();
    alt.add((Parser) a.pop());
    alt.add((Parser) top);
    a.push(alt);
}
}
```

8.5 A Regular Expression Parser

The class RegularParser holds a collection of methods that return the subparsers for a regular expression grammar. Figure 8.4 shows this class.

To use this class, you can apply RegularParser.start() to match a character assembly. As with the ArithmeticParser class, the RegularParser class provides a value() method, which simplifies using the class. The following example uses the RegularParser class's value() method to match a variety of regular expressions:

```
package sjm.examples.regular;

import sjm.parse.*;
import sjm.parse.chars.*;
```

```
                    ┌─────────────────────────────────┐
                    │          RegularParser          │
                    ├─────────────────────────────────┤
                    │ #expression:Sequence            │
                    ├─────────────────────────────────┤
                    │ +start():Parser                 │
                    │ +expression():Parser            │
                    │ #term():Parser                  │
                    │ #orTerm():Parser                │
                    │ #factor():Parser                │
                    │ #nextFactor():Parser            │
                    │ #phrase():Parser                │
                    │ #phraseStar():Parser            │
                    │ +value(s:String):Parser         │
                    └─────────────────────────────────┘
```

Figure 8.4 The RegularParser class. This class holds a collection of methods that compose into a parser for regular expressions.

```java
/**
 * Show how to use the <code>RegularParser</code> class.
 */

public class ShowRegularParser {

/*
 * Just a little help for main().
 */
private static void showMatch(Parser p, String s) {
    System.out.print(p);
    Assembly a = p.completeMatch(new CharacterAssembly(s));
    if (a != null) {
        System.out.print(" matches ");
    } else {
        System.out.print(" does not match ");
    }
    System.out.println(s);
}

public static void main(String args[])
    throws RegularExpressionException {

    // a*
    Parser aStar = RegularParser.value("a*");
    showMatch(aStar, "");
    showMatch(aStar, "a");
    showMatch(aStar, "aa");
    showMatch(aStar, "aaaaaaaaaaaaaaaaaaaaaaaaaaaaaaaaaa");
```

```
// (a|b)*
Parser abStar = RegularParser.value("(a|b)*");
showMatch(abStar, "aabbaabaabba");
showMatch(abStar, "aabbaabaabbaZ");

// a few other examples
showMatch(RegularParser.value("a*a*"), "aaaa");
showMatch(RegularParser.value("a|bc"), "bc");
showMatch(RegularParser.value("a|bc|d"), "bc");

// four letters
Parser L = new Letter();
Parser L4 =
    new Sequence("LLLL").add(L).add(L).add(L).add(L);
showMatch(L4, "java");
showMatch(L4, "joe");
showMatch(new Repetition(L), "coffee");
    }
}
```

The first example in the `main()` method is

```
// a*
Parser aStar = RegularParser.value("a*");
showMatch(aStar, "");
showMatch(aStar, "a");
showMatch(aStar, "aa");
showMatch(aStar, "aaaaaaaaaaaaaaaaaaaaaaaaaaaaaaaaa")
```

When this section of code runs, it prints the following:

```
a* matches
a* matches a
a* matches aa
a* matches aaaaaaaaaaaaaaaaaaaaaaaaaaaaaaaaa
```

This demonstrates that the parser built from "a*" will match any number of a characters. The next stretch of code is

```
// (a|b)*
Parser abStar = RegularParser.value("(a|b)*");
showMatch(abStar, "aabbaabaabba");
showMatch(abStar, "aabbaabaabbaZ");
```

When this code runs, it prints the following:

```
<a|b>* matches aabbaabaabba
<a|b>* does not match aabbaabaabbaZ
```

The parser abStar prints itself as <a|b>*. The angle brackets are part of how Alternation and Sequence objects represent themselves as strings: by showing their subparsers in angle brackets. The separator between alternative subparsers is a vertical bar, and between sequence elements is an empty string. The output shows that a parser built from "(a|b)*" matches strings of as and bs, but not if such a string ends with a Z.

The next few examples are

```
showMatch(RegularParser.value("a*a*"), "aaaa");
showMatch(RegularParser.value("a|bc"), "bc");
showMatch(RegularParser.value("a|bc|d"), "bc");
```

These examples demonstrate operator precedence, and they print the following:

```
<a*a*> matches aaaa
<a|<bc>> matches bc
<<a|<bc>>|d> matches bc
```

The last set of sample code is

```
// four letters
Parser L = new Letter();
Parser L4 =
    new Sequence("LLLL").add(L).add(L).add(L).add(L);
showMatch(L4, "java");
showMatch(L4, "joe");
showMatch(new Repetition(L), "coffee");
```

This code creates the parser L4 to match a sequence of four letters and names this parser "LLLL". When this code runs, it prints the following:

```
LLLL matches java
LLLL does not match joe
L* matches coffee
```

8.6 Summary

Regular expressions let your users define patterns of characters. Any pattern of text is a language, so regular expressions form a metalanguage—a language for defining languages. Despite the word *regular*, there is no standard for how to parse regular expressions. You can craft a regular expression parser to meet the needs of your users.

CHAPTER 9

Advanced Tokenizing

Tokenizing a string means dividing the string into logical chunks, or *tokens*. This lets you define a grammar in terms of token terminals, something that is much simpler than defining a grammar in terms of every character in an input stream. Simpler grammars translate into simpler parsers, so tokenizing reduces the complexity of a parser. This chapter explains how tokenizing works and describes techniques for controlling in detail how sequences of characters form tokens.

9.1 The Role of a Tokenizer

Most languages are easier to describe as patterns of tokens than as patterns of characters. A token represents a logical piece of a string. For example, a typical tokenizer would divide the string "1.23 <= 12.3" into three tokens: the number 1.23, a less-than-or-equal symbol, and the number 12.3. A token is a receptacle; it relies on a tokenizer to decide precisely how to divide a string into tokens. In addition to building up numbers from the characters of a string, a tokenizer provides other services that divide a string into tokens. A tokenizer typically does the following:

- Parse numbers.
- Build up "words" from letters and potentially other characters.
- Treat characters such as "<" as one-character symbols.
- Allow multicharacter symbols, such as "<=" and "=:=".
- Treat whitespace as a token separator.
- Respect quoted strings, "like this".
- Strip out comments.

For example, here is a short program that exercises most of these features in a tokenizer. This program uses the `Tokenizer` class from `sjm.parse.tokens`, which we later compare to the tokenizers in the standard Java libraries.

```
package sjm.examples.tokens;

import java.io.*;
import sjm.parse.tokens.*;

/**
 * Show a default <code>Tokenizer</code> object at work.
 */
public class ShowTokenizer {

public static void main(String args[]) throws IOException {

    String s =

    "\"It's 123 blast-off!\", she said, // watch out!\n" +
    "and <= 3 'ticks' later /* wince */ , it's blast-off!";

    System.out.println(s);
    System.out.println();

    Tokenizer t = new Tokenizer(s);

    while (true) {
        Token tok = t.nextToken();
        if (tok.equals(Token.EOF)) {
            break;
        }
        System.out.println("(" + tok + ")");
    }
}
}
```

Running this class prints the following:

```
"It's 123 blast-off!", she said, // watch out!
and <= 3 "ticks" later /* wince */ , it's blast-off!

("It's 123 blast-off!")
(,)
(she)
(said)
(,)
(and)
(<=)
(3.0)
('ticks')
(later)
```

```
(,)
(it's)
(blast-off)
(!)
```

The tokenizer respects the quoted strings, ignores Java-style comments, and otherwise gathers characters into roughly the same chunks as would a human reader, separating words, numbers, and punctuation.

9.2 Acquiring a Tokenizer

You have several choices regarding how you acquire a tokenizer to use for your parsers. For one thing, you can use a tokenizer that comes with the freely available Java software development kit (JDK). However, as of this writing, these tokenizers lack features that the languages in this book require. To overcome these limitations, a new tokenizer was developed for this book, and this chapter explains how to use it.

This discussion opens other approaches to acquiring a tokenizer. You can use the tokenizer that comes with this book as is, without changing its code. The `Tokenizer` class in `sjm.parse.tokens` is highly customizable, and you may find that it meets all your needs for tokenization. Another choice is to compare `StreamTokenizer` in `java.io` with `Tokenizer` in `sjm.parse.tokens` to develop ideas for writing your own tokenizer. You can learn from the strengths and weaknesses of existing tokenizers if you choose to design your own.

9.3 Tokenizers in Standard Java

The standard Java libraries include two tokenizers: `StringTokenizer` in `java.util` and `StreamTokenizer` in `java.io`.

The `StringTokenizer` class does not parse numbers, and it allows little customization. This tokenizer is suitable only for simple tokenization, and this book does not discuss it further.

The `StreamTokenizer` class is more customizable than `StringTokenizer` but lacks some desirable features. In particular, `StreamTokenizer` in Java 1.1.7 does not provide

- A Token class to encapsulate token results
- Customization of how to recognize numbers
- The ability to define new token types

- Differentiation of allowable characters for the start of a word from allowable characters within a word

- Handling of multicharacter symbols such as "<="

For example, the following program uses `StreamTokenizer` from `java.io` to tokenize the "blast-off" line from the preceding section:

```java
package sjm.examples.tokens;

import java.io.*;

/**
 * Show a <code>StreamTokenizer</code> object at work
 */
public class ShowTokenizer2 {

public static void main(String args[]) throws IOException {

    String s =

    "\"It's 123 blast-off!\", she said, // watch out!\n" +
    "and <= 3 'ticks' later /* wince */ , it's blast-off!";

    System.out.println(s);
    System.out.println();

    StreamTokenizer t =
        new StreamTokenizer(new StringReader(s));
    t.ordinaryChar('/');
    t.slashSlashComments(true);
    t.slashStarComments(true);

    boolean done = false;
    while (!done) {
        t.nextToken();
        switch (t.ttype) {
            case StreamTokenizer.TT_EOF :
                done = true;
                break;

            case StreamTokenizer.TT_WORD :
            case '\"' :
            case '\'' :
                System.out.println("(" + t.sval + ")");
                break;

            case StreamTokenizer.TT_NUMBER :
                System.out.println("(" + t.nval + ")");
                break;
```

```
        default :
            System.out.println(
                "(" + (char) t.ttype + ")");
            break;
        }
    }
}
}
```

To initialize a `StreamTokenizer` object to ignore Java-style comments, this code uses these statements:

```
StreamTokenizer t =
    new StreamTokenizer(new StringReader(s));
t.ordinaryChar('/');
t.slashSlashComments(true);
t.slashStarComments(true);
```

The default behavior of `StreamTokenizer` is to ignore all characters on a line after an initial slash, so this code makes a slash an "ordinary" character.

The code in `main()` also shows how to handle quoted strings and symbols with `StreamTokenizer`. When a `StreamTokenizer` object finds a quoted string, it places the quote symbol in its ttype attribute and places the value of the string in its sval attribute. Two `case` statements in the example lead to the same output behavior for words and for quoted strings.

By default, the `switch` statement in the example shows as a symbol any token that is not a word, quoted string, or number. In this case, the `StreamTokenizer` object stores the symbol characters in its ttype attribute. The sample code casts ttype to a char in this case, so symbols print as characters rather than as numeric values. Running `ShowTokenizer2` prints the following:

```
"It's 123 blast-off!", she said, // watch out!
and <= 3 'ticks' later /* wince */ , it's blast-off!

(It's 123 blast-off!)
(,)
(she)
(said)
(,)
(and)
(<)
(=)
(3.0)
(ticks)
(later)
(,)
```

```
(it)
(s blast-off!)
```

This is similar to the earlier output except that StreamTokenizer does not include the quote character as part of the quoted string. The output also shows that StreamTokenizer divides the <= symbol into two tokens. This makes it more difficult to write a grammar because the grammar must comprehend that some comparisons use one symbol and other comparisons use two symbols. This also means that your language will allow whitespace to appear inside a two-character symbol. One solution to this problem is to wrap StreamTokenizer with a class that looks ahead and combines the two symbols "<" and "=" into one.

Another problem with this example is that the tokenizer mistakes the apostrophe in "it's" for the beginning of a quoted string. There is no corresponding mate for this character, so the tokenizer consumes the rest of the input, returning it as a quoted string. You could ask the tokenizer to treat the single quote as a word character, but then the tokenizer would return 'ticks' as a word with the quotes embedded in it. Worse, if the input included 'wee ticks', this approach would tokenize 'wee as one word and ticks' as the next. The problem is that you want an apostrophe to occur inside a word as part of that word, and you want a single quote after some whitespace to mean the beginning of a quoted string. To achieve this, you need to separate the event of entering a tokenizer state from the mechanics of how that state builds a token. This is a primary motivation for writing a new Tokenizer class.

This example is longer than the preceding example, primarily because of the printing logic that handles the different token types. This illustrates the advantage of introducing a separate Token class that knows how to display itself.

9.4 A Token Class

A token is a receptacle that holds a number or a morsel of text. A tokenizer is an object whose job is to define precisely how to build a number and to define where morsels of text begin and end. For example, a typical tokenizer (such as a StreamTokenizer object) will view the string ">give 2receive" as containing four tokens: a symbol, a word, a number, and another word. A tokenizer class might not create special objects for each token. In particular, the StreamTokenizer class in java.io holds token information in its own state and does not create instances of a Token class. The tokenizer in sjm.parse.tokens uses instances of a Token class to hold the results of tokenizing a string.

The Token class does not determine what is or is not a token. Instances of class Token are containers that hold the results of whatever the tokenizer decides is a token. The Token class does introduce a constraint that a token is definable in terms of a token

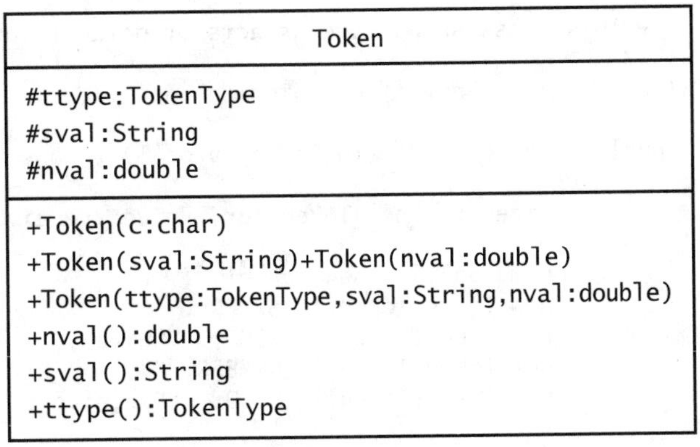

Token
#ttype:TokenType #sval:String #nval:double
+Token(c:char) +Token(sval:String)+Token(nval:double) +Token(ttype:TokenType,sval:String,nval:double) +nval():double +sval():String +ttype():TokenType

Figure 9.1 The Token class. A Token is a receptacle for the results of reading a typically small amount of text, such as a word or a number.

type and an associated `String` or `double` value. Figure 9.1 shows the `Token` class in `sjm.parse.tokens`.

Class `Token` defines the following constants as token types:

```
TT_EOF
TT_NUMBER
TT_WORD
TT_SYMBOL
TT_QUOTED
```

These types help a parser to distinguish between common types of language elements. For example, although words as well as symbols are strings of one or more characters, most programming languages allow words, but not symbols, as variable names. By default, the `Tokenizer` class in `sjm.parse.tokens` tokenizes the string `">give 2receive"` as these four tokens:

```
new Token(Token.TT_SYMBOL, ">",         0)
new Token(Token.TT_WORD,   "give",      0)
new Token(Token.TT_NUMBER, "",        2.0)
new Token(Token.TT_WORD,   "receive",   0)
```

To demonstrate this, the following class creates these four tokens individually and compares them to the results of tokenizing the string:

```
package sjm.examples.tokens;
import java.io.*;
import sjm.parse.tokens.*;
```

```
/**
 * This class shows some aspects of default tokenization.
 */
public class ShowDefaultTokenization {

public static void main(String args[]) throws IOException {

    Tokenizer t = new Tokenizer(">give 2receive");

    Token manual[] = new Token[] {
        new Token(Token.TT_SYMBOL, ">",        0),
        new Token(Token.TT_WORD,   "give",     0),
        new Token(Token.TT_NUMBER, "",       2.0),
        new Token(Token.TT_WORD,   "receive", 0)};

    for (int i = 0; i < 4; i++) {
        Token tok = t.nextToken();
        if (tok.equals(manual[i])) {
            System.out.print("ok! ");
        }
    }
}
}
```

This code prints:

    ok! ok! ok! ok!

This code uses the `Token.equals()` method, shown in Figure 9.2 along with other methods of Token. The `value()` method returns either a `String` or a `Double` to represent the token. The various `is` methods verify the token's type.

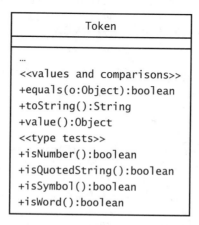

Figure 9.2 Other methods in class Token. Class Token includes methods that return or compare a token's value, and methods that check a token's type.

9.5 A Tokenizer Class

The `Tokenizer` class in `sjm.parse.tokens` uses a set of states to recognize different types of tokens. Each state is a subclass of `TokenizerState`, a class in the same package. A `Tokenizer` object reads a character of an input string and uses this character to decide which state to use to find the next token. The design of `Tokenizer` in `sjm.parse.tokens` is as follows:

1. Read a character and use it to look up which `TokenizerState` object to use.

2. Send the `TokenizerState` object the initial character, and ask the `TokenizerState` to return a `Token`. The `TokenizerState` reads as many characters as it needs to produce a `Token`.

3. Repeat until there are no more characters.

Figure 9.3 shows a state diagram of the classes in `sjm.parse.tokens`.

The tokenizer state classes follow the *state* pattern [Gamma et al.], providing different implementations of the `nextToken()` method depending on the tokenizer's state. Tokenizer states generally consume text, produce a token, and return the token. For example, if a string to tokenize is `"123 blastoff"`, the tokenizer sees the "1" and

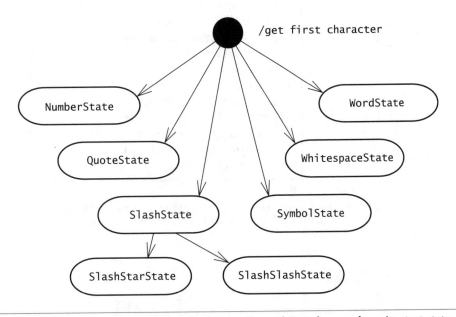

Figure 9.3 Tokenizer state transitions. A `Tokenizer` object changes from its start state into a `TokenizerState` object that returns a token.

transfers control to a NumberState object. The NumberState object consumes all three characters of the number and then returns a token that represents the number 123.

Some states cannot produce a token themselves but rather have the role of ignoring input. All objects of class WhitespaceState, SlashStarState, and SlashSlashState discard some sequence of characters and then ask the tokenizer to return the next token. One job that the states share is the ability to produce the next token in support of the Tokenizer class's nextToken() method. Figure 9.4 shows the Tokenizer class.

The Tokenizer class creates a default set of states, makes them accessible, and plugs them in to its lookup table, which it calls characterState. You can create new states and plug them in to the lookup table, giving you complete control over how the tokenizer works.

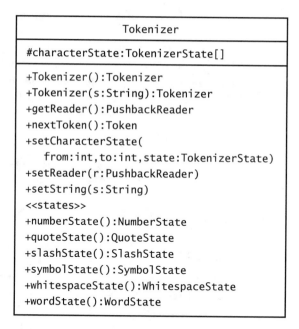

Figure 9.4 The Tokenizer class. A Tokenizer returns a series of tokens using various TokenizerState objects to build different types of tokens.

9.6 Tokenizer Lookup Tables

Both the `Tokenizer` class in `sjm.parse.tokens` and `StreamTokenizer` in `java.io` use lookup tables to decide how to build a token. The classes are similar in that the first character of a token determines the tokenizer's state. The classes differ in that `Tokenizer` transfers control to a `TokenizerState` object, whereas the state of `StreamTokenizer` is internal to the `StreamTokenizer` class. Figure 9.5 shows the table that a default `Tokenizer` object uses to determine which state to use to build a token.

	0	1	2	3	4	5	6	7	8	9	a	b	c	d	e	f
0																
10																
20		!	"	#	$	%	&	'	(	)	*	+	,	-	.	/
30	0	1	2	3	4	5	6	7	8	9	:	;	<	=	>	?
40	@	A	B	C	D	E	F	G	H	I	J	K	L	M	N	O
50	P	Q	R	S	T	U	V	W	X	Y	Z	[	\	]	^	_
60	`	a	b	c	d	e	f	g	h	i	j	k	l	m	n	o
70	p	q	r	s	t	u	v	w	x	y	z	{	|	}	~	
80																
90																
a0		¡	¢	£	¤	¥	¦	§	¨	©	ª	«	¬		®	¯
b0	°	±	²	³	´	µ	¶	·	¸	¹	º	»	¼	½	¼	¿
c0	À	Á	Â	Ã	Ä	Å	Æ	Ç	È	É	Ê	Ë	Ì	Í	Î	Ï
d0	Ð	Ñ	Ò	Ó	Ô	Õ	Ö	×	Ø	Ù	Ú	Û	Ü	Ý	Þ	ß
e0	à	á	â	ã	ä	å	æ	ç	è	é	ê	ë	ì	í	î	ï
f0	ð	ñ	ò	ó	ô	õ	ö	÷	ø	ù	ú	û	ü	ý	þ	ÿ

Figure 9.5 This table depicts the default lookup table used by the class `Tokenizer` in `sjm.parse.tokens` to determine which `TokenizerState` can produce a `Token`. The Unicode value of each character is the sum of its row number value and column value, which appear in hexadecimal format.

Figure 9.5 shows the Unicode encoding that maps numbers to characters. This encoding handles characters from most written languages. The Tokenizer class in sjm.parse.tokens, however, handles only the first 256 characters of Unicode. If you are working with languages other than English and the European languages, you may need to modify Tokenizer to handle a broader array of characters. See http://unicode.org for more information about Unicode.

The sum of the encoding table's row and column labels indicates the numeric value, in hexadecimal (base 16), of each character. For example, row 40, column 1 contains A, meaning that 41 in hexadecimal format represents an A. There are several reasons for showing the numeric value of characters in base 16. First, there is some periodicity around the number 16 in the table, which shows the standard Unicode values of characters. For example, lowercase letters appear 32 positions after their uppercase counterparts. A deeper reason for showing character values in hexadecimal is that developers who work with characters at the low level required by tokenizers tend to acquire an understanding of exactly how the bits and bytes of characters translate into either numbers or text. A final reason for using hexadecimal is that Unicode escape sequences must appear in Java in hexadecimal format.

Java lets you represent hexadecimal numbers by preceding them with 0x. For example, you can write the numeric value of A as 0x41. Java also expects Unicode escape values to appear in hexadecimal, so the Unicode escape of A is \u0041. Each of the following lines prints an A:

```
System.out.println('A');
System.out.println((char) 0x41);
System.out.println((char) 65);
System.out.println("\u0041");
```

The casts to char are important because a char value prints as a character rather than as a number. A char is essentially an integer that knows how to print as a character. For this reason, you can use a char as an index into an array. The lookup table that Tokenizer objects use to determine which TokenizerState to use is an array. Its declaration is

```
protected TokenizerState[] characterState =
    new TokenizerState[256];
```

The Tokenizer class provides access to this array through the method setCharacterState(), which takes two int arguments followed by a TokenizerState argument. The constructor for Tokenizer uses this method to set its default states. For example, the constructor includes the line

```
// ...
setCharacterState('0', '9', numberState());
// ...
```

This statement in the constructor uses the method `numberState()` to access a default number-recognizing state, and it places this state in positions `'0'` through `'9'` of the lookup table. Here, the `char` values work as indexes, delineating locations 48 through 57 (or 0x30 through 0x39) of the array.

The default states that `Tokenizer` uses are as follows:

```
From     To     State

   0     ' '    whitespaceState
  'a'    'z'    wordState
  'A'    'Z'    wordState
 0xc0    0xff   wordState
  '0'    '9'    numberState
  '-'    '-'    numberState
  '.'    '.'    numberState
  '"'    '"'    quoteState
  '\'    '\'    quoteState
  '/'    '/'    slashState
```

For any index not in this list, such as `'<'`, a default `Tokenizer` uses a `SymbolState` object to consume a token.

9.7 Tokenizer States

A tokenizer state is an object that can return a token from an input reader. The `Tokenizer` class in `sjm.parse.tokens` uses, by default, the classes that Figure 9.6 shows.

Each subclass implements the `nextToken()` method of the abstract class `TokenizerState`, which Figure 9.7 shows.

The `PushbackReader` is usually created in the `Tokenizer` constructor, although you can override this with the `Tokenizer` class's `setReader()` method. Section 9.8, "Setting a Tokenizer's Source," shows how. A `PushbackReader` object provides the ability to *unread* characters. This is especially useful when your parser is reading symbols; the tokenizer state may read several characters in pursuit of a long symbol and then must push them back if the entire symbol is not found.

When the `Tokenizer` object is deciding which state to use, it looks at the next character of the input and uses this character as an index into the `Tokenizer` object's character table. Rather than push this back and let the state reread it, the `Tokenizer` object

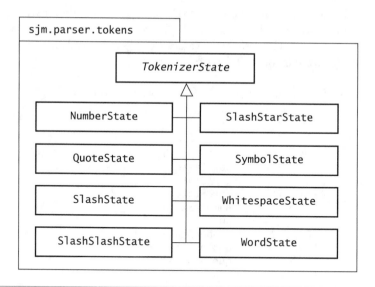

Figure 9.6 The `TokenizerState` hierarchy. This diagram shows the hierarchy of `TokenizerState` in `sjm.parse.tokens`. A `Tokenizer` object can use these states to consume tokens from a string.

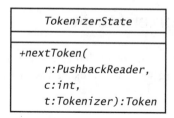

Figure 9.7 The `TokenizerState` class. `TokenizerState` is an abstract class that defines the minimal behavior of an object that can read characters and build a corresponding `Token` object.

passes the character it reads to the `TokenizerState` object. The `Tokenizer` object also passes a copy of itself. This allows states to discard characters from the input and eventually call back the `Tokenizer` object to find the next token. Whitespace and comment states work this way.

9.7.1 QuoteState

One of the simpler tokenizer states is `QuoteState`, which Figure 9.8 depicts.

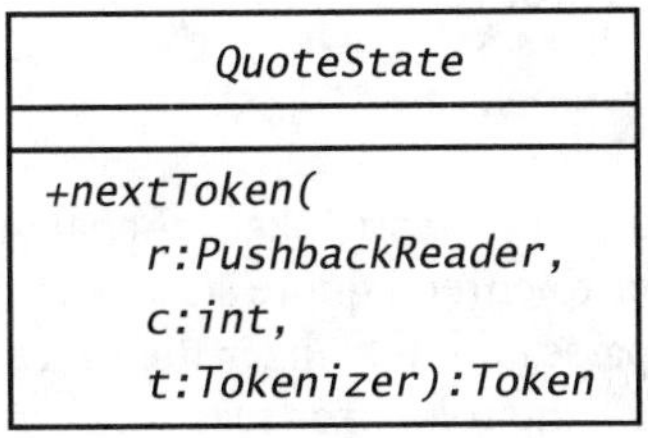

Figure 9.8 The QuoteState class. A QuoteState object reads characters until it matches the initial character c that it receives in nextToken().

The method QuoteState.nextToken() reads characters until it finds a match for the initial character it receives as its int c argument, or until it finds the end of the string. Here is an example that tokenizes out quoted strings:

```
package sjm.examples.tokens;

import java.io.*;
import sjm.parse.tokens.*;

/**
 * This class demonstrates how <code>QuoteState</code>
 * works.
 */
public class ShowQuoteState {

public static void main(String args[]) throws IOException {
    Tokenizer t = new Tokenizer(
        "Hamlet says #Alas, poor Yorick!# and " +
        "#To be, or not...");

    t.setCharacterState('#', '#', t.quoteState());

    while (true) {
        Token tok = t.nextToken();
        if (tok.equals(Token.EOF)) {
            break;
        }
        System.out.println(tok);
    }
}
}
```

This prints out:

```
Hamlet
says
```

```
#Alas, poor Yorick!#
and
#To be, or not...#
```

The main() method creates a Tokenizer, giving it a string to tokenize. Next, main()
tells the tokenizer to enter a quote state when the tokenizer sees a "#" character. The
main() method passes the tokenizer the tokenizer's own, default quote state object to
use. The first time the tokenizer sees a "#", it uses the quote state to read up to the
next "#", producing a token whose string is "Alas, poor Yorick!" Next, the tokenizer finds the word "and" amidst some whitespace, and then it finds another "#". The
tokenizer calls its QuoteState object a second time, and this time it consumes all the
text up to the end of the string. Because there is no closing quote, the QuoteState
object appends a quote symbol that matches the initial one. This ensures that quoted
strings always appear between a pair of quote symbols.

The QuoteState class's task of reading text until it matches a specific character is relatively simple. The only subtlety is that QuoteState must use some caution to make
sure its buffer of characters is large enough. Here is the code in QuoteState.java:

```java
package sjm.parse.tokens;

import java.io.*;

/**
 * A quoteState returns a quoted string token from a reader.
 * This state will collect characters until it sees a match
 * to the character that the tokenizer used to switch to
 * this state. For example, if a tokenizer uses a double-
 * quote character to enter this state, then <code>
 * nextToken()</code> will search for another double-quote
 * until it finds one or finds the end of the reader.
 */
public class QuoteState extends TokenizerState {
    protected char charbuf[] = new char[16];

/*
 * Fatten up charbuf as necessary.
 */
protected void checkBufLength(int i) {
    if (i >= charbuf.length) {
        char nb[] = new char[charbuf.length * 2];
        System.arraycopy(charbuf, 0, nb, 0, charbuf.length);
        charbuf = nb;
    }
}

/**
 * Return a quoted string token from a reader. This method
 * will collect characters until it sees a match to the
```

```
 * character that the tokenizer used to switch to this
 * state.
 */
public Token nextToken(
    PushbackReader r, int cin, Tokenizer t)
    throws IOException {

    int i = 0;
    charbuf[i++] = (char) cin;
    int c;
    do {
        c = r.read();
        if (c < 0) {
            c = cin;
        }
        checkBufLength(i);
        charbuf[i++] = (char) c;
    } while (c != cin);

    String sval = String.copyValueOf(charbuf, 0, i);
    return new Token(Token.TT_QUOTED, sval, 0);
    }
}
```

This code performs its own memory management, expanding the size of charbuf as necessary. You could delegate this to an existing class, particularly StringBuffer. In fact, in Java 1.1.7, StringBuffer uses a memory management technique similar to the approach taken here. When tokenizing, however, you are concerned with efficiency and with the details of how characters become tokens, and tokenizers typically retain fine-grained control of this conversion.

9.7.2 NumberState

A NumberState object builds a double value that corresponds to the digits and decimal point in a string of characters. It divides its task primarily into two parts: Read the number to the left of a decimal point, and read the remaining digits after the decimal point. This state also has to handle negative numbers and two special cases that result from reading only a minus sign and only a dot. Figure 9.9 shows the Number-State class.

To construct a token, NumberState.nextToken() takes the following steps:

1. Set the initial value of the number to 0.

2. Note whether there is a minus sign.

3. Absorb digits until there are no more. For each digit, multiply value by 10 and add the new digit.

```
┌─────────────────────────────────────────┐
│              NumberState                 │
├─────────────────────────────────────────┤
│ +nextToken(                             │
│     r:PushbackReader,                   │
│     c:int,                              │
│     t:Tokenizer):Token                  │
│ #absorbDigits(                          │
│     r:PushbackReader,                   │
│     fraction:boolean)                   │
│ #parseLeftSide(r:PushbackReader)        │
│ #parseRightSide(r:PushbackReader)       │
│ #reset(c:int)                           │
│ #value():Token                          │
└─────────────────────────────────────────┘
```

Figure 9.9 The NumberState class. A NumberState object builds a token that contains a number.

4. If the next character is a decimal point, again absorb digits until there are no more. For each digit, multiply value by 10 and add the new digit's value. Also keep track of a divisor, multiplying it by 10 for each digit. After consuming all remaining digits, divide value by this divisor.

5. Negate value if the number began with a minus sign, and return value.

Consider tokenizing the string "123.456". A NumberState object sets value to 0 and stores the initial character it receives from the Tokenizer in the variable c. Then the NumberState object consumes the digits up to the decimal point with the following code:

```java
/*
 * Convert a stream of digits into a number, making this
 * number a fraction if the boolean parameter is true.
 */
protected double absorbDigits(
    PushbackReader r, boolean fraction) throws IOException {

    int divideBy = 1;
    double v = 0;
    while ('0' <= c && c <= '9') {
        gotAdigit = true;
        v = v * 10 + (c - '0');
        c = r.read();
        if (fraction) {
            divideBy *= 10;
        }
    }
```

```
        if (fraction) {
            v = v / divideBy;
        }
        return v;
}
```

A `NumberState` object uses this method to absorb digits on both sides of a decimal point. If the object has seen a decimal point, then `fraction` is true. The `NumberState` object records, in `gotADigit`, that at least one digit appears in the number. This allows an evaluation method to recognize that a stand-alone "`.`" is a symbol and not a number.

After reading the left side of the number, the `NumberState` object reuses the preceding logic to read the right side. After reading both sides of the number, the `NumberState` object unreads the last character it read and evaluates a token. The value of the token depends on whether the input string had a leading minus and whether it had any digits. If the input had no digits, the input is not a number at all, and the `NumberState` object passes control to a `SymbolState` object to create a symbol token.

9.7.3 SlashState

By default, a `Tokenizer` passes read control to a `SlashState` object when the `Tokenizer` sees a "`/`" character. Incidentally, you can change this behavior by informing the `Tokenizer` object to treat the "`/`" as a symbol. For example,

```java
package sjm.examples.tokens;

import java.io.*;
import sjm.parse.tokens.*;

/**
 * This class shows how to <i>not</i> ignore Java-style
 * comments.
 */
public class ShowNoComment {

public static void main(String args[]) throws IOException {
    Tokenizer t = new Tokenizer("Show /* all */ // this");

    t.setCharacterState('/', '/', t.symbolState());

    while (true) {
        Token tok = t.nextToken();
        if (tok.equals(Token.EOF)) {
            break;
        }
        System.out.println(tok);
    }
}
}
```

This prints the following:

```
Show
/
*
all
*
/
/
/
this
```

The default behavior is for a Tokenizer to ignore these Java-style comments. By default, a Tokenizer object passes control to a SlashState object upon seeing a "/". Figure 9.10 shows the slash states.

A SlashState handles three possibilities. It may need to ignore either type of comment, or it may be that the character read is only a slash. To decide the proper course, a SlashState object reads the next character and dispatches further responsibility to either a SlashSlashState object or a SlashStarState object. Or, if the next character is neither a "/" nor a "*", the SlashState object returns the initial "/" as a symbol.

If the character following a slash is an asterisk, a SlashStarState object consumes characters up to the next "*/". The nextToken() method still needs to return a token, but SlashStarState delegates this responsibility back to the tokenizer. As Figure 9.7 shows, the signature of nextToken() includes a Tokenizer object. The SlashStarState implementation of nextToken() consumes a comment and then returns tokenizer.nextToken().

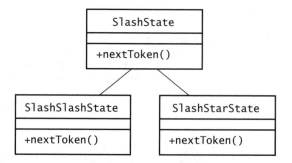

Figure 9.10   Three states for slash. Note that the diagram shows attributes of class SlashState and not inheritance. A SlashState object uses the other states to consume a comment.

If the character following a slash is another slash, a SlashState object uses its SlashSlashState to ignore characters up to the end of the line. As with SlashStarState, this state consumes the comment and uses the tokenizer to find and return the next actual token.

Comments bring out a weakness of the design of Tokenizer, which assumes that a single character is sufficient to determine which state to use to consume the next token. When this assumption is incorrect, the state must read further and must pass control to a substate. This design works reasonably well, because typically only one extra character at most is necessary for deciding which state to use. Another state that must sometimes peek ahead is SymbolState.

9.7.4 SymbolState

Speaking loosely, a symbol is a character that typically should stand alone as a single token. Consider the string "(432+321)>(321+432)" and note that the middle of the string has the characters ")>(". Most human readers will think of these three characters as three separate symbols and not as a string of related characters. The opposite applies to the characters "432", which look like a single number and thus a single token. Given the string "(432+321)>(321+432)", a default Tokenizer object returns tokens for a left parenthesis, the number 432, a plus sign, the number 321, a right parenthesis, a greater-than symbol, a left parenthesis, the number 321, a plus sign, the number 432, and a right parenthesis.

A symbol is usually a single character that stands alone as its own token, such as a colon or comma. On seeing a symbol character, a Tokenizer object passes control to a SymbolState object. Typically, the SymbolState object reads no further and returns a Token object that represents a single character. For example, a typical tokenizer returns a less-than character in the input as a Token object of type TT_SYMBOL and a value of "<".

A problem arises when a language designer wants to allow multicharacter symbols. For example, in the string "cat<=dog", the characters "<=" indicate a single symbol, with the meaning of less-than-or-equal. To allow for this, the class SymbolState provides a method for establishing strings of characters that together form a single symbol and should appear in a single Token:

```
public void add(String s)
```

Figure 9.11 shows the SymbolState class.

```
                      ┌────────────────────────────────┐
                      │           SymbolState          │
                      ├────────────────────────────────┤
                      │ +SymbolState():SymbolState     │
                      │ +nextToken(                    │
                      │      r:PushbackReader,          │
                      │      c:int,                     │
                      │      t:Tokenizer):Token         │
                      │ +add(s:String)                 │
                      └────────────────────────────────┘
```

Figure 9.11 The SymbolState class. A SymbolState object typically returns the single character that a tokenizer passes it as a symbol, such as "<".

The SymbolState constructor uses this method to establish the following character strings as symbols:

```
!=
:-
<=
>=
```

Three of these symbols appear as operators in Java. The ":-" symbol, sometimes called if, is the predicate symbol of logic languages such as Prolog and Logikus. The following code gives an example of adding a new multicharacter symbol:

```java
package sjm.examples.tokens;

import java.io.*;
import sjm.parse.tokens.*;

/**
 * This class shows how to add a new multicharacter symbol.
 */
public class ShowNewSymbol {

public static void main(String args[]) throws IOException {
    Tokenizer t = new Tokenizer("42.001 =~= 42");

    t.symbolState().add("=~=");

    while (true) {
        Token tok = t.nextToken();
        if (tok.equals(Token.EOF)) {
            break;
        }
        System.out.println(tok);
    }
}
}
```

This prints the following:

```
42.001
=~=
42.0
```

This output shows that the tokenizer has changed from the default, viewing "=~=" as a single symbol.

To allow multicharacter symbols, the SymbolState class maintains a tree of SymbolNode objects. A SymbolNode object is a member of a tree that contains all possible prefixes of allowable symbols. Multicharacter symbols appear in a SymbolNode tree with one node for each character.

For example, the symbol "=:~" appears in a tree as three nodes, as Figure 9.12 shows. The first node contains an equal sign and has a child; that child contains a colon and has a child; this third child contains a tilde and has no children of its own. In this tree, the colon node has another child for a dollar sign character, so the tree contains the symbol "=:$".

A tree of SymbolNode objects collaborate to read a potential multicharacter symbol from an input stream. A root node with no character of its own finds an initial node that represents the first character in the input. This node looks to see whether the next character in the input stream matches one of its children. If it matches, the node delegates its reading task to its child. This approach walks down the tree, pulling symbols from the input that match the path down the tree.

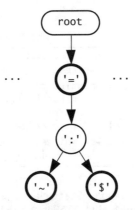

Figure 9.12   A SymbolNode tree. A SymbolNode tree contains all symbol prefixes, including many single character symbols such as "=". The tree shown also contains the multicharacter symbols "=:~" and "=:$". This diagram shows bold nodes that represent complete symbols.

When a node does not have a child that matches the next character, it will have read the longest possible symbol prefix from the input stream. This prefix may or may not be a valid symbol. Consider a symbol tree that has had "=:~" added and has not had "=:" added, as in Figure 9.12. In this tree, of the three nodes that represent "=:~", only the first and third contain complete symbols. If, say, the input contains "=:a", the colon node will not have a child that matches the a, so it will stop reading. The colon node must unread. It must push back its character and ask its parent to unread. Unreading continues until it reaches an ancestor that represents a valid symbol.

The root node of a symbol node tree is a special case of a `SymbolNode` object. The class `SymbolRootNode` subclasses `SymbolNode` and overrides certain behaviors. A `SymbolRootNode` object has no symbol of its own, but it has children that represent all possible symbols. It keeps its children in an array and sets all its children to be valid symbols. The decision as to which characters are valid one-character symbols lies outside this tree. If a tokenizer asks a symbol tree to produce a symbol, the tree assumes that the first available character is a valid symbol.

9.7.5 WhitespaceState

The term *whitespace* refers to a sequence of one or more *whitespace characters*. A whitespace character is subject to definition, but it usually includes at least spaces, tabs, and newlines. Figure 9.13 shows the `WhitespaceState` class.

For an example of whitespace, consider this declaration:

```
int        i;
```

```
                    WhitespaceState
─────────────────────────────────────────────

+WhitespaceState()
+nextToken(
      r:PushbackReader,
      c:int,
      t:Tokenizer):Token
+setWhitespaceChars(
      from:int,to:int,b:boolean)
```

Figure 9.13 The `WhitespaceState` class. A `Whitespace` object ignores whitespace characters, such as spaces and tabs, and uses the tokenizer passed in `nextToken()` to find the actual next token.

In this declaration, whitespace must occur between the type int and the variable i. Any combination of spaces, tabs, and other whitespace characters may appear as long as there is at least one whitespace character.

By default, the Tokenizer class sets all characters with numeric values between 0 and 32 to be whitespace characters. Upon seeing one of these characters, a Tokenizer object transfers control to its default WhitespaceState object. The characters between 0 and 32 include all of Java's escape sequences. The lines

```
System.out.println((int) '\b'); // backspace
System.out.println((int) '\f'); // form feed
System.out.println((int) '\n'); // newline
System.out.println((int) '\r'); // carriage return
System.out.println((int) '\t'); // tab
System.out.println((int) ' ');  // space
```

print the following:

```
8
12
10
13
9
32
```

These numbers are the numeric values of the escape sequences. Each is less than or equal to 32, and by default the Tokenizer class treats them all as whitespace. The WhitespaceState.nextToken() method reads and ignores all whitespace characters and then, to return the next token, calls back the tokenizer object that called it.

9.7.6 WordState

The decision that a character begins a word is the Tokenizer class's decision. The decision that a character belongs inside a word is the WordState class's decision. If you want to customize the characters that can make a word, you may need to customize the Tokenizer object, and you may need to customize the WordState object that the Tokenizer uses.

To change how words may begin, update the Tokenizer object with a call to setCharacterState(). To change the characters that may appear inside a word, retrieve the Tokenizer object's WordState object with a call to wordState(), and update the WordState object with a call to setWordChars(). Figure 9.14 shows the WordState class.

It's common to distinguish between the first character and the remaining characters of a word, especially in computer programming. In particular, words may conventionally

```
┌─────────────────────────────────────────┐
│                 WordState               │
├─────────────────────────────────────────┤
│ +WordState():WordState                  │
│ +nextToken(                             │
│     r:PushbackReader,                   │
│     c:int,                              │
│     t:Tokenizer):Token                  │
│ +setWordChars(                          │
│     from:int,to:int,b:boolean)          │
└─────────────────────────────────────────┘
```

Figure 9.14   The WordState class. A WordState object builds a token that contains a word.

contain digits but may not begin with a digit because the Tokenizer class (by default) does not transfer reading control to a WordState upon seeing a numeric digit. WordState objects do (by default) consider digits to be allowable characters within a word, so a word can *contain* digits.

The WordState constructor contains these lines:

```
setWordChars('a', 'z', true);
setWordChars('A', 'Z', true);
setWordChars('0', '9', true);
setWordChars('-', '-', true);
setWordChars('_', '_', true);
setWordChars('\'', '\'', true);
setWordChars(0xc0, 0xff, true);
```

These calls to setWordChars() establish that, by default, a word can contain digits, minus signs (or hyphens), underscores, apostrophes, and most of the characters of European languages. You can change these defaults to suit the language you are tokenizing for.

9.8 Setting a Tokenizer's Source

Most of the examples in this chapter create a tokenizer and use it once. Because this is a common practice, the Tokenizer class lets you pass a string to tokenize into its constructor. For example, the following line creates a Tokenizer object and gives it the string to tokenize:

```
Tokenizer t = new Tokenizer(">give 2receive");
```

You can also create a tokenizer without a string and then set the string later. This approach lets you create a customized tokenizer and reuse it for many strings. For example, the CoffeeParser class in Chapter 5, "Parsing Data Languages," creates a special tokenizer that allows spaces to appear inside words. Here is the tokenizer() method of CoffeeParser:

```java
/**
 * Returns a tokenizer that allows spaces to appear inside
 * the "words" that identify a coffee's name.
 */
public static Tokenizer tokenizer() {
    Tokenizer t = new Tokenizer();
    t.wordState().setWordChars(' ', ' ', true);
    return t;
}
```

This code creates a default tokenizer and asks its word state to allow spaces. A calling method can retrieve this tokenizer, set the tokenizer's string to be a string that describes a type of coffee, and then feed the tokenizer to a parser. Here, again, is ShowCoffee.java:

```java
package sjm.examples.coffee;

import java.io.*;
import sjm.parse.*;
import sjm.parse.tokens.*;

/**
 * Show the recognition of a list of types of coffee,
 * reading from a file.
 */
public class ShowCoffee {

public static void main(String args[]) throws Exception {

    InputStream is =
        ClassLoader.getSystemResourceAsStream("coffee.txt");
    BufferedReader r =
        new BufferedReader(new InputStreamReader(is));

    Tokenizer t = CoffeeParser.tokenizer();
    Parser p = CoffeeParser.start();

    while (true) {
        String s = r.readLine();
        if (s == null) {
            break;
        }
        t.setString(s);
        Assembly in = new TokenAssembly(t);
```

```
                Assembly out = p.bestMatch(in);
                System.out.println(out.getTarget());
            }
        }
    }
```

The `main()` method of `ShowCoffee` retrieves a tokenizer from the `CoffeeParser` class's static `tokenizer()` method and retrieves the parser itself. The method reuses these two objects to parse each line of input. For each coffee line, the method passes the string to the tokenizer, forms a `TokenAssembly` object from the tokenizer, and uses the parser to match the token assembly.

You can also set a tokenizer's source by passing it a `PushbackReader` object to read from. Java character streams follow the *decorator* pattern [Gamma et al.], meaning that you can wrap one reader around another. For example, you can construct a `PushbackReader` object from a `FileReader` object:

```java
package sjm.examples.tokens;

import java.io.*;
import sjm.parse.tokens.*;

/**
 * This class shows that you can supply your own reader to
 * a tokenizer.
 */
public class ShowSuppliedReader {

public static void main(String[] args) throws IOException {
    String s = "Let's file this away.";
    FileWriter fw = new FileWriter("temp.txt");
    fw.write(s);
    fw.close();

    FileReader fr = new FileReader("temp.txt");
    PushbackReader pr = new PushbackReader(fr, 4);

    Tokenizer t = new Tokenizer();
    t.setReader(pr);

    while (true) {
        Token tok = t.nextToken();
        if (tok.equals(Token.EOF)) {
            break;
        }
        System.out.println(tok);
    }
}
}
```

Running this class prints the following:

```
Let's
file
this
away
.
```

The `main()` method in `ShowSuppliedReader` creates a `FileReader`, wraps a `PushbackReader` around it, and provides this reader to the tokenizer. The code supplies the reader with an ample (four-character) pushback buffer, which lets the reader handle multicharacter symbols.

The design of the `Tokenizer` class allows you to construct a `Tokenizer` object without having a string or reader to read from. This allows you to create a customized tokenizer that is independent of any particular string.

9.9 Customizing a Tokenizer

You can customize a tokenizer in three ways: by customizing one of the tokenizer's states, by changing which state the tokenizer enters given an initial character, or by adding an entirely new state.

9.9.1 Customizing a State

The preceding section shows how the `CoffeeParser` class creates a special tokenizer that allows spaces to appear in words. The `tokenizer()` method of this class retrieves a `WordState` object from a tokenizer `t` and updates it:

```
t.wordState().setWordChars(' ', ' ', true);
```

9.9.2 Changing Which State the Tokenizer Enters

The example in Section 9.7.1 changes the state the tokenizer enters on seeing a "#" to a quote state. It uses this line:

```
t.setCharacterState('#', '#', t.quoteState());
```

9.9.3 Adding a State

As an example of creating and using a new tokenizer state, consider how to change the default tokenizer to recognize scientific notation. For example, in your language you might want to allow exponential notation for numbers. That is, given a line of text such as:

```
"2.998e8 meters per second"
```

your language might recognize the number as 2,998,000,000, or 2.998 times 10 to the eighth power. To achieve this, you must change how you tokenize numbers. Figure 9.15 shows a ScientificNumberState class. This class subclasses from NumberState and reuses some of its superclass's logic.

To use the scientific notation tokenizer with a parser, follow these steps:

1. Create the tokenizer.

2. Feed the tokenizer a string to tokenize.

3. Create a token assembly from the tokenizer.

4. Ask the parser to parse this assembly.

Here's an example:

```
package sjm.examples.tokens;

import sjm.parse.*;
import sjm.parse.tokens.*;
import sjm.examples.arithmetic.*;
```

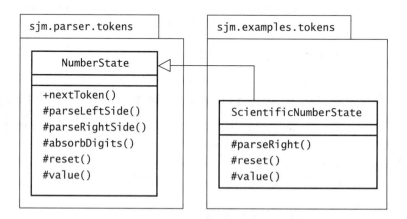

Figure 9.15 The ScientificNumberState. The ScientificNumber class overrides some of the methods in NumberState to allow for exponential notation.

```
/**
 * This class shows how to use a tokenizer that accepts
 * scientific notation with an arithmetic parser.
 */
public class ShowScientific {

public static void main(String[] args) throws Exception {

    Tokenizer t = new Tokenizer();
    ScientificNumberState sns = new ScientificNumberState();
    t.setCharacterState('0', '9', sns);
    t.setCharacterState('.', '.', sns);
    t.setCharacterState('-', '-', sns);

    t.setString("1e2 + 1e1 + 1e0 + 1e-1 + 1e-2 + 1e-3");

    Parser p = ArithmeticParser.start();
    Assembly a = p.bestMatch(new TokenAssembly(t));
    System.out.println(a.pop());
}
}
```

This example evaluates

```
"1e2 + 1e1 + 1e0 + 1e-1 + 1e-2 + 1e-3"
```

Running the class prints the correct answer:

```
111.111
```

9.10 The TokenStringSource Utility

The TokenStringSource class in sjm.parse.tokens is a utility that helps divide an input stream into lines that a parser can parse one at a time. Figure 9.16 shows this class.

```
┌─────────────────────────────────────┐
│          TokenStringSource           │
├─────────────────────────────────────┤
├─────────────────────────────────────┤
│ +TokenStringSource(                  │
│     t: Tokenizer,                    │
│     delimiter:String)                │
│ +hasMoreTokenStrings():boolean       │
│ +nextTokenString():TokenString       │
└─────────────────────────────────────┘
```

Figure 9.16 The TokenStringSource class. The TokenStringSource nextTokenString() method returns all the tokens up to the specified delimiter as a TokenString.

This class provides an enumeration over the tokens of a tokenizer. Each call to nextTokenString() results in a TokenString that contains all the tokens up to a specified delimiter. This is useful for languages that consist of statements that are separated by a delimiter, such as ";". By using a TokenStringSource, the author of a parser need only parse individual statements of the language. The main() method of TokenStringSource gives the following example:

```
public static void main(String args[]) {

    String s = "I came; I saw; I left in peace;";

    TokenStringSource tss =
        new TokenStringSource(new Tokenizer(s), ";");

    while (tss.hasMoreTokenStrings()) {
        System.out.println(tss.nextTokenString());
    }
}
```

This prints the following:

```
I came
I saw
I left in peace
```

The Logikus parser in Chapter 14, "Parsing a Logic Language," uses TokenStringSource to break up lines of input. Statements in a Logikus program are rules and facts, separated by semicolons. The Logikus parser does not parse an entire program. Instead, it parses a single statement and relies on a TokenStringSource object to divide the input into statements. Using TokenStringSource can make your parser easier to write and faster, too.

9.11 Token Strings

The package sjm.parse.tokens uses a TokenString class to hold the results of tokenizing a string. A TokenString is similar to a String, but it contains a series of tokens rather than a series of characters. Like String objects, TokenString objects are immutable, meaning that they cannot change after they are created. Figure 9.17 shows the TokenString class.

The TokenAssembly class hides the fact that it relies on class TokenString. The TokenStringSource class, on the other hand, returns TokenString objects. If you use TokenStringSource to break up an input stream, you must understand the collaboration of several token-related classes. This example shows a collaboration of instances of these classes:

```
                    ┌─────────────────────────────────────┐
                    │           TokenString               │
                    ├─────────────────────────────────────┤
                    │ +TokenString(tokens[]:Token)        │
                    │ +TokenString(                       │
                    │     r:PushbackReader,               │
                    │     t:Tokenizer)                    │
                    │ +TokenString(s:String)              │
                    │ +length():int                       │
                    │ +tokenAt(i:int):Token               │
                    │ +toString():String                  │
                    │ ...                                 │
                    └─────────────────────────────────────┘
```

Figure 9.17 The TokenString class. A TokenString is essentially an array of Tokens.
Like String, TokenString is immutable, so there is never a need to copy a
TokenString.

```java
package sjm.examples.tokens;

import sjm.parse.*;
import sjm.parse.tokens.*;

/**
 * This class shows a collaboration of objects from classes
 * <code>Tokenizer</code>, <code>TokenStringSource</code>,
 * <code>TokenString</code>, <code>TokenAssembly</code>.
 */

public class ShowTokenString

public static void main(String args[]) {

    // a parser that counts words

    Parser w = new Word().discard();
    w.setAssembler(new Assembler() {
        public void workOn(Assembly a) {
            if (a.stackIsEmpty()) {
                a.push(new Integer(1));
            } else {
                Integer i = (Integer) a.pop();
                a.push(new Integer(i.intValue() + 1));
            }
        }
    });

    // a repetition of the word counter

    Parser p = new Repetition(w);
```

```
        // consume token strings separated by semicolons

        String s = "I came; I saw; I left in peace;";
        Tokenizer t = new Tokenizer(s);
        TokenStringSource tss = new TokenStringSource(t, ";");

        // count the words in each token string

        while (tss.hasMoreTokenStrings()) {
            TokenString ts = tss.nextTokenString();
            TokenAssembly ta = new TokenAssembly(ts);
            Assembly a = p.completeMatch(ta);
            System.out.println(
                ts + " (" + a.pop() + " words)");
        }
    }
}
```

Running this class shows the word count of each semicolon-delimited section:

```
I came (2 words)
I saw (2 words)
I left in peace (4 words)
```

In this example,

- A `Tokenizer` object breaks the input into tokens.

- A `TokenStringSource` object divides the tokens into `TokenString` objects.

- A `TokenString` variable holds a succession of `TokenString` objects from the input.

- A `TokenAssembly` variable holds a `TokenAssembly` object that wraps around a `TokenString` object.

9.12 Summary

Tokenizing text lets you simplify grammars so that they define patterns of tokens instead of patterns of individual characters. A tokenizer must have a default state along with a set of other states to enter, depending on the next character to consume. Once entered, a tokenizing state needs to arrange to consume and return one token, although it can delegate this task to another state. You can customize which state a tokenizer enters given an initial character, and you can customize how a state builds a token. You can also create your own tokenizing states, so you have a great deal of freedom in customizing a tokenizer to meet the needs of your language.

CHAPTER 10

Matching Mechanics

The parsers in this book depend on a few classes that bring a grammar to life, recognizing text and assembling results. Earlier chapters explain how to use these classes without explaining how the classes work. This chapter explains the mechanics of how `Sequence`, `Alternation`, and `Repetition` make their matches.

10.1 Introduction

Given a package of classes and their interfaces, would you ever want to look within, to see how the classes work? Indeed, there are several reasons *not* to look beneath the method signatures of the classes. By relying strictly on the interface and not on how the code supports it, you free your code from dependencies on how another package works. The separation of interface and execution is a cornerstone of several advances in applied computer science, especially distributed computing and component development.

On the other hand, professional developers often want to look beneath the signatures of methods they rely on. In the general case, this examination may help you to understand in detail the exact performance of a method. The code is the final arbiter of what a class actually does.

In the case of parsers, there are many reasons to look under the hood to see how the fundamental classes work. When you write your own parsers, you may encounter surprises and subtleties that pull you into looking at the mechanics of these classes. You may find that you want to write a faster engine, or you may want to add a new type of terminal or a new subhierarchy of `Parser`. Even if you have no intention of tinkering with the workings of the fundamental parser classes, familiarizing yourself with their operation will increase your understanding of how to use them.

10.2 Parser Matching

The main goals of a parser are to match text and to use assemblers to build a result in an assembly. Matching is what differentiates, say, a sequence from an alternation from a repetition. As you'll soon see, a parser that contains alternations or repetitions does not always know which way or how many times to perform a match. The solution used in this book is to add *all* possible alternatives into an output set. Some alternative algorithms for matching are faster, but they impose constraints on allowable grammars. For a thorough analysis of approaches to matching, see *Compilers* [Aho et al.].

Each parser in the hierarchy beneath Parser implements matching in a different way. Figure 10.1 shows the aspects of the Parser class that relate to establishing an assembler and to matching.

The Parser hierarchy relies on the Vector class for managing sets of assemblies. To be compatible with early versions of Java that did not have a Set class, the classes in sjm.parse use Vector as if it were Set. The Parser class provides two static methods that facilitate the manipulation of vectors. The add() method appends the elements of a second vector to the first vector in its parameter list. The elementClone() method returns a vector that contains clones of the elements of a given vector. Subclasses use these methods in implementing match().

The match() method, which is abstract, and the matchAndAssemble() method form the heart of matching. The mechanics of matching are different for every subclass of Parser, but the collaboration of parsers, assemblies, and assemblers is the same for every parser. So even though every subclass of Parser must implement match(), only Parser itself has a matchAndAssemble() method.

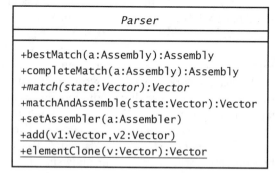

```
                        Parser

+bestMatch(a:Assembly):Assembly
+completeMatch(a:Assembly):Assembly
+match(state:Vector):Vector
+matchAndAssemble(state:Vector):Vector
+setAssembler(a:Assembler)
+add(v1:Vector,v2:Vector)
+elementClone(v:Vector):Vector
```

Figure 10.1 Parser matching and assembling. The methods bestMatch() and completeMatch() hide the fact that the Parser class's matching algorithm works with a set (or Vector) of assemblies.

The matchAndAssemble() method follows the *template method* pattern [Gamma et al.], implementing an algorithm but deferring some steps to subclasses. Specifically, this method accepts a vector of input assemblies, applies the abstract match() method against these, and applies the parser's assembler against each result. Here is the code for matchAndAssemble():

```
/**
 * Match this parser against an input state, and then
 * apply this parser's assembler against the resulting
 * state.
 *
 */
public Vector matchAndAssemble(Vector in) {
    Vector out = match(in);
    if (assembler != null) {
        Enumeration e = out.elements();
        while (e.hasMoreElements()) {
            assembler.workOn((Assembly) e.nextElement());
        }
    }
    return out;
}
```

This method establishes the mechanics of matching and then assembling, although it relies on the abstract match() method, which subclasses must implement.

10.3 Repetition Matching

The Repetition class earns its name through the way it implements the match() method. A repetition parser takes another parser and matches it repeatedly against each assembly in a set. The parser that a repetition repeats may be a simple terminal, such as the object new Word(). The parser that a repetition repeats may also be an arbitrarily complex composite parser. Figure 10.2 shows that the constructors of the Repetition class require the creator of a Repetition object to specify this subparser.

The idea of a Repetition object is that it produces many matches against a single assembly. The match() method's input parameter, however, is not a single assembly but rather a collection of assemblies in a vector. The responsibility of Repetition.match() is to produce zero or more matches against each assembly in the input vector, gathering all the matches into a final output state, which is another vector.

The Repetition class provides for a preassembler that it applies to every assembly in an input state before matching. Unlike Sequence and Alternation objects, a Repetition object matches every assembly in an input state at least once. If the

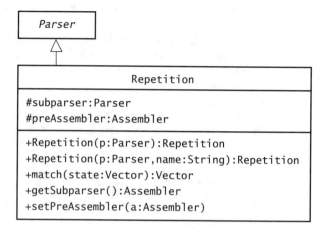

Figure 10.2   The Repetition class. A Repetition object represents a repetition of another parser, so the constructors of this class require this parser to be specified.

subparser cannot match the assembly even once, it counts as zero matches and the match succeeds. Because every input state carries through to the output state, it is safe and occasionally useful to apply a *preassembler*. For example, the code in sjm.examples.pretty uses a preassembler to stack a fence object before matching a repetition and uses a regular assembler to pop down to this fence after matching.

In pseudocode, you can let s be a working state that contains the results of successive applications of the repetition's subparser to the input state. Here is the algorithm for a repetition match:

```
// pseudocode
out = in;
apply preassembler
s = in; // a working state
while (!s.isEmpty()) {
    s = subparser.matchAndAssemble(s);
    out = out + s;
}
```

The actual code must take care that the initial value of out is a deep copy of the input state. If out were a simple clone of the input vector, it would contain the same objects as the input. Then if you applied an assembler to the out vector, you would modify the elements of the input set. Here is the code for Repetition.match():

```
public Vector match(Vector in) {
    if (preAssembler != null) {
```

```
            Enumeration e = in.elements();
            while (e.hasMoreElements()) {
                preAssembler.workOn((Assembly) e.nextElement());
            }
        }
        Vector out = elementClone(in);
        Vector s = in; // a working state
        while (!s.isEmpty()) {
            s = subparser.matchAndAssemble(s);
            add(out, s);
        }
        return out;
    }
```

Note that the code uses `matchAndAssemble()` rather than `match()`. The general responsibility of any implementation of `match()` is for the parser to match each subparser and apply the subparser's assembler, if it has one.

10.4 Collection Parsers

The `Sequence` and `Alternation` classes are subclasses of `CollectionParser`, as Figure 10.3 shows. These classes have a common way of adding and storing their subparsers. They differ primarily in how they match a set of assemblies.

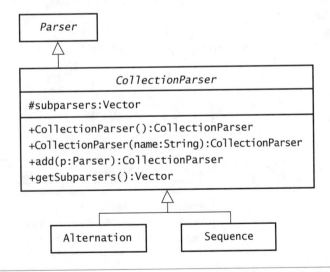

Figure 10.3 The `CollectionParser` class. `CollectionParser` is the abstract superclass of the two fundamental types of collection parsers: `Alternation` and `Sequence`.

The main behavior that `CollectionParser` provides to its subclasses is the ability to add a parser to a collection.

10.5 Sequence Matching

A `Sequence` parser holds a collection of parsers that must each, in turn, match against an assembly. Matching is the main service that the `Sequence` class provides, as Figure 10.4 shows.

When a sequence matches, it matches against an input collection of assemblies. To perform the match, the sequence matches its first subparser against each assembly in the collection. The result is a new collection of assemblies, all having one property in common: They all are assemblies that have just survived a match of the first subparser. If the input collection is a variable `in` and you call the first subparser `p1`, the new state of the match is

```
state1 = p1.match(in); // pseudocode
```

Here, `state1` is a collection of assemblies that have all matched `p1`. Continuing down the path, calling the second subparser `p2`, you could write

```
state2 = p2.match(state1); // also pseudocode
```

Here, `state2` is a collection of assemblies that have all matched `p1` and `p2`. You could also write

```
state2 = p2.match(p1.match(state1));
```

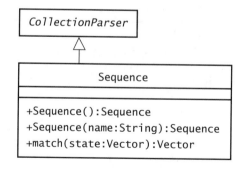

Figure 10.4   The Sequence class. Sequence implements match() so that matching succeeds only if all the parsers in its collection match in succession.

If the sequence has three subparsers—p1, p2, and p3—you could write

```
out = p3.match(p2.match(p1.match(state)));
```

To continue this approach, you must loop over all the subparsers of the sequence. Here is the pseudocode for this:

```
out = in;
for each subparser p[i] {
    out = p[i].match(out);
}
return out;
```

This pseudocode overwrites out in each pass, with the intermediate result of matching one subparser against the previous intermediate result. The actual code for this `Sequence.match()` is not much different:

```
public Vector match(Vector in) {
    Vector out = in;
    Enumeration e = subparsers.elements();
    while (e.hasMoreElements()) {
        Parser p = (Parser) e.nextElement();
        out = p.matchAndAssemble(out);
        if (out.isEmpty()) {
            return out;
        }
    }
    return out;
}
```

10.6 Alternation Matching

An alternation is a collection of parsers, any of which may match against an assembly. As with the `Sequence` class, the primary service of the `Alternation` class is matching, as Figure 10.5 shows.

An `Alternation` object matches each of its subparsers against the collection of assemblies that `match()` receives. The `Alternation` object accumulates the results of each match into an output final state. Here it is in pseudocode:

```
out = new state;
for each subparser p {
    out = out + p.match(in);
}
return out;
```

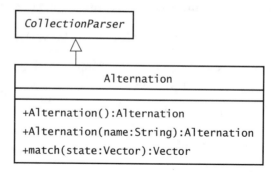

Figure 10.5 The Alternation class. Alternation implements match() so that matching succeeds against any of the parsers in the collection of parsers it
inherits from CollectionParser.

The actual code for alternation matching follows this design, but it walks the results
of intermediate results more manually. Here is the code for Alternation.match():

```
public Vector match(Vector in) {
    Vector out = new Vector();
    Enumeration e = subparsers.elements();
    while (e.hasMoreElements()) {
        Parser p = (Parser) e.nextElement();
        add(out, p.matchAndAssemble(in));
    }
    return out;
}
```

10.7 Empty Matching

An empty parser matches a collection of assemblies by returning the collection with
no changes whatsoever. Here is the code for Empty.match():

```
public Vector match(Vector in) {
    return elementClone(in);
}
```

The match() methods must not change the input state. An Empty parser does not
consume text from an assembly, but it may alter an assembly's state by applying an
assembler to it in matchAndAssemble(). The code here makes a copy to ensure that
matching does not affect the input state.

10.8 Terminal Matching

The parsers discussed to this point have been compositions of other parsers. Each of them matches a collection of assemblies by delegating the matching job to its sub-parsers. This structural composition and runtime delegation ends with Terminal and its subclasses. Terminal objects are the leaves of a parser composition and thus "terminate" the composition. They also terminate the matching process by deciding themselves whether or not they match a given assembly. Figure 10.6 shows the Terminal class.

Any Terminal object can decide whether it matches any assembly, so the job of matching a collection of assemblies reduces to the job of matching each assembly individually. Subclasses of Terminal typically override matchOneAssembly() or qualifies(), but they need not override match(). Here is the code for Terminal.match():

```
public Vector match(Vector in) {
    Vector out = new Vector();
    Enumeration e = in.elements();
    while (e.hasMoreElements()) {
        Assembly a = (Assembly) e.nextElement();
        Assembly b = matchOneAssembly(a);
        if (b != null) {
            out.addElement(b);
        }
    }
    return out;
}
```

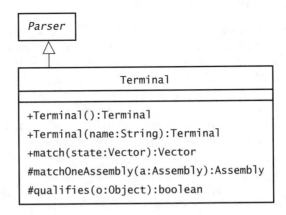

Figure 10.6 The Terminal class. A Terminal object is a parser that is not a composition of other parsers.

This code gathers into an output collection the results of matching the `Terminal` object against each assembly in the input collection. Here is the code for `matchOneAssembly()`:

```
protected Assembly matchOneAssembly(Assembly in) {
    if (!in.hasMoreElements()) {
        return null;
    }
    if (qualifies(in.peek())) {
        Assembly out = (Assembly) in.clone();
        Object o = out.nextElement();
        if (!discard) {
            out.push(o);
        }
        return out;
    }
    return null;
}
```

This code peeks at the next element of the input assembly to see whether it "qualifies." The `Terminal` class has a default implementation of `qualifies()`, but subclasses typically override it. The `qualifies()` method determines whether the terminal matches the next element.

`Terminal` objects by default push the element they match from an assembly onto the assembly's stack. You can prevent this by sending the `Terminal` object a `discard()` message. In practice, you usually want to prevent the pushing of symbols, literals, and any other terminals when you know the exact value of the match in advance.

10.8.1 Token Terminals

One result of tokenization is that when a `Terminal` parser must determine whether it matches the next chunk of text, a tokenizer has already made decisions about how to compose the next token. For example, a tokenizer decides whether scientific notation is allowable in numbers.

A `Terminal` parser can make further decisions about what it matches, but as a practical matter it cannot undo decisions the tokenizer makes. A good strategy is to keep tokenization simple, adding specialization in `Terminal` subclasses.

For example, this book has a single token type for word tokens and has three subclasses of `Terminal` that match against word tokens. Classes `Word`, `Literal`, and `CaselessLiteral` are all `Terminal` subclasses that match against a token of type `Token.TT_WORD`. Objects of class `Word` successfully match any word token. Objects of class `Literal` recognize only a specific word; a `Literal` object fails to match any token that does not contain the same string the object receives in its constructor. The CaselessLiteral subclass of Literal relaxes this selectivity, matching a specific string but ignoring case. Figure 10.7 shows the subclasses of Terminal that match word tokens.

These classes must say whether they match a given object. In other words, they must say whether a given object qualifies as the specific type of terminal. For example, here is Literal.qualifies():

```
/**
 * Returns true if the literal this object represents equals
 * an assembly's next element.
 */
protected boolean qualifies (Object o) {
    return literal.equals((Token) o);
}
```

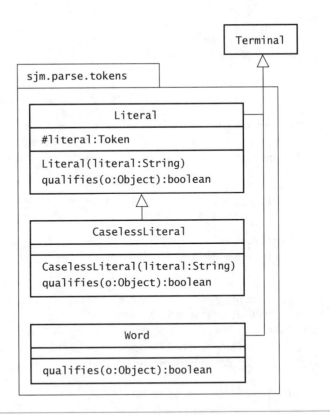

Figure 10.7   Token terminals. Typical token terminals simply say whether a given object qualifies as the type of terminal sought.

The Literal class accepts a string in its constructor but builds a Token from this string and saves it in its literal instance variable. The Literal.qualifies() method determines that a token qualifies as a match if the token contains the same string.

CaselessLiteral is a subclass of Literal that allows the desired string to match regardless of case, as its qualifies() method shows:

```
/**
 * Returns true if the literal this object represents equals
 * an assembly's next element, disregarding case.
 */
protected boolean qualifies(Object o) {
    return literal.equalsIgnoreCase((Token) o);
}
```

The qualifies() methods for Num, QuotedString, and Word use the is methods of Token. For example, here is Word.qualifies():

```
/**
 * Returns true if an assembly's next element is a word.
 */
protected boolean qualifies(Object o) {
    Token t = (Token) o;
    return t.isWord();
}
```

The Symbol class typically recognizes a single character, such as "<". However, class Tokenizer in sjm.parse.tokens also provides for multicharacter symbols, such as "<=" to appear as single tokens. Here is Symbol.qualifies():

```
/**
 * Returns true if the symbol this object represents equals
 * an assembly's next element.
 */
protected boolean qualifies (Object o) {
    return symbol.equals((Token) o);
}
```

This code is nearly identical to the qualifies() method for Literal, but it matches symbol tokens rather than word tokens. The difference between literals and symbols lies mainly in the tokenizer. For example, a default Tokenizer object tokenizes the string: "<<<" as three tokens of type Token.TT_SYMBOL. No Literal object could match this string, but the following object would:

```
new Repetition(new Symbol('<'))
```

10.8.2 Character Terminals

Classes for the character-based terminals in `sjm.parse.chars` are as simple as those of the token terminals. Any terminal has the primary task of saying whether it matches the next element of an assembly. For example, here is `Digit.qualifies()`:

```
/**
 * Returns true if an assembly's next element is a digit.
 */
public boolean qualifies(Object o) {
    Character c = (Character) o;
    return Character.isDigit(c.charValue());
}
```

10.8.3 Terminals Summary

Creating new `Terminal` subclasses is usually easy. The mechanics of matching belong to the `Terminal` class, and the new subclass needs only to decide which tokens or characters qualify as a match.

10.9 Parser Matching Utilities

Figure 10.1 shows two methods that support matching: `bestMatch()` and `completeMatch()`. The `bestMatch()` method accepts a single assembly, puts it in a vector, and matches against the vector. Then `bestMatch()` returns one assembly from the output vector of assemblies, choosing the one whose index is advanced furthest. If a grammar matches only part of an input, `bestMatch()` returns an assembly that shows the progress made. For example, consider matching the grammar

```
adjectives = ("steaming" | "hot")*;
```

against the string

```
"hot hot steaming hot coffee"
```

The following code sends `bestMatch()` to a parser for `adjectives`, showing that the parser can match up to the word "coffee":

```
package sjm.examples.mechanics;

import sjm.parse.*;
import sjm.parse.tokens.*;
```

```
/**
 * Show that <code>Parser.bestMatch()</code> matches a
 * parser against an input as far as possible.
 */
public class ShowBestMatch {

public static void main(String[] args) {

    Alternation a = new Alternation();

    a.add(new Literal("steaming"));
    a.add(new Literal("hot"));

    Repetition adjectives = new Repetition(a);

    TokenAssembly ta =
        new TokenAssembly("hot hot steaming hot coffee");

    System.out.println(adjectives.bestMatch(ta));
    }
}
```

This prints the following:

```
[hot, hot, steaming, hot]hot/hot/steaming/hot^coffee
```

The bestMatch() method performs three tasks that a user of a parser typically needs: placing an assembly in a vector, matching against that vector, and choosing the longest match. Here is the code for this method:

```
/**
 * Returns an assembly with the greatest possible number of
 * elements consumed by matches of this parser.
 */
public Assembly bestMatch(Assembly a) {
    Vector initialState = new Vector();
    initialState.addElement(a);
    Vector finalState = matchAndAssemble(initialState);
    return best(finalState);
}
```

Here is the supporting method, best():

```
/**
 * Returns the most-matched assembly in a collection.
 */
public Assembly best(Vector v) {
    Assembly best = null;
    Enumeration e = v.elements();
```

```
        while (e.hasMoreElements()) {
            Assembly a = (Assembly) e.nextElement();
            if (!a.hasMoreElements()) {
                return a;
            }
            if (best == null) {
                best = a;
            } else
                if (   a.elementsConsumed() >
                       best.elementsConsumed()) {

                    best = a;
                }
        }
        return best;
}
```

You usually want to require that a parser consume all of the input text. For example, an arithmetic parser recognizes

```
3 * 4 + 5 and more
```

as an arithmetic expression followed by unrecognizable text. To ensure that the best match is a complete match, the `Parser` class provides a `completeMatch()` method. Here is the code for `completeMatch()`:

```
/**
 * Returns either null or a completely matched version of
 * the supplied assembly.
 */
public Assembly completeMatch(Assembly a) {
    Assembly best = bestMatch(a);
    if (best != null && !best.hasMoreElements()) {
        return best;
    }
    return null;
}
```

This method returns either a complete match or `null`. Here is an example:

```
package sjm.examples.mechanics;

import sjm.parse.*;
import sjm.parse.tokens.*;
import sjm.examples.arithmetic.*;

/**
 * This class shows that <code>Parser.completeMatch()</code>
 * returns a complete match or null.
 */
```

```
public class ShowCompleteMatch {

public static void main(String[] args)
    throws ArithmeticException {

    Parser p = ArithmeticParser.start();

    TokenAssembly ta =
        new TokenAssembly("3 * 4 + 5 and more");

    System.out.println(p.bestMatch(ta));
    System.out.println(p.completeMatch(ta));
}
}
```

Running this class prints the following:

```
[17.0]3.0/*/4.0/+/5.0^and/more
null
```

This shows that bestMatch() matches as much input as possible, whereas completeMatch() returns null unless the parser can match all of the input.

10.10 Summary

A central problem of parser construction is nondeterminism: Parsers do not always know which path to take as they recognize text. The solution used in this book is to handle recognition at a "set" level. Given a set of partially recognized text strings, each fundamental parser type produces a new set:

- A repetition creates a copy of the initial set, adds a set that results from matching a subparser once, and repeats this process until the subparser can match nothing in the preceding set.

- A sequence matches its subparsers in sequence, starting with the input set. It matches each subparser to the result of the preceding subparser and returns the final set.

- An alternation applies each of its subparsers to each member of the input set and returns an accumulation of the resulting sets.

- A terminal finds assemblies in the input set that start with some element. The terminal creates an output set from copies of these assemblies, removing the sought element from each copy.

These set operations empower the parsing of an infinite variety of languages, including the query, logic, and imperative languages that lie ahead in this book.

CHAPTER 11

Extending the Parser Toolkit

This chapter explains how you can extend the parser toolkit by introducing new types of terminals or completely new parser types.

11.1 The Role of New Types of Parsers

The basic parser tools of repetition, sequence, and alternation are sufficient for building an infinite variety of parsers. You may find that you never need to extend this fundamental suite of tools. However, cases do arise in which new parser types are needed, and this section looks at several ways to extend the parser hierarchy.

The most common need is for a new type of terminal. For example, a new terminal might distinguish an integer from a floating point number, or a lowercase word from an uppercase word. You may also need to adjust the tokenizer to change how it forms elements, and in conjunction create one or more new `Terminal` subclasses that recognize the new token types.

In general, there is no way to predict the new types of parsers you might want to create. This section includes an example that shows how to add a new kind of sequence that complains intelligently when it fails to find the conclusion of a sequence.

The sections that follow cover three ways in which you may want to extend the parser hierarchy: creating a new subclass of `Terminal`, creating a new token or terminal design, and creating a completely new parser type.

11.2 New Terminals

Terminals use some judgment about whether the next element in an assembly qualifies as the type of element sought. You can refine this judgment by introducing new
subclasses of `Terminal`. For example, consider a language that differentiates between
known values and unknown values by using lowercase and uppercase letters. In this
language, a structure might appear that looks like this:

```
member(X, [republican, democrat])
```

This structure might imply that the unknown X can take on either of the known values in the list. A partial grammar for this language might look something like this:

```
//...
term     = variable | known;
variable = UppercaseWord;
known    = LowercaseWord;
```

Here is a sample program that depends on `UppercaseWord` and `LowercaseWord` to
detect the difference between variables and known values:

```java
package sjm.examples.mechanics;

import sjm.parse.*;
import sjm.parse.tokens.*;

/**
 * Show the use of new subclasses of <code>Terminal</code>.
 */
public class ShowNewTerminals {

public static void main(String[] args) {

    /*  term     = variable | known;
     *  variable = UppercaseWord;
     *  known    = LowercaseWord;
     */

    Parser variable = new UppercaseWord();
    Parser known    = new LowercaseWord();

    Parser term = new Alternation()
        .add(variable)
        .add(known);

    // anonymous Assembler subclasses note element type

    variable.setAssembler(
        new Assembler() {
```

```
            public void workOn(Assembly a) {
                Object o = a.pop();
                a.push("VAR(" + o + ")");
            }
        });

    known.setAssembler(
        new Assembler() {
            public void workOn(Assembly a) {
                Object o = a.pop();
                a.push("KNOWN(" + o + ")");
            }
        });

    // term* matching against knowns and variables:

    System.out.println(
        new Repetition(term).bestMatch(
            new TokenAssembly(
                "member X republican democrat")));
    }
}
```

This sample program uses anonymous subclasses of Assembler to suggest how, in practice, you can react differently to different types of matches. Running this class prints the following:

```
[KNOWN(member), VAR(X), KNOWN(republican), KNOWN(democrat)]
member/X/republican/democrat^
```

In practice, your assemblers will perform some useful function. For example, you might have Variable objects and KnownValue objects, and your assemblers might create these and pass them to the overall target of the assembly. The point here is that you can add new types of terminals to trigger these different types of actions.

Implementations of LowercaseWord and UppercaseWord (in package sjm.examples.mechanics) require only overriding qualifies() from Word. Here is the code for LowercaseWord.qualifies():

```
/**
 * Returns true if an assembly's next element is a
 * lowercase word.
 */
protected boolean qualifies (Object o) {
    Token t = (Token) o;
    if (!t.isWord()) {
        return false;
    }
    String word = t.sval();
```

```
        return word.length() > 0 &&
            Character.isLowerCase(word.charAt(0));
    }
```

In this example, you could take a different design approach and push the job of distinguishing lowercase and uppercase words down to the tokenizer. You could create new token types and modify the tokenizer class to separate lowercase tokens from uppercase tokens. To distinguish lowercase from uppercase words, the approach of introducing new `Terminal` subclasses is simple and effective. However, there are times when you will want to modify your tokenizer, particularly when there is potential overlap and ambiguity surrounding token types.

In an earlier example (in Chapter 4, "Testing a Parser"), the word "cups" was seen by the parser both as a regular word and as a reserved word. In this case, it would be helpful to have the tokenizer make the distinction between reserved and nonreserved words.

11.3 New Token Types

A tokenizer is responsible for breaking text into logical elements. Your idea of what a "logical" element is may differ from the defaults provided by class `Tokenizer` in `sjm.parse.tokens`. For example, you may want to distinguish real numbers from imaginary numbers, or HTML tags from other kinds of text, or reserved and nonreserved words. Often, when you create a new type of token, you will create one or more new `Terminal` types to recognize it.

One important reason for changing a tokenizer is to avoid ambiguity. Section 4.2.2, "Terminal Ambiguity," shows the ambiguity of the following grammar:

```
query  = (Word | volume)* '?';
volume = "cups" | "gallon" | "liter";
```

This grammar is ambiguous because a word such as "cups" is both a `Word` and a `volume`. To prevent this ambiguity without modifying the tokenizer, you can introduce new terminals. You could create new subclasses of `Terminal`, perhaps `ReservedWord` and `NonReservedWord`, having each one keep a list of known reserved words. `ReservedWord` would succeed in matching a word only if the word were on the list; `NonReservedWord` would succeed only for words not on the reserved word list. This design has the disadvantage of your having to invent a way of passing around a list of reserved words. An alternative is to push the job of distinguishing types of words down to the tokenizer.

To provide for unambiguous parsing of the `query` grammar, you can create a new token type—say, `TT_RESERVED`—and have the tokenizer return each word as either a `TT_WORD` token or a `TT_RESERVED` token. Figure 11.1 shows a new tokenizer state and a new terminal type that can work together to tokenize text, distinguishing reserved words from nonreserved words.

The default behavior of class `Tokenizer` in `sjm.parse.tokens` is to transfer control to a `WordState` object when the input stream starts with a word character. By default, a `Tokenizer` constructor sets words to begin with characters using the following messages:

```
//...
setCharacterState( 'a',   'z', wordState());
setCharacterState( 'A',   'Z', wordState());
setCharacterState(0xc0,  0xff, wordState());
```

The last line here allows words to begin with characters that do not typically appear in English. Figure 9.5 in Chapter 9, "Advanced Tokenizing," shows the values of characters.

To craft a tokenizer that returns reserved words as distinct from nonreserved words, you can replace the `WordState` tokenizer state with an object of the new class

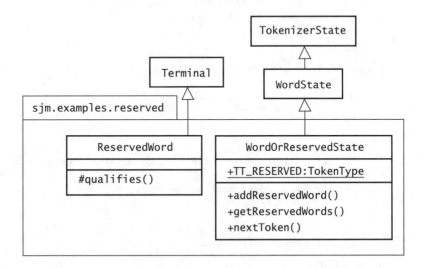

Figure 11.1   The `reserved` package. A new class for tokenizing, `WordOrReservedState`, allows an input string to produce elements that are either plain words or reserved words. A new terminal class, `ReservedWord`, recognizes the reserved tokens that the tokenizer produces.

WordOrReservedState. This class subclasses WordState, introduces a static variable TT_RESERVED, and overrides nextToken() to consult a list of known reserved words. Here is WordOrReservedState.java:

```java
package sjm.examples.reserved;

import java.io.*;
import java.util.*;
import sjm.parse.*;
import sjm.parse.tokens.*;

/**
 * Override WordState to return known reserved words as
 * tokens of type TT_RESERVED.
 */
public class WordOrReservedState extends WordState {
    Vector reserved = new Vector();

    /**
     * A constant indicating that a token is a reserved word.
     */
    public static final TokenType TT_RESERVED =
        new TokenType("reserved");

/**
 * Adds the specified string as a known reserved word.
 */
public void addReservedWord(String word) {
    reserved.addElement(word);
}

/**
 * Return all the known reserved words.
 */
public Vector getReservedWords() {
    return reserved;
}

/**
 * Return a reserved token or a word token from a reader.
 */
public Token nextToken(PushbackReader r, int c, Tokenizer t)
    throws IOException {

    Token tok = super.nextToken(r, c, t);
    if (reserved.contains(tok.sval())) {
        return new Token(TT_RESERVED, tok.sval(), 0);
    }
    return tok;
}
}
```

The `WordOrReservedState` class maintains a list of known reserved words and checks this list after the superclass builds a word from the reader. To use this state, you will create a `Tokenizer` object and direct it to use a `WordOrReservedState` object wherever it would have used a `WordState` object. First, to recognize the new type of token that the tokenizer will return, you need the class `ReservedWord`:

```
package sjm.examples.reserved;

import java.util.*;
import sjm.parse.*;
import sjm.parse.tokens.*;

/**
 * A Word matches a word from a token assembly.
 */
public class ReservedWord extends Terminal {

/**
 * Returns true if an assembly's next element is a reserved
 * word.
 */
protected boolean qualifies (Object o) {
    Token t = (Token) o;
    return t.ttype() == WordOrReservedState.TT_RESERVED;
}
}
```

This class is similar to the `Word` class, whose notion of whether an element "qualifies" depends entirely on the token type. Here is a demonstration of this class, and `WordOrReservedState`, in action:

```
package sjm.examples.reserved;

import java.io.*;
import java.util.*;
import sjm.parse.*;
import sjm.parse.tokens.*;

/**
 * This class shows the use of a customized tokenizer and
 * the use of a terminal that looks for the new token type.
 */
public class ShowReserved {

/**
 * Return a customized tokenizer that uses
 * WordOrReservedState in place of WordState.
 */
public static Tokenizer tokenizer() {
```

```
        Tokenizer t = new Tokenizer();

        WordOrReservedState wors = new WordOrReservedState();
        wors.addReservedWord("cups");
        wors.addReservedWord("gallon");
        wors.addReservedWord("liter");

        t.setCharacterState( 'a',    'z', wors);
        t.setCharacterState( 'A',    'Z', wors);
        t.setCharacterState(0xc0,  0xff, wors);

        return t;
    }

    public static void main(String[] args) {

        // volume = "cups" | "gallon" | "liter";

        Parser volume = new ReservedWord();

        // an anonymous Assembler subclass notes volume matches

        volume.setAssembler(
            new Assembler() {
                public void workOn(Assembly a) {
                    Object o = a.pop();
                    a.push("VOL(" + o + ")");
                }
            });

        // query = (Word | volume)* '?';

        Parser wordOrVolume = new Alternation()
            .add(new Word())
            .add(volume);

        Parser query = new Sequence()
            .add(new Repetition(wordOrVolume))
            .add(new Symbol('?'));

        Tokenizer t = tokenizer();
        t.setString("How many cups are in a gallon?");

        Vector v = new Vector();
        v.addElement(new TokenAssembly(t));

        System.out.println(query.match(v));
    }
}
```

This sample class contains the static method `tokenizer()`, which returns a special tokenizer that looks for reserved words. The sample hard-codes three reserved words: "cups", "gallon", and "liter". A more comprehensive example would have the names of perhaps 100 to 200 units. The tokenizer() method changed the default Tokenizer object to use the WordOrReservedState object for elements that begin with a letter.

The main() method in the example builds a parser for the grammar:

```
query  = (Word | volume)* '?';
volume = "cups" | "gallon" | "liter";
```

The example uses a ReservedWord terminal for volume. Because the main() method uses the class's customized tokenizer, a word such as "cups" is a token of type TT_RESERVED and not TT_WORD. A Word terminal does not recognize "cups" as a word, but a ReservedWord terminal recognizes "cups" as a reserved word. Section 4.2.2, "Terminal Ambiguity," shows a sample program that prints four parses of the input "How many cups are in a gallon?". Now, running ShowReserved prints the following:

```
[
 [How, many, VOL(cups), are, in, a, VOL(gallon), ?]
 How/many/cups/are/in/a/gallon/?^
 ]
```

The anonymous assemblers in ShowReserved.main() wrap the characters "VOL()" around the reserved words "cups" and "gallon". Parsing the query is no longer ambiguous. This means that there is only one way to parse the input phrase.

The connection between tokens and terminals is tight. A tokenizer changes input text into a series of tokens, and a terminal either matches the whole token or it does not. This implies that for every token there must be at least one terminal in a parser that can match it, or else the parser can never match an input string. When you create a new token type, as in this section, you generally must create one or more terminals to match the new type.

11.4 New Parser Features

With the classes Sequence, Alternation, and Repetition, along with a hierarchy of Terminal classes, you can build an infinite variety of parsers. These classes form a complete toolkit, and so you could argue that they need never be extended. History has shown, however, that no toolkit is ever complete in the sense that it cannot profitably be extended. Toolkit developers should strive both for comprehensiveness and extensibility.

Software that is extensible has the following features:

- Classes have short methods that perform a single service.

- Methods and instance variables are generally protected rather than private, allowing subclasses more flexibility in how they extend a class.

- Documentation is accurate and complete at the class level and at the design and architectural levels.

The software in the sjm packages that come with this book generally meets these criteria. An exception is that classes that begin with "Show" are not designed for reuse; they just implement examples. All the classes in sjm.parse, sjm.parse.tokens, and sjm.parse.chars are designed with the goal of being extensible. Although these classes provide a complete kit for composing an unbounded assortment of new parsers, you can easily add to or extend these tools.

There are many reasons that you might want to extend the sjm.parse toolkit. For example, you might want to create subclasses that execute more quickly, parsers that have associated visual components, or parsers that provide helpful information when they fail to match. In each of these examples, the new behaviors follow a different line of thought than merely matching input text. Although the toolkit is complete in meeting its original objectives, it is wide open to enhancements in meeting new objectives.

11.4.1 An Error-Handling Parser

This section gives an example of how to extend the basic toolset with a new type of parser that helps explain why a match failed. The context is that you have written a parser, and your user is attempting to enter a language element that your parser will match. For example, imagine that you have written a parser that recognizes lists according to this grammar:

```
list       = '(' contents ')';
contents   = Empty | actualList;
actualList = Word (',' Word)*;
```

Suppose your user enters

```
(burgle, filch, pilfer, pinch,, purloin, steal, thieve)
```

Your parser fails to match this input because there is a double comma after pinch. The tools in sjm.parse note that a list parser cannot match the input, but they say nothing about where the match failed.

To create a parser that is more helpful when matches fail, you can create a subclass of Sequence that throws an exception at the moment of failure. For example, an object of this class could throw an exception upon seeing a second comma after pinch.

A subtlety here is that it is usually acceptable for a Sequence object to fail entirely, but not after the sequence begins. For example, consider the contents rule in the preceding grammar. This rule allows a list to be either empty or an actual list. When an input list is empty, the actualList sequence fails entirely, and that is what you want. On the other hand, it is usually not acceptable for a Sequence object to begin and not complete. For example, the list sequence begins matching input that starts with an open parenthesis. If the input does not contain a corresponding closing parenthesis, then the input is not a member of the grammar's language, and we can say the input is in error.

There are two sequences in the list grammar that, once started, must complete for the input to be valid. The first sequence is list itself, which must complete after seeing an opening parenthesis. The second place is the sequence (',' Word) that appears in actualList. After seeing a comma for this sequence, the input must contain a following word. For these two sequences, it is useful to have a Track class that throws an exception if a sequence begins but does not complete. Figure 11.2 shows this class.

The class Track overrides the match() method it inherits from Sequence. Recall the pseudocode for Sequence.match():

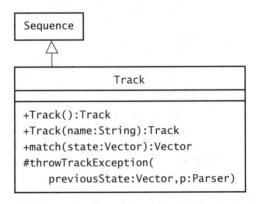

Figure 11.2 The Track class. A Track object is like a Sequence object, except that a track throws an exception if its first subparser matches without all of its subparsers also matching.

```
out = in;
for each subparser p[i] {
    out = p[i].match(out);
}
return out;
```

A Track object notes whether its first subparser matches the input state vector. If it does, all the remaining subparsers must match for the Track object to succeed. If any subparser after the first one fails to match, the Track object throws an exception. Here is the pseudocode for Track.match():

```
inTrack = false;
out = in;
for each subparser p[i]{
    out = p[i].match(out);
    if (out isEmpty && inTrack)
        throw exception;
    inTrack = true;
}
return out;
```

The code for Track.match() follows almost directly from the design:

```
public Vector match(Vector in) {
    boolean inTrack = false;
    Vector last = in;
    Vector out = in;
    Enumeration e = subparsers.elements();
    while (e.hasMoreElements()) {
        Parser p = (Parser) e.nextElement();
        out = p.matchAndAssemble(last);
        if (out.isEmpty()) {
            if (inTrack) {
                throwTrackException(last, p);
            }
            return out;
        }
        inTrack = true;
        last = out;
    }
    return out;
}
```

If the match() method does not throw an exception, it must return a complete state. This includes a responsibility to apply a subparser's assemblers to the results of a match, and that is why this method calls matchAndAssemble() for each subparser.

If any subparser after the first one fails to match, the match() method throws an exception. The method keeps a copy of the last successful match state to help create an informative message if the track fails. Here is the code for throwTrackException():

```
protected void throwTrackException(
    Vector previousState, Parser p) {

    Assembly best = best(previousState);
    String after = best.consumed(" ");
    if (after.equals("")) {
        after = "-nothing-";
    }

    String expected = p.toString();

    Object next = best.peek();
    String found =
        (next == null) ? "-nothing-" : next.toString();

    throw new TrackException(after, expected, found);
}
```

This code prepares an error message that explains where the parser was, what it was looking for, and what it found instead. To explain where the parser was, this method picks the most advanced (the "best") assembly in the last successful matching set. For example, a `Track` object might be matching a list of synonyms for *steal*, and the input string might be `"(pilfer, pinch,, purloin)"`. In `throwTrackException()`, the best assembly would be `"(pilfer, pinch,"`. The parser this method receives is the parser that was trying to match the last set. In this case, the parser might be a `Word` parser. An error message can say that you "expected" a `Word`. To show what the parser found instead of what it sought, the `throwTrackException()` method peeks at the next element in the best assembly. In this example, the next element is an extra comma. The `TrackException` object uses its `after`, `expected`, and `found` strings to compose a message string such as

```
After   : ( pilfer , pinch ,
Expected: Word
Found   : ,
```

The `TrackException` class includes newline (\n) characters in its message, something that is unusual for an exception. Figure 11.3 shows the `TrackException` class.

The constructor for `TrackException` requires three input strings: `after`, `expected`, and `found`. The `after` string is an indication of which text was parsed. The `expected` string is an indication of the kind of text that was expected, such as a `term`. The `found` string is the textual element the thrower actually found. The `get-` methods return the values set in the constructor.

The `TrackException` class, a subclass of `RuntimeException`, allows methods that call `throwTrackException()` not to declare that they may throw this exception. This is important because `Track.match()` calls `throwTrackException()`, and thus it may throw a `TrackException`. If `TrackException` were not a `RuntimeException`,

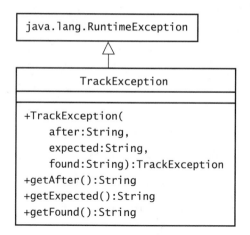

Figure 11.3   The TrackException class. A TrackException object contains the reasons that a track started but did not complete.

Track.match() would have a different signature than does the method in its superclass, Sequence.match(). Java does not allow this. In general, a method that overrides a superclass method cannot introduce a new exception unless the new exception is a subclass of RuntimeException.

11.4.2 Tracks in Action

The following sample class has a static method that returns a list parser. The list grammar is:

```
list       = '(' contents ')';
contents   = empty | actualList;
actualList = Word (',' Word)*;
```

The sample code uses two Track objects: one to parse the sequence (',' Word) in actualList, and a second one to parse the list sequence. The example applies the list parser to attempt to parse a mixture of valid and invalid inputs.

```
package sjm.examples.track;

import sjm.parse.*;
import sjm.parse.tokens.*;

/**
 * Show some examples of using a <code>Track</code>.
 */
```

```java
public class ShowTrack {

public static Parser list() {

    Parser empty, commaWord, actualList, contents, list;

    empty = new Empty();

    commaWord = new Track()
        .add(new Symbol(',').discard())
        .add(new Word());

    actualList = new Sequence()
        .add(new Word())
        .add(new Repetition(commaWord));

    contents = new Alternation()
        .add(empty)
        .add(actualList);

    list = new Track()
        .add(new Symbol('(').discard())
        .add(contents)
        .add(new Symbol(')').discard());

    return list;
}

public static void main(String args[]) {

    Parser list = list();

    String test[] = new String[] {
        "()",
        "(pilfer)",
        "(pilfer, pinch)",
        "(pilfer, pinch, purloin)",
        "(pilfer, pinch,, purloin)",
        "(",
        "(pilfer",
        "(pilfer, ",
        "(, pinch, purloin)",
        "pilfer, pinch"};

    System.out.println("Using parser: " + list);
    for (int i = 0; i < test.length; i++) {
        System.out.println("---\ntesting: " + test[i]);
        TokenAssembly a = new TokenAssembly(test[i]);
        try {
            Assembly out = list.completeMatch(a);
            if (out == null) {
                System.out.println(
```

```
                                "list.completeMatch() returns null");
                        }
                        else {
                            Object s = list.completeMatch(a).getStack();
                            System.out.println("Ok, stack is: " + s);
                        }
                    } catch (TrackException e) {
                        System.out.println(e.getMessage());
                    }
                }
            }
        }
```

The main() method uses list to parse an assortment of input strings. If list can consume the entire input, the main() method prints "Ok...". If parsing the input causes a Track object to throw a TrackException, main() catches it and prints the exception's message.

Running this class initially prints a string representation of list:

```
Using parser: <(< empty |<Word<,Word>*>>)>
```

Lists that are empty, or that contain one, two, or three words are all acceptable:

```
---
testing: ()
Ok, stack is: []

---
testing: (pilfer)
Ok, stack is: [pilfer]

---
testing: (pilfer, pinch)
Ok, stack is: [pilfer, pinch]

---
testing: (pilfer, pinch, purloin)
Ok, stack is: [pilfer, pinch, purloin]
```

After a comma, list expects a Word and not another comma:

```
---
testing: (pilfer, pinch,, purloin)
After   : ( pilfer , pinch ,
Expected: Word
Found   : ,
```

If the input starts with an opening parenthesis but ends before the `list` track finds contents and a closing parenthesis, `list` throws an exception saying what it expected and what it found:

```
---
testing: (
After   : (
Expected: )
Found   : -nothing-


---
testing: (pilfer
After   : ( pilfer
Expected: )
Found   : -nothing-


---
testing: (pilfer,
After   : ( pilfer ,
Expected: Word
Found   : -nothing-
```

After an opening parenthesis, a `list` expects contents, which may be empty. If actual contents do not follow the parenthesis, the `list` must be empty, which is acceptable, but then `list` expects a closing parenthesis:

```
---
testing: (, pinch, purloin)
After   : (
Expected: )
Found   : ,
```

Without an opening parenthesis, the match fails entirely, the list track never begins, and it does not throw an exception. The result is that `list.completeMatch()` returns `null`:

```
---
testing: pilfer, pinch
list.completeMatch() returns null
```

The `Track` class helps a language user determine what is wrong with an input string a parser cannot recognize. As a language developer, you'll find that it is easy to overlook the importance of helping your user stalk input errors. In practice, new language users spend most of their energy trying to enter text that a parser will accept. The parsers for the larger languages in this book (Jaql, Logikus, and Sling) use `Track` objects to help users produce proper programs.

11.5 Summary

The most common motivation for extending the parser toolkit in sjm.parse is to provide a new Terminal subclass that recognizes a subset of tokens of an existing type, or that recognizes a new token type that you create. In addition, you may want to add behavior to the Parser hierarchy that provides a feature other than matching. The Track class is an example of an extension to the parsers in sjm.parse that does not increase the ability to match but adds value when the match fails.

In your own projects, you should feel free to extend, override, and replace the classes in any of the sjm packages. The same is true of the java packages and object-oriented programming in general. In the object-oriented era, the practice of programming has shifted from creating new programs from scratch to creating new programs by extending an existing set of software.

CHAPTER 12

Engines

An *engine* is an object that powers query languages and logic languages. Engines accept queries and execute them by looking through a collection of data and rules. An engine returns objects or combinations of objects that match a query. This chapter introduces an engine that later chapters use to power a new logic language (Logikus) and a new query language (Jaql).

12.1 Engines versus Interpreters

In some contexts, especially logic programming, the word *interpreter* describes what this book calls an engine. In this same context the word *interpreter* may also refer to the combination of the engine and the parser that accepts a programmer's commands. This book uses *engine* rather than *interpreter* to refer specifically to the object that can sift through data looking for matches to a query.

Another reason this book avoids the word *interpreter* is that the *interpreter pattern*, as [Gamma et al.] document it, associates interpreters with languages. The engine that this book develops is language-independent, and it does not follow the interpreter pattern.

For these reasons, this book describes the object that powers logic and query languages as an engine.

12.2 The Role of Engines

Some languages rely on an engine to perform a useful service. In particular, logic languages and query languages need an engine in order to work. For example, Prolog is a leading logic programming language that needs an engine to prove its logical statements. SQL, or Structured Query Language, is a popular query language that also uses an engine to do the work that a query requests. A parser can parse a statement such as:

```
"select status from sales where city = 'Istanbul'"
```

However, a parser needs an engine to actually find the results. The engine is the part of the software in a database that decides which records fulfill the demands of a query.

Writing code to directly access an engine is usually complicated. It is safe to say that most people who use SQL never dream of accessing the engine directly from a programming language. In fact, many SQL users are unaware that the engine exists. If your only interaction with a database is through its query language, it might not occur to you to ponder the mechanics that allow the query language to function. A more realistic view of a database is that the database *is* the engine, and the engine comes with a language that provides a simple interface to the engine.

Engines and parsers are natural partners. Parsers provide a simple interface to an engine. The engine powers the language. This chapter introduces a logic engine used in the next three chapters. Chapter 13 introduces logic programming, giving examples in the Logikus programming language. Chapter 14 shows how to create a parser for Logikus. Chapter 15 shows how to create a query language using the engine from this chapter in place of a commercial database engine.

12.3 Building Blocks

All the code for the engine described in this chapter lies within the package `sjm.engine`. In this package, there is no `Engine` class; instead, there are a few collaborating classes that together produce an engine. The essential classes that make up the engine are `Structure`, `Variable`, `Rule`, and `Program`. The classes `Structure` and `Variable` are the fundamental building blocks of the engine. Classes `Program` and `Rule` are aggregations; a `Program` object is an aggregation of `Rule` objects, and a `Rule` object is an aggregation of `Structure` objects. You'll visit all these classes, starting with the fundamentals shown in Figure 12.1.

12.3.1 Structures

The `Structure` class provides the basic repository, or *data structure*, in a logic engine. A structure is a *functor* associated with a group of *terms*. A functor can be any object, and a term is either a structure or a variable. A structure is an aggregation of other structures, much as an object in an object-oriented system can be an aggregation of

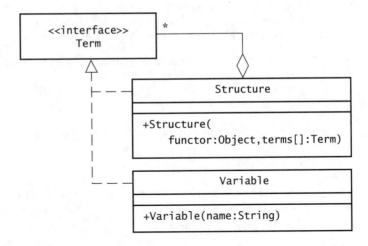

Figure 12.1 Terms, structures, and variables. The classes `Structure` and `Variable` implement the `Term` interface. A structure has a functor, which can be any object, and has zero or more terms, which may be other structures or variables.

other objects. In the same way that "everything is an object" in an object-oriented language, everything is a structure in a logic engine.

The simplest structure has only a functor and no terms and is called an *atom*. For example, the following code fragment creates an atom:

```
Structure denver = new Structure("denver");
```

The functor of a structure must be an object, such as an instance of `String` or `Integer`. Here's an example:

```
Structure altitude = new Structure(new Integer(5280));
```

This assignment statement creates a structure having no terms and having a functor that is the `Integer` object 5280. Here is a complete program that combines the denver and 5280 atoms:

```
package sjm.examples.engine;

import sjm.engine.*;

/**
 * This class shows a simple structure.
 */
public class ShowStructure {
```

```
public static void main(String args[]) {
    Structure denver = new Structure("denver");
    Structure altitude = new Structure(new Integer(5280));
    Structure city = new Structure(
        "city", new Structure[]{denver, altitude});
    System.out.println(city);
}
}
```

Compiling and running this program prints the following:

```
city(denver, 5280)
```

The city structure represents an assertion about reality, and that qualifies it as a *fact* in logic terminology. In logic, a *fact* is a structure that contains no variables. Thus, in the preceding program, the objects denver, altitude, and city are all facts.

The code in this chapter follows a convention of writing facts with initial lowercase letters and variables with initial uppercase letters. This convention aids languages, such as Logikus and Prolog, that choose not to allow the declaration of types.

12.3.2 Variables

A *variable* is an object that has a name and can bind (or *instantiate*) to structures or other variables. Here is a program that creates a structure with two variables:

```
package sjm.examples.engine;

import sjm.engine.*;

/**
 * This class shows some variables.
 */
public class ShowVariable {

public static void main(String args[]) {

    Variable name = new Variable("Name");
    Variable alt = new Variable("Altitude");
    Structure vCity = new Structure(
        "city",
        new Term[]{name, alt});
    System.out.println(vCity);
}
}
```

This class prints the following:

```
city(Name, Altitude)
```

This code creates the vCity structure using an array of Term rather than an array of Variable. This code could have used an array of Variable with equivalent results. Note that this code follows the convention of using uppercase strings to name variables.

12.4 Unification

Suppose that you would like to be able to match a structure such as:

    city(Name, Altitude)

with a structure such as:

    city(denver, 5280)

so that you can extract a structure's data into variables. Logic engines provide just this kind of matching in a behavior called *unification*. Unification lets a variable bind to a value. It also allows entire structures to bind, with all the terms in a structure binding to their counterparts in another structure. For example, if you ask the two structures here to unify, the variables Name and Altitude will unify with denver and 5280, as the following program shows:

```
package sjm.examples.engine;

import sjm.engine.*;

/**
 * Show two structures unifying.
 */
public class ShowStructureUnification {

public static void main(String args[]) {

    // city(denver, 5280)

    Structure denver = new Structure("denver");
    Structure altitude = new Structure(new Integer(5280));
    Structure city = new Structure(
        "city", new Structure[]{denver, altitude});

    // city(Name, Altitude)

    Variable name = new Variable("Name");
    Variable alt = new Variable("Altitude");
    Structure vCity = new Structure(
        "city",
        new Term[]{name, alt});
```

```
                    // show the cities

                    System.out.println(city);
                    System.out.println(vCity);

                    // unify, and show the variables

                    vCity.unify(city);

                    System.out.println("\n     After unifying: \n");

                    System.out.println("Name = " + name);
                    System.out.println("Alt  = " + alt);
            }
    }
```

Running this program prints the following:

```
city(denver, 5280)
city(Name, Altitude)

    After unifying:

Name = denver
Alt  = 5280
```

The code creates the two structures `city` and `vCity` and then unifies them. The unification succeeds because the structures have the same functor and the same number of terms, and their terms are able to unify. After unification, the variables in `vCity` take on the values of the corresponding terms in `city`.

The rule for unifying structures is as follows:

> ▪ A structure can unify with another structure if the structures have equal functors and an equal number of terms, and if these terms can unify.

When the `vCity` structure unifies with the `city` structure, it verifies that both structures have the same functor ("city") and the same number of terms (two). Then it asks these terms to unify. For example, the variable `Name` unifies with the structure `denver`. The rule for unifying uninstantiated variables is as follows:

> ▪ An uninstantiated variable unifies with a structure by taking the structure as its value.

By taking a structure as its value, a variable in a logic program acts somewhat like a variable in an assignment statement in a Java program. However, in a Java program each new assignment overwrites the previous value of a variable. Consider these Java statements:

```
String x = null, y = null;
x = "denver";
x = y;
```

These lines leave x with the value null. Unification differs from assignment in that, after unifying with a term, a variable uses that term in future unifications. For example, a variable X can unify with a structure denver and can then unify with another variable Y. In this second unification, X is instantiated and Y is not, so Y takes on the value of X. The following code shows this:

```
package sjm.examples.engine;

import sjm.engine.*;

/**
 * Show a variable unifying with a structure and then
 * another variable.
 */
public class ShowVariableUnification2 {

public static void main(String args[]) {

    Variable x = new Variable("X");
    Variable y = new Variable("Y");
    Structure denver = new Structure("denver");

    x.unify(denver);
    x.unify(y);

    System.out.println("X = " + x);
    System.out.println("Y = " + y);
}
}
```

This program unifies X with denver and then unifies X with Y. Running the class prints:

```
X = denver
Y = denver
```

When a variable has unified with a term (either a structure or another variable) and then attempts to unify with another term, the variable passes the unification request to the term to which it has instantiated.

- An instantiated variable unifies by asking its instantiated value to unify.

In the preceding example, when X unifies with Y, X has already instantiated with denver. To attempt to unify with Y, X passes the unification request to denver so that denver unifies with Y. This has the same effect of Y unifying with denver, and so the previously uninstantiated Y takes on denver as its value.

In short, when a variable attempts to unify with a structure, if the variable is uninstantiated it takes the structure as its instantiated value. If the variable is already instantiated, it delegates the unification request to the value that it is holding.

12.5 Facts

With structures, variables, and unification in place, you might think that the next logical step is to collect groups of structures and then to unify a variable structure with each one. However, logic programming introduces notions that veer from this course. The first notion is that a structure can represent a statement of truth, or what logic programming calls an *axiom*. For example, you can regard

```
city(denver, 5280)
```

as a model of the true statement that Denver's elevation is about 5,280 feet. A structure that contains no variables is a fact, which is one type of axiom. The other type of axiom is a rule, which you will meet shortly. In the classes in package sjm.engine, class Fact is a subclass of Structure, as Figure 12.2 shows.

The constructors for the Fact class that accept objects as terms wrap these objects as other facts. A Fact object is always a composition of facts. In other words, a structure that contains only data is a composition of structures that contain only data. The

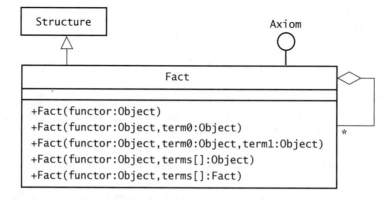

Figure 12.2 The Fact class. A Fact object is a Structure object that contains no variables. If a fact has terms at all, they must be other facts.

variety of constructors provided by the Fact class makes it easier to create new Fact objects. For example, you can create city facts as follows:

```
package sjm.examples.engine;

import sjm.engine.*;

/**
 * This class shows the construction of a couple of facts.
 */
public class ShowFacts {

public static void main(String[] args) {
    Fact d = new Fact(
        "city",
        new Fact[]{
            new Fact("denver"),
            new Fact(new Integer(5280))});

    Fact j = new Fact(
        "city", "jacksonville", new Integer(8));

    System.out.println(d + "\n" + j);
}
}
```

This prints

```
city(denver, 5280)
city(jacksonville, 8)
```

You can build a logic program from facts because facts are axioms.

12.6 Programs and Queries

A *program* is a collection of axioms, which are facts or rules (which you have yet to meet). A *query* is a structure that can prove itself against a program. Figure 12.3 shows the Program and Query classes.

The following Java program creates a logic program, loads it with facts, and uses a query to extract all its results:

```
package sjm.examples.engine;

import sjm.engine.*;
/**
 * Show the construction and use of a simple program.
 */
```

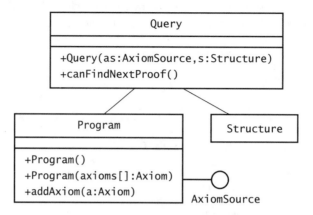

Figure 12.3 The Program and Query classes. A program is a collection of axioms and an implementation of the AxiomSource interface. The Query class has a constructor that accepts a source of axioms and a structure to unify with the axioms.

```
public class ShowProgram {

/**
 * Return a small database of cities and their altitudes.
 */
public static Program altitudes() {
    Fact [] facts = new Fact[]{
        new Fact("city", "abilene",      new Integer(1718)),
        new Fact("city", "addis ababa",  new Integer(8000)),
        new Fact("city", "denver",       new Integer(5280)),
        new Fact("city", "flagstaff",    new Integer(6970)),
        new Fact("city", "jacksonville", new Integer(8)),
        new Fact("city", "leadville",    new Integer(10200)),
        new Fact("city", "madrid",       new Integer(1305)),
        new Fact("city", "richmond",     new Integer(19)),
        new Fact("city", "spokane",      new Integer(1909)),
        new Fact("city", "wichita",      new Integer(1305))
    };

    Program p = new Program();
    for (int i = 0; i < facts.length; i++) {
        p.addAxiom(facts[i]);
    }
    return p;

}

/**
 * Show the construction and use of a simple program.
 */
public static void main(String[] args) {
```

```
Program p = altitudes();

Variable name = new Variable("Name");
Variable height = new Variable("Height");
Structure s = new Structure(
    "city", new Term[]{name, height});
Query q = new Query(p, s);

while (q.canFindNextProof()) {
    System.out.println(
        name + " is about " +
        height + " feet above sea level.");
}
}
}
```

This program prints the following:

```
abilene is about 1718 feet above sea level.
addis ababa is about 8000 feet above sea level.
denver is about 5280 feet above sea level.
flagstaff is about 6970 feet above sea level.
jacksonville is about 8 feet above sea level.
leadville is about 10200 feet above sea level.
madrid is about 1305 feet above sea level.
richmond is about 19 feet above sea level.
spokane is about 1909 feet above sea level.
wichita is about 1305 feet above sea level.
```

The program works by loading a program with facts and then querying the program.
ShowProgram.main() constructs a Query object with this code:

```
Variable name = new Variable("Name");
Variable height = new Variable("Height");
Structure s = new Structure(
    "city", new Term[]{name, height});
Query q = new Query(p, s);
```

If the query structure s printed itself, it would appear as

```
city(Name, Height)
```

ShowProgram.main() creates a query by combining this structure with a logic program to prove against. In a while loop, the program repeatedly asks the Query object q whether it can find another proof:

```
while (q.canFindNextProof()) {
    System.out.println(
        name + " is about " +
        height + " feet above sea level.");
}
```

Each time the `Query` object q finds a proof, it unifies its structure with one of the program's facts. When this structure unifies, its variables unify. When `Variable` objects are printed, they show the value with which they have unified.

12.7 Proofs

The engine *proves* a query by unifying the query's structures with facts in a program. Queries can contain a series of structures, each of which must be true for the query to succeed. When a query has multiple structures, its first structure unifies with some axiom in the program, which typically establishes values for some of the query's variables. The remaining structures attempt to establish their truth with these variable values in place.

Consider a collection of facts about construction companies and a supplier's fees (in drachmas) for delivery to their locations:

```
charge(athens, 23);
charge(sparta, 13);
charge(milos, 17);

customer("Marathon Marble", sparta);
customer("Acropolis Construction", athens);
customer("Agora Imports", sparta);
```

To see the shipping charge for each customer, you can create a query from two structures so that the query would print itself as

```
charge(City, Fee), customer(Name, City)
```

A variable's scope is the query in which it appears. In this query the variable `City` is the same variable in both structures. As a result, the query *joins* on the `City` variable.

When the query first proves itself, it unifies its `charge` structure with the first `charge` fact in the program. This unification causes the `City` variable to unify with `athens`. The query continues its proof, trying to prove

```
customer(Name, athens)
```

This structure succeeds when it unifies with

```
customer("Acropolis Construction", athens);
```

When the query's last structure succeeds, the proof succeeds. At this point, you could print the query's variables to see the values they unified with during the proof:

```
City: athens
Fee:  23
Name: Acropolis Construction
```

Here is a program that loads the shipping facts and queries them:

```
package sjm.examples.engine;

import sjm.engine.*;

/**
 * Show a simple query proving itself.
 */
public class ShowProof {
/**
 * Return a small database of shipping charges.
 */
public static Program charges() {

    Fact [] facts = new Fact[]{
        new Fact("charge", "athens", new Integer(23)),
        new Fact("charge", "sparta", new Integer(13)),
        new Fact("charge", "milos", new Integer(17))
    };

    return new Program(facts);
}


/**
 * Return a small database of customers.
 */
public static Program customers() {

    Fact [] facts = new Fact[]{
        new Fact("customer", "Marathon Marble", "sparta"),
        new Fact("customer", "Acropolis Construction",
            "athens"),
        new Fact("customer", "Agora Imports", "sparta")
    };

    return new Program(facts);
}

/**
 * Show a simple query proving itself.
 */

public static void main(String[] args) {
    Program p = new Program();
    p.append(charges());
    p.append(customers());
```

```
System.out.println("Program:");
System.out.println(p);

Variable city = new Variable("City");
Variable fee  = new Variable("Fee");
Variable name = new Variable("Name");

Structure s1 = new Structure(
    "charge", new Term[] {city, fee});

Structure s2 = new Structure(
    "customer", new Term[] {name, city});

// charge(City, Fee), customer(Name, City)
Query q = new Query(p, new Structure[] {s1, s2});

System.out.println("\nQuery:");
System.out.println(q);

System.out.println("\nProofs:");
while (q.canFindNextProof()) {
    System.out.println("City: " + city);
    System.out.println("Fee:  " + fee);
    System.out.println("Name: " + name);
    System.out.println();
}
    }
}
```

This class has static methods that create `Program` objects that contain facts about charges and customers. The `main()` method creates one `Program` object as a collection of all these facts, constructs a query, and proves it repeatedly. Running this program prints the following:

```
Program:
charge(athens, 23);
charge(sparta, 13);
charge(milos, 17);
customer(Marathon Marble, sparta);
customer(Acropolis Construction, athens);
customer(Agora Imports, sparta);

Query:
charge(City, Fee), customer(Name, City)

Proofs:
City: athens
Fee:  23
Name: Acropolis Construction
```

```
City: sparta
Fee:  13
Name: Marathon Marble

City: sparta
Fee:  13
Name: Agora Imports
```

The first proof results from proving the `charge` structure and then the `customer` structure. The remaining proofs depend on the engine's ability to backtrack.

12.7.1 Backtracking

The power of a logic engine lies in its ability to find multiple proofs. After a query finds one proof, you can ask it to find another. The query relays this request to its last structure. In the shipping company example, the first proof of the query finds

```
City: athens
Fee:  23
Name: Acropolis Construction
```

If you ask the query for another proof, the query asks its last structure for another proof. When a structure seeks a new proof, it unbinds any variables it bound in proving itself previously. In this case, the last structure of the query unbinds the `Name` variable. Thus, the query's last structure searches for a new proof of

```
customer(Name, athens)
```

The `City` variable remains bound to `athens` because the last structure neither bound nor unbound that variable in its proof.

Because there is no other customer in Athens, this structure's proof fails. The query does not give up but rather *backtracks*, or asks the preceding structure for a new proof. In this example, the query backtracks to its `charge` structure. This structure unbinds its `City` variable and finds the next axiom it can unify with:

```
charge(sparta, 13)
```

Because this structure succeeds, the query starts proving forward again. Now the query asks the structure

```
customer(Name, sparta)
```

for a proof, which succeeds by unifying with

```
customer("Marathon Marble", sparta)
```

Because this succeeds, the query succeeds and you can again print the query's variables:

```
City: sparta
Fee:  13
Name: Marathon Marble
```

Now if you ask the query for another proof, the query again asks its last structure for a new proof. This time the structure succeeds by finding a new proof for

```
customer(Name, sparta)
```

This structure unifies with

```
customer("Agora Imports", sparta)
```

The query succeeds and the program prints

```
City: sparta
Fee:  13
Name: Agora Imports
```

Pressing on, you ask the query for another proof. There are no more customers in Sparta, so the last structure fails. The query's first structure finds that you know the fee for shipping to Milos, and the query tries to prove forward. There are no customers in Milos at present, and so the `customer` structure in the query fails. The query backtracks to its `charge` structure, looking for a new proof. There are no other `charge` axioms to unify with, so the first structure of the query fails, and the entire query fails.

To summarize, a query proves itself by proving each structure in turn. When a structure fails to find a proof, the query backtracks to a preceding structure to look for a new proof. If this fails, the query backtracks again until the first structure fails and the entire proof fails. If, after backtracking, a query finds a proof of a structure, this structure usually binds new values for some of the query's variables. This means that there are new chances for the later structures to find new proofs. The proof again moves forward, trying to prove each of the following structures. A query backtracks and proves forward until it proves all its structures or until all its structures fail.

Rules prove themselves in the almost same way that queries do. A structure can prove itself by unifying with a rule and asking the tail of the rule to prove itself. The tail is a series of structures that proves itself exactly the way a query would.

12.8 Rules

A rule is an axiom, or statement of truth, that has more than one structure. In a rule, the truth of the first structure follows from the ability to prove the remaining structures. For example, you could add to a program a rule that displays itself as

```
custCharge (Name, Fee) :-
    charge(City, Fee), customer(Name, City);
```

The ":-" symbol is the "if" symbol. Prolog and Logikus use this symbol rather than a comma after the first structure in a rule. This convention emphasizes the meaning of rules: The first structure is true if the latter structures are provable. Figure 12.4 shows the Rule class.

The custCharge rule means that you can find customer charges by proving the charge and customer structures. As with queries, a variable's scope is the rule in which it appears. Thus, the custCharge rule joins charge and customer on the City variable.

To this point, you have seen structures prove themselves by unifying with facts in a program. A more comprehensive explanation of how structures prove themselves is that they unify with the first structure of an axiom in a program and prove the axiom's remaining structures. The first structure of an axiom is its *head*; the remainder is its *tail*. One view of a fact is that it is an axiom that has no tail. Because there is no tail to prove, a structure can prove itself simply by unifying with a fact in a program. In the case of a rule, a structure unifies with the head of the rule and asks the tail to prove itself.

For example, if you added the custCharge rule to the shipping charges program, you could query the program with a query that would display itself as

```
custCharge(Name, 23)
```

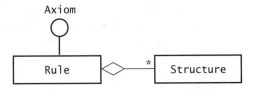

Figure 12.4   The Rule class. A rule is a sequence of structures. A query can prove itself by unifying with the first structure in a rule and then proving the remaining structures.

When this query proves itself, it unifies with the `custCharge` rule and asks the rule's tail to prove itself. This proof succeeds, binding the `Name` variable to `"Acropolis Construction"`.

Speaking somewhat loosely, rules provide the logic in a logic program. They allow flexible modeling of the relationships between objects such as customers and shipping charges. They also allow modeling of logical concepts such as the observation that if Yarmouth is in Maine and Maine is in the United States, then Yarmouth must be in the United States. Rules can also model arbitrary definitions, such as a business's definition of a "good" customer. Chapter 13, "Logic Programming," gives many examples of the use of rules in a logic program. Before turning to that chapter, however, we'll consider several other features of the logic engine.

12.9 Additional Features of the Engine

At this point, we have covered the fundamentals that make a logic engine work. If you understand structures, variables, facts, rules, and programs, you can create query or logic languages that use the engine these objects create. In practice, you may want several additional features, including

- Comparisons
- Arithmetic
- Evaluation
- Not
- Anonymous variables
- Lists

12.9.1 Comparisons

A `Comparison` object compares the values of two terms. These terms can be either variables or structures, but if they are structures, they must be atoms. This restriction follows from the fact that there is no conventional way to compare two structures, such as

```
city(denver, 5280)
city(richmond, 19)
```

If you compare these facts by an alphabetic ordering of city name, you will find `richmond > denver`. If you compare them by altitude, you will find `denver > richmond`.

To ensure that comparisons apply only to atoms, the package `sjm.engine` has an `Atom` class. Class `Atom`, a subclass of `Fact`, allows no terms. The engine can compare `5280` and `19`, or `denver` and `richmond`, but not `city(denver, 5280)` and `city(richmond, 19)`.

The `Comparison` class applies the standard Java meaning to these comparison operators:

```
> < >= <= !=
```

The `Comparison` class differs from Java in requiring the operator "`=`" to effect the results of the Java operator "`==`". Figure 12.5 shows the `Comparison` class.

A comparison can function without reference to a program. Here's an example:

```
package sjm.examples.engine;

import sjm.engine.*;

/**
 * Show a couple of comparisons.
 */
public class ShowComparison {

public static void main(String[] args) {
    Atom alt1 = new Atom(new Integer(5280));
    Atom alt2 = new Atom(new Integer(19));

    Query q1 = new Query(
        null, // no axiom source
        new Comparison(">", alt1, alt2));
```

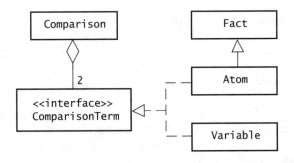

Figure 12.5 The relationship of `Comparison` and `Atom`. The terms of a `Comparison` object must be implementations of `ComparisonTerm`, specifically `Atom` objects or `Variable` objects.

```
        System.out.println(q1 + " : " + q1.canFindNextProof());

        Query q2 = new Query(
            null,
            new Comparison(">",
                new Atom("denver"),
                new Atom("richmond")));

        System.out.println(q2 + " : " + q2.canFindNextProof());
    }
}
```

This prints the comparisons of 5280 > 19 and "denver" > "richmond":

```
>(5280, 19) : true
>(denver, richmond) : false
```

The second comparison is false because the Comparison class relies internally on the
compareTo() method of the String class. This method compares the Unicode values
of characters. The Unicode value of d is less than the Unicode value of r, so "denver"
is less than "richmond". Both queries in this program specify null as the axiom
source because these queries need no access to a logic program to prove their results.

12.9.2 Arithmetic

It is useful for a logic engine to provide a mechanism for representing arithmetic
expressions, such as the amount of tax on a coffee order. Figure 12.6 shows the composition of arithmetic operators.

The NumberFact class simplifies the creation of atoms that are numbers. Without
NumberFact, creating a structure that holds the number two requires a statement
such as

```
Atom two = new Atom(new Integer(2));
```

With the NumberFact class, an equivalent but shorter statement is

```
NumberFact two = new NumberFact(2);
```

Such simplifications have a limited return. Ultimately, you want to create new languages that replace both statements with simply the character 2. No amount of refactoring, simplified constructors, or new subclasses will match the power of creating a
parser to feed the engine.

An ArithmeticOperator object always has two terms, both of which must be
implementations of ArithmeticTerm. Three classes in the engine implement

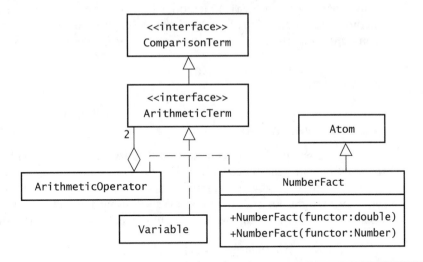

Figure 12.6 The ArithmeticOperator class. An ArithmeticOperator object has two arithmetic terms, which may be variables, number facts, or other arithmetic operators.

ArithmeticTerm: NumberFact, Variable, and ArithmeticOperator. An arithmetic operator can contain other arithmetic operators, and that makes it possible to compose any arithmetic expression. Here is an example:

```
package sjm.examples.engine;

import sjm.engine.*;

/**
 * Show how to perform arithmetic within the engine.
 */
public class ShowArithmetic {

public static void main(String[] args) {
    NumberFact a, b;
    a = new NumberFact(1000);
    b = new NumberFact(999);

    ArithmeticOperator x, y;
    x = new ArithmeticOperator('*', a, b);
    y = new ArithmeticOperator('+', x, b);

    System.out.println(y);
    System.out.println(y.eval());
}
}
```

This program uses the `eval()` method, which is part of the `Term` interface. This method returns the value of the `Term` that the engine will use in arithmetic expressions and comparison functions. Running this program prints the following:

```
+(*(1000.0, 999.0), 999.0)
999999.0
```

12.9.3 Evaluation

An `Evaluation` object unifies one term with the value of another. This capability is most useful when combined with arithmetic. For example, you might want to evaluate the weight of a baby by weighing yourself holding the baby and then subtracting your own weight. An evaluation displays itself using a pound sign ("#") as its functor, so an evaluation that computes the weight of a baby might look like this:

```
#(Baby, -(YouAndBaby, You))
```

Here is a program that shows this evaluation in action:

```java
package sjm.examples.engine;

import sjm.engine.*;

/**
 * Show an evaluation.
 */
public class ShowEvaluation {

public static void main(String[] args) {
    Variable you       = new Variable("You");
    Variable youAndBaby = new Variable("YouAndBaby");
    Variable baby      = new Variable("Baby");

    ArithmeticOperator diff;
    diff = new ArithmeticOperator('-', youAndBaby, you);

    Evaluation e = new Evaluation(baby, diff);
    System.out.println("Before weighing:");
    System.out.println(e);

    you.unify(new NumberFact(185));
    youAndBaby.unify(new NumberFact(199));

    System.out.println("\nAfter weighing:");
    System.out.println(e);

    e.canFindNextProof();
```

```
        System.out.println(
            "\nThat baby weighs about " + baby + " pounds.");
    }
}
```

This program creates three variables, an arithmetic operation, and an evaluation that ties them together. To force the evaluation to execute, the program asks the evaluation to prove itself. The results are

```
Before weighing:
#(Baby, -(YouAndBaby, You))

After weighing:
#(Baby, -(199.0, 185.0))

That baby weighs about 14.0 pounds.
```

12.9.4 Not

It can be useful to determine that the engine cannot prove a structure. A Not object is a structure that fails if it can prove itself against a program, and succeeds if it cannot prove itself. The Not class has the same constructors as the Structure class, but it proves itself differently. For an example of how a Not object behaves in a logic program, see Section 13.8.3, "Negation," in Chapter 13, "Logic Programming."

12.9.5 Anonymous Variables

An anonymous variable unifies successfully with any other term without binding to the term. This is useful for screening out unwanted terms. See Chapter 13 for an example of anonymous variables in action.

In sjm.engine, class Anonymous is a subclass of Variable, as Figure 12.7 shows. Anonymous variables print themselves as an underscore ("_").

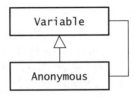

Figure 12.7 The Anonymous class. Anonymous variables unify successfully without binding to a value.

12.9.6 Lists

A list is a structure that contains a list of terms. Objects of class List can represent sequences of any length, but internally lists always have two terms. The first term of a list can be any term, and the second term of a list is another list. This definition suffices to define a sequence of terms. For example, a list that represents ten items actually contains only two terms. The first term of a ten-item list contains the first item, and the second term contains a nine-item list. The engine manages lists this way because it minimizes the extent to which lists are a special case.

The functor of a list is always ".". Because lists are structures, they need a functor, although in practice you will be more interested in the terms of a list than its functor. You could use any standard value as the functor for lists, and "." is conventional.

The recursive definition of lists requires a termination mechanism, and that is a special object: the empty list. The empty list displays itself as "[]".

For example, a list that contains cobra, garter, and python stores itself internally as .(cobra, .(garter, .(python, []))). Note that this list contains only two terms: the cobra term and a list of two other snakes. The inner, two-snake list contains garter and a one-snake list. The one-snake list contains python and the empty list. Every list except the empty list contains two terms.

The toString() method of class Structure treats lists as a special case so that lists print themselves in a manner that makes them more readable. The list that internally is .(cobra, .(garter, .(python, []))) displays itself as

    [cobra, garter, python]

The power of lists is one of the greatest advantages of logic languages over simple query languages. Chapter 13, "Logic Programming," gives many examples of the use of lists.

12.10 Summary

An engine is an object that performs a well-defined service against a collection of data. A database engine typically scans data in files stored in a proprietary format. A logic engine typically must be fed data in the form of facts, and it retrieves data by matching query structures against the facts. This matching, or unification, provides a basic ability to see whether two structures can match, potentially unifying variables and values in the structures. A logic engine also provides the ability to model rules, which are a sequence of structures in which the truth of the latter structures can confirm the truth of the first structure. In addition to these basic abilities, a well-rounded logic engine needs a provision for handling arithmetic, evaluations, comparisons, negation, and lists. A query language might ignore some these facilities, but a logic programming language such as Prolog or Logikus puts these features to work.

Chapters 13 and 14 show that a logic engine can power both logic languages and query languages. Query languages use the engine's matching ability to check whether a table row matches a SQL "where" clause. A logic language is essentially a facade, a thin veneer over the engine itself.

CHAPTER 13

Logic Programming

This book aims to show that you can create computer languages that differ radically from Java. Toward that end, Chapter 14 shows how to create a parser for a logic language. However, this book does not assume that you are familiar with logic programming. It is probably impossible to understand how to parse a logic programming language if you do not understand logic programming, so this chapter provides a rapid introduction to logic programming, using Logikus, a logic programming language developed for this book.

This chapter covers many of the same topics as Chapter 12, "Engines," but does not assume that you have read that chapter. This repetition stems from the fact that Logikus is essentially an interface to the logic engine. If you have read Chapter 12, you can skim sections of this chapter that appear redundant.

Logic programming lets you concentrate on modeling the relations between objects instead of on modeling the objects themselves. This difference in focus results in logic programming having strengths that are different from (and in fact orthogonal to) object-oriented languages such as Java.

13.1 The Role of Logic Languages

Developers vary in their enthusiasm for logic languages. One author of a book about the logic language Prolog claims that Prolog is able to provide a better solution to the problem that object orientation was designed to solve. This seems to suggest that Prolog is more powerful than Java—a difficult view to defend. Although it is unlikely that a logic language will *displace* Java, there is strong evidence that logic languages can *augment* Java.

The primary motivation for creating a logic language is to let your users program using rules. By incorporating a logic language in a system, you can bring rules to the surface, where a logic programmer can manipulate them directly. In practice, that logic programmer may be you. In this case your logic programming language will let you model business rules quickly, with no rebuilding and redeployment of your Java code. You may also be able to train a member of the user community to be the logic programmer. The simpler you keep your language, the more likely it is that you will succeed in delegating business rule programming to one of your users.

The business logic in most companies changes every day as businesses adjust their strategies and practices in pursuit of profits. By augmenting your system with a logic language, you can empower your users with the ability to model their evolving business logic.

13.2 Building Blocks

The fundamental elements of Logikus are structures and variables. As a logic programmer, you will learn to weave structures and variables together into rules and then to combine rules to form logic programs.

13.2.1 Structures

A *structure* is the basic data repository in a logic language. A structure is a *functor* associated with a group of *terms*. A functor can be a lowercase string, a quoted string, or a number. Some acceptable functors are

```
jamesCagney

starred

"Yankee Doodle Dandy"

1942
```

In addition to having a functor, each structure possesses a collection of zero or more terms. A structure with no terms is an *atom*. When a structure has terms, they must be structures and variables, separated by commas and enclosed in parentheses. For example, here is a valid structure:

```
starred(jamesCagney, "Yankee Doodle Dandy", 1942)
```

This structure models the fact that James Cagney starred in "Yankee Doodle Dandy," which debuted in 1942. This structure contains no variables, and so it is a *fact*. Its functor is starred, and it has three terms, each of which is an atom. For example, within the starred structure,

```
jamesCagney
```

is an atom. This structure's functor is jamesCagney, and it has no associated terms.

To write James Cagney's name with proper capitalization, you can put it in double quotes:

```
starred("James Cagney", "Yankee Doodle Dandy", 1942)
```

Numbers in Logikus must be atoms, and they can be integers or reals but not exponents or other descriptive forms. For example, the following is a valid atom:

```
1942.0
```

But the following expressions are not valid in Logikus:

```
19.42e2          // invalid - uses an exponent
3.14(symbol, pi) // invalid - nonatomic
```

Structures can have nonatomic structures as terms. For example,

```
person(
    jim,
    address(
        "2240 A Street",
        "Yourtown",
        "YS"),
    23)
```

is a valid structure having three terms. Its middle term, the `address` structure, serves to group information for a single term in `person`. Practical logic programmers use nested structures sparingly because these structures can make a logic model harder to use.

13.2.2 Variables

A Logikus variable is an object that has a name and can bind to structures or other variables. The Logikus parser distinguishes variables from structures using case, treating any string beginning with an uppercase letter as a variable. For example, valid variable names include

```
X

Y

Title

WhoDoneIt
```

Given the structure

```
starred(jamesCagney, Title, Year)
```

the Logikus parser creates the `starred` structure with three terms. Those terms are the atom `jamesCagney` and the variables `Title` and `Year`. The terms `Title` and `Year` are variables because they begin with capital letters.

You might like to match a structure such as this one with a structure such as

```
starred(jamesCagney, "Yankee Doodle Dandy", 1942)
```

so that you can extract a structure's data into variables. Logikus provides this kind of matching in a behavior called *unification*. You can use the Logikus development environment to see unification in action.

13.3 A Logikus Interactive Development Environment

The Logikus interactive development environment (IDE) lets you experiment with logic programming. You can launch the environment by running the `LogikusIde` class:

```
> java sjm.examples.logic.LogikusIde
```

The `LogikusIde` class launches a Swing-based user interface that provides a programming area, a query area, and an area for results. When the IDE comes up, you can enter the program and query shown in Figure 13.1. If you do not want to type in the data, you can find the file `starred.txt` on the CD and copy and paste its contents into the program area. (This file actually lists 68 of James Cagney's films, four of which appear in Figure 13.1.)

With the program in place as Figure 13.1 shows, you can experiment with the **Next** and **Rest** buttons. These buttons ask the query to prove itself by unifying with the facts in the program.

13.4 Unification

Unification lets variables bind to values. Unification also lets structures unify if they have the same functor and the same number of terms, and if their terms can unify. When a query structure wants to prove itself, it can do so by unifying with a fact in the program. For example, the query

```
starred(jamesCagney, Title, Year)
```

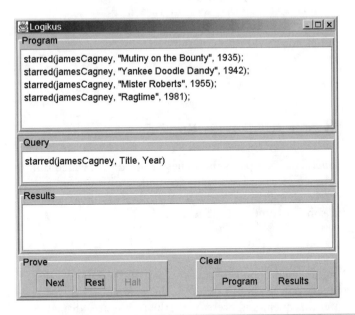

Figure 13.1 The Logikus interactive development environment. The class that is running here is LogikusIde, although it titles itself "Logikus".

can prove itself by unifying with the facts in the program in Figure 13.1. If you enter the program and query in Figure 13.1 and then click the **Next** button, the query unifies with the first fact in the program. The results area displays

```
Title = Mutiny on the Bounty, Year = 1935.0
```

This shows that the variables in the query have unified with the values in the program's first fact. The unification succeeds because the query and the fact have the same functor (starred) and the same number of terms (three), and their terms can unify. Specifically, the atom jamesCagney in the query unifies with its counterpart in the fact because both structures have the same functor (jamesCagney) and the same number of terms (zero). The variables in the query unify with their counterparts by binding to them. After the query proves itself, the environment displays the query's variables.

If you press **Next** again, the query unbinds its variables and unifies with the next fact in the program. The results area displays

```
Title = Yankee Doodle Dandy, Year = 1942.0
```

By pressing the **Rest** button, you can ask the query to prove itself until no more proofs exist. The results are

```
Title = Ragtime, Year = 1981.0
Title = Yankee Doodle Dandy, Year = 1942.0
no
```

The results area displays no when there is no further proof of a query.

13.5 Comparisons

A *comparison* compares the values of two terms, which can be variables, atoms, or arithmetic terms. The comparison operator is the functor of a comparison structure, and the comparison's terms are the terms of this structure. For example, a valid comparison can compare 9*11 to 100:

```
<(9*11, 100)
```

You can issue a comparison as a query to the Logikus IDE. Regardless of the program that is present in the IDE, this comparison is true—99 is less than 100. If you enter this query and press **Next**, the results area displays yes. If you press **Next** again, the results area displays no. There is only one proof of the comparison, and thus there is no other way to prove its truth.

Logikus recognizes the following operators in comparisons:

```
<, >, =, <=, >=, !=
```

The terms in a comparison can be atoms. For example,

```
>= (volleyball, golfball)
```

is a valid comparison, and it is true because the Unicode value of v is greater than the Unicode value of g. (We might also say that "volleyball" comes alphabetically, or lexicographically, after "golfball".)

Comparisons can also contain variables, a useful capability when a comparison appears in a rule.

13.6 Rules, Axioms, and Programs

A rule is a series of structures in which the truth of the first structure follows from the ability to prove the remaining structures. For example, in Logikus the following rule defines "high" cities:

```
highCity(Name, Alt) :- city(Name, Alt), >(Alt, 5000);
```

This rule states that highCity(Name, Alt) is true for any known city whose altitude is greater than 5,000. A rule's first structure is its *head*; its other structure is its *tail*. Between its head and its tail a rule has the "if" (":-") symbol. The head is true if the tail is provable.

An *axiom* is a model of truth, and in Logikus an axiom is either a fact or a rule. A Logikus *program* is a collection of axioms, and this means that a program is an extended model of some truth in some context. For example, a collection of facts about city altitudes combined in a program with the highCity rule lets you query the program to ask which cities are high. Figure 13.2 shows such a program using data from the CD file city.txt.

In Figure 13.2, the query succeeds because it is able to unify with the head of a rule whose tail can, in turn, prove itself. In the figure, the user has pressed the **Rest** button,

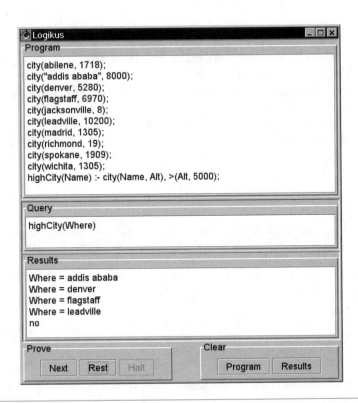

Figure 13.2 A rule in action. The highCity rule lets a query find which cities in a collection are, in fact, high.

asking for all the proofs. The behavior of the query and the rule depends primarily on the mechanics of proofs.

13.7 Proofs

As mentioned, this chapter covers many of the same topics as Chapter 12, "Engines," although a few differences arise when you implement a language. For example, the engine accepts any object as a functor, whereas Logikus allows only lowercase strings, quoted strings, or numbers. The engine accepts any string as the name of a variable, whereas Logikus variable names must begin with a capital letter and may not contain whitespace. Because of these subtle differences, an explanation of Logikus is a somewhat different discussion than an explanation of the engine. However, on the topic of proofs, Logikus behaves exactly as the engine does. As a result, this section covers the same information as Section 12.7, "Proofs." If you have read that section, you can skip ahead here to Section 13.7.4, "Looping and Halting."

13.7.1 Variable Scope

Structures generally prove themselves by unifying with an axiom in a program and then proving that axiom's tail, if any. The behavior of structures in the tail of a rule or in a query depends on the fact that variables in a query or rule share the same *scope*.

A variable's scope is the rule or query in which it appears. Another variable with the same name in another rule is a different variable. For example, a program might contain the following two rules:

```
highCity(Name) :- city(Name, Alt), >(Alt, 5000);
largeCountry(Name) :- country(Name, Pop), >(Pop, 10000000);
```

The Name variable in the first rule is the same variable throughout that rule, and it is completely independent of the Name variable in the second rule. In a query, a variable's scope is the query. So, for example, the query

```
city(X, X)
```

cannot match

```
city(denver, 5280)
```

because X can take on only one of the two values: denver or 5280.

13.7.2 Variable Joins

The fact that all the variables in a rule have the same scope allows the construction of *relational joins*. A relational join connects two facts according to a common element. For example, consider a collection of facts about coffee types, customers, and their orders from a coffee company:

```
coffee("Launch Mi", french, kenya, 6.95);
coffee("Simple Best", regular, colombia, 5.95);
coffee("Revit", italian, guatemala, 7.95);
coffee("Brimful", regular, kenya, 6.95);
coffee("Smackin", french, colombia, 7.95);

customer("Jim Johnson", 2024);
customer("Jane Jerrod", 2077);
customer("Jasmine Jones", 2093);

order(2024, "Simple Best", 1);
order(2077, "Launch Mi", 3);
order(2077, "Smackin", 3);
order(2093, "Brimful", 2);
```

In this data, a `coffee` structure contains the name of a type of coffee, the roast, the country of origin, and the price per pound. The `customer` facts include the name of the customer and the customer number. The `order` facts record a standing order that the company ships monthly. They show the customer number, the type of coffee, and the number of pounds to ship each month.

As Figure 13.3 shows, to see the types of coffee each customer has ordered, you can use the query

```
customer(Name, Cnum), order(Cnum, Type, Pounds)
```

Queries and rules prove themselves in the same way: by proving each of their structures in turn. Each structure may find multiple successful proofs of itself, and each structure unifies its variables with each proof. For example, the query

```
customer(Name, Cnum), order(Cnum, Type, Pounds)
```

proves itself by proving `customer` and then `order`. When this rule proves itself, it first asks `customer` to prove itself. The `customer` structure looks through the program and unifies with the fact

```
customer("Jim Johnson", 2024)
```

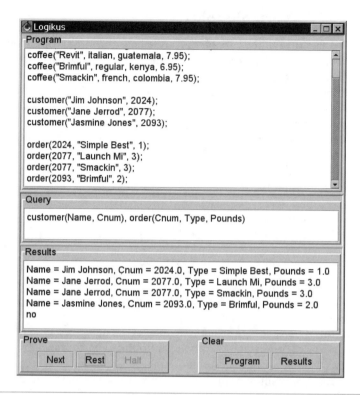

Figure 13.3 A join. All the variables in a query are in the same scope, so this query joins `customer` and `order` facts on customer number.

The structure proves itself by unifying with a fact in the program. This structure succeeds, and so the rule asks its next structure to prove itself. This structure shares variables with the first structure; all the structures in a rule have a common scope. So this structure must effectively prove

```
order(2024, Type, Pounds)
```

The customer number is fixed at this point. This screens out all possible proofs except one. The structure proves itself by unifying with the fact

```
order(2024, "Simple Best", 1)
```

By unifying with this fact, the `order` structure of the query succeeds. Because this is the last structure in the query, the entire query succeeds, with its variables unified with values that make the query true. After a successful proof, the IDE prints the query's variables.

13.7.3 Backtracking

In Figure 13.3, the user has pressed the **Rest** button. After its first success, the IDE asks the query to prove itself again. The query does not begin its proof anew. To find another proof, the query asks its last structure to find another proof. In this case, there is no other `order` fact with customer number 2024, and the last structure in the query fails to find another proof. The query then *backtracks*, which means that the query asks the preceding structure to find a new proof. In this example, the preceding structure is `customer`.

When a structure looks for a new proof, it first unbinds any variables it bound in its previous proof. In this example, the `customer` structure is able to find a new proof, unifying with the fact

```
customer("Jane Jerrod", 2077)
```

This proof unifies the query's variables with new values, and that produces new chances for the latter structures to prove themselves. The query moves forward again and asks its order structure to prove itself. This amounts to proving

```
order(2077, Type, Pounds)
```

There are two possible proofs because there are two orders for customer number 2077. The structure first unifies with the fact

```
order(2077, "Launch Mi", 3)
```

This unification completes a second successful proof of the query, and the IDE prints the new values of the variables. The IDE then asks the query for another proof. The query searches for a new proof by asking its last structure whether it can find another proof. In this case it can. First, the structure unbinds the variables it bound in finding its last proof. Specifically, the order structure unbinds the variables `Type` and `Pounds`. The structure unbinds only the variables it bound; it does not unbind `Cnum` because an earlier structure bound that variable.

With its `Cnum` variable still unified with 2077, the `order` structure finds another fact to unify with:

```
order(2077, "Smackin", 3)
```

This results in a new proof, and the IDE prints the result. The IDE keeps asking for more proofs. The query fails to find another proof for order 2077, and the query backtracks to the `customer` structure. This structure unbinds its variables and unifies with the fact

```
customer("Jasmine Jones", 2093)
```

The order structure then unifies with

```
order(2093, "Brimful", 2)
```

This constitutes the last successful proof. When the IDE asks for yet another proof, the query tries to find another order for customer number 2093. When this fails, the query tries to find another customer with which to unify. There are none, so the first structure of the query fails, the entire query fails, and the IDE prints no.

13.7.4 Looping and Halting

Logikus rules can refer to other rules, including themselves. This capability lets you construct powerful, recursive algorithms. In addition, this ability lets you create loops, which may compute until your program runs out of available memory. To help handle this prospect, the Logikus IDE provides a **Halt** button. The IDE executes Logikus proofs in a separate thread, which you can stop if you think the proof will not complete. For example, consider a program that contains the rule

```
loop :- loop;
```

This rule says, "to prove loop, prove loop." If this rule executes, it will loop forever, or until your program runs out of memory.

Try entering this rule in a Logikus program and issuing the query "loop". While the query futilely pursues its proof, you can click the **Halt** button to stop it. However, if your program runs out of memory resources, this button may not be able to execute.

13.7.5 Gateways

Compared with other structures, comparisons behave differently in proofs. First, their truth or falsity depends on their terms, so they need not consult a program. Second, a comparison can be true no more than once. After a comparison participates in a successful proof, it does not search for alternative proofs. For example, consider the query

```
coffee(Name, Roast, Country, Price),
    >(Price, 6),
    order(Cnum, Name, Pounds);
```

In this query, the comparison on price acts as a *gateway*, which is a structure that can be true no more than once. When the coffee structure unifies with a fact in a program, the Price variable unifies with the coffee price. At this point, the price is either greater than 6 or it is not. Unlike the coffee and order structures, the comparison structure can be true no more than once. If the comparison is true, the query moves on and finds proofs of the order structure. When the order structure runs out of proofs, the rule backtracks to the comparison and asks for another proof, and the comparison returns false; there is no other way to prove that the comparison is true. You'll meet two other gateways—evaluations and negations—when we look into additional features of Logikus.

13.8 Additional Features of Logikus

At this point, we have covered the fundamentals of logic programming. If you understand structures, variables, facts, and rules, you can create logic programs to model logical problems in the real world. In practice, several other features enhance this modeling, including

- Comments
- Evaluations
- Negation
- Anonymous variables
- Lists

13.8.1 Comments

The Logikus parser that comes with this book accepts comments in the same format that Java does. A comment that begins with // extends to the end of the line on which it appears. For example, the line

```
founded(rome, bc750); // according to legend...
```

provides a comment on the stated fact.

A comment that begins with /* comments out all text until the next */. If there is no matching */ comment terminator, the Logikus parser accepts the end of the program as the end of the comment.

13.8.2 Evaluations

Logikus provides an evaluation structure that unifies its first term with an evaluation of its second term. The functor for the evaluation structure is "#". For example, if you enter the query

```
#(X, (100 - 1)*(100 + 1))
```

and click **Next**, the Results area displays

```
X = 9999.0
```

As with comparisons, evaluations are gateways, which can be true no more than once in a proof. If you click **Next** again, the Results area displays

```
no
```

The second term in an evaluation can be a string or an arithmetic expression. Logikus recognizes arithmetic operators for multiplication ("*"), division ("/"), addition ("+") and subtraction ("-").

You can use evaluation structures as parts of queries or rules. Figure 13.4 shows an evaluation in action. (This Logikus program is on the CD in the file `art.txt`.)

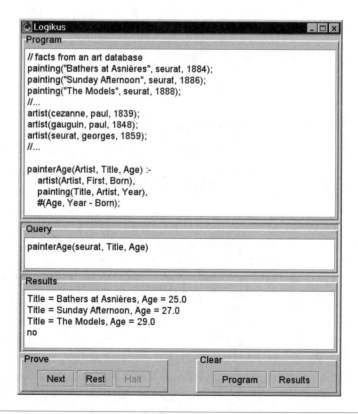

Figure 13.4 An evaluation structure in action. The `painterAge` rule calculates an artist's age at the time he or she completed a particular painting.

If the first term in an evaluation is an unbound variable, the evaluation acts as if it were an assignment command: The variable in the first term binds to the value of the second term. However, it is not always correct to think of evaluation as assignment. The evaluation structure *unifies* its first term with the value of its second term. For example, consider the evaluation

```
#(X, X + 1)
```

This evaluation can never succeed. If X has a value, the evaluation attempts to unify X with the value of X + 1. For example, if X is bound to 7, the evaluation attempts to unify 7 with 8. On the other hand, if X is not bound to a value, the evaluation fails when it attempts to evaluate X + 1.

Given that the evaluation #(X, X + 1) always fails, you might think that it is impossible to achieve iteration in a Logikus program. Perhaps this would be no great loss because iteration goes against the grain of logic programming. Rather than direct the flow of execution, a logic program models truth and works with a query to find variable values that make the query true. However, it turns out that you can effect iteration in a logic program. Section 13.12.5, "Altitude Bands," gives an example.

13.8.3 Negation

It can be useful to determine that the engine cannot prove a structure. The not qualifier in Logikus modifies the proof of a structure so that the proof fails if the structure can prove itself against a program and succeeds if the structure cannot prove itself. For example, consider the following logic program:

```
bachelor(X) :- male (X), not married(X);
married(jim);
male(jeremy);
male(jim);
```

Against this program, the query

```
bachelor(B)
```

finds that the only bachelor in the program is jeremy. The query unifies with the program's bachelor rule, unifying the query's B variable with the rule's X variable. The query asks the rule to prove its remaining structures. The rule proves male(X) by unifying with the fact male(jeremy). Then the rule attempts to prove not married(jeremy). This proof proceeds by trying to prove married(jeremy). This fails, and so not married(jeremy) succeeds.

If asked for another proof, the query begins by asking the rule it unified with for another proof. This rule in turn asks its last structure for another proof. Not structures are gateways (and thus true no more than once), so the not structure fails, and the rule backtracks to the male structure. This structure successfully unifies with male(jim), and the rule moves forward again. The rule asks the structure not married(jim) to prove itself. This not structure tries to prove married(jim) and succeeds because the program contains this exact fact. The structure not married(X) fails if X has unified with jim, because Jim is married.

Like comparisons and evaluations, not structures are gateways. If a not structure succeeds as part of a proof, when the rule or query it is in backtracks to the not structure, it automatically fails.

13.8.4 Not Dangerous

The meaning of not leads to subtleties. For example, the engine query

```
not dangerous
```

usually returns true. This means that the engine cannot find the fact dangerous in the program.

The fact that not declares that a structure is unprovable can lead to mystifying results. For example, suppose you change the bachelor program to read

```
badBachelor(X) :- not married(X), male(X);
married(jim);
male(jeremy);
male(jim);
```

Then the query

```
badBachelor(B)
```

finds no bachelors at all. The engine matches this query with the badBachelor rule and then attempts to prove not married(X). Because X is unbound, this is a request to prove that *no one* is married. The structure married(X) succeeds with the binding X = jim. Because married(X) succeeds, not married(X) is false, and badBachelor(X) is false.

Negations usually make sense only if they appear later in a rule's body than other structures that establish values for variables on which the negated structure relies. In the original bachelor program, not married(X) appears later than male(X). Thus, not married(X) tries to prove itself only after X has unified with a value, such as jim or jeremy.

13.8.5 Anonymous Variables

Anonymous variables let you avoid creating variable names for variables that you are not interested in. To indicate that you want an anonymous variable, you use an underscore ("_"). For example, Figure 13.5 shows a query that uses anonymous variables with data from `coffee.txt`.

Anonymous variables do not unify with corresponding terms in other structures, but they do allow unification to succeed. Note that the following query finds no coffee:

```
coffee(Name, X, X, Price) // bad
```

For the coffees in Figure 13.5, this query fails because the variable X first unifies with a coffee's roast, and then it tries to unify with a coffee's country, which is different in every case. (You *could* use this query to find coffees whose roast and country are identical, but no such coffees exist in the given program.)

You can use anonymous variables in rules to provide *projections*, or views of relations, including relational joins. For example, suppose that you are modeling a family tree with these facts:

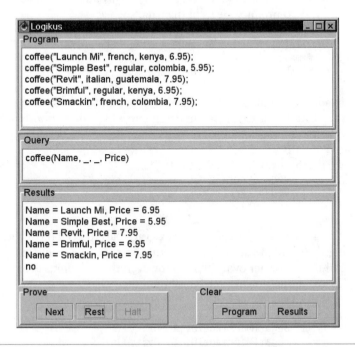

Figure 13.5 Anonymous variables. The query in this figure uses two anonymous variables to reduce the information it retrieves from the program.

```
begat(900, jim, 19350801, male);
begat(901, janie, 19370310, female);

begat(902, kyle, 19600829, male);
begat(903, kirk, 19550404, male);
begat(904, kevin, 19580815, male);

marriage(001, jim, janie, 19560512, present);
begat(001, karla, 19570114, female);
begat(001, katie, 19590712, female);

marriage(002, kevin, karla, 19790623, 19831112);
begat(002, leo, 19800115, male);
begat(002, lisa, 19810226, female);

marriage(003, kirk, karla, 19900114, present);

marriage(004, katie, kyle, 19951203, present);
begat(004, laura, 19980217, female);
```

These facts are a subset of the sample Logikus program contained in the CD file family.txt. The facts model each child as the product of a marriage; marriage structures have an ID, the names of the parents, and the dates of the marriage. In this model, begat structures refer to the marriage that begat the individual; they have the person's name, birth date, and sex. With this foundation, you can use anonymous variables to produce views of the data, such as

```
male(X)        :- begat(_, X, _, male);
female(X)      :- begat(_, X, _, female);
birthdate(X, D) :- begat(_, X, D, _);
```

In addition to simplifying the creation of logical views, anonymous variables can help keep extraneous data from interfering in a logical relationship. For example, here is a rule for defining siblings:

```
siblings(X, Y) :-
    begat(MarriageID, X, _, _),
    begat(MarriageID, Y, _, _),
    !=(X, Y);
```

The siblings rule uses anonymous variables to keep birth date and sex from affecting the sibling relationship. This rule uses the "!=" comparison to avoid counting a child as his or her own sibling. However, this rule finds every pair of siblings twice. To avoid this, you can introduce the rule

```
siblingPair(X, Y) :-
    begat(MarriageID, X, Dx, _),
    begat(MarriageID, Y, Dy, _),
    <(Dx, Dy);
```

This rule finds only sibling pairs in which one child is born first. In the case of twins, that requires more precision in modeling birth times.

13.9 Lists

The basic collection class in Logikus is the list. You can write a list as a pair of brackets containing a series of terms. For example, here is a list of synonyms for French roasted coffee:

```
[dark, full, high, viennese, continental]
```

There are many ways to write a list that unifies with this one. First, any list that contains the same number of elements will unify with this list if each term unifies with its corresponding element. For example, each of the following lists unifies with the list of synonyms:

```
[A, B, C, D, E]

[dark, full, A, B, continental]
```

You can also describe a list in terms of its head elements and its tail, indicating the tail after a vertical bar. The tail of a list is always itself a list. For example, the following list also unifies with the list of synonyms:

```
[A | B]
```

Unifying this structure with the synonyms unifies A with dark, and B with the list

```
[full, high, viennese, continental].
```

You can specify more than one head element, separating them with commas. Consider the list

```
[A, B | C]
```

This unifies A with dark, B with full, and C with

```
[high, viennese, continental].
```

Figure 13.6 shows examples of successful and unsuccessful list unifications. (This Logikus program is in the file french.txt.)

The query in Figure 13.6 tries to prove itself by unifying with ok rules and proving them. The program first establishes a list of synonyms for French roasted coffee.

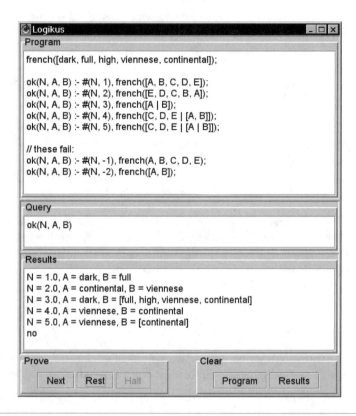

Figure 13.6 List unifications. In this example, the ok query proves itself against the ok rules, which identify themselves by number. As the output shows, only rules 1 through 5 can unify with the query.

The program then specifies a series of ok rules, which unify the variable N with a number and then specify a list that may unify with the given list of synonyms. The first five rules specify lists that unify with the synonyms, and the last two rules do not.

The first ok rule declares

```
ok(N, A, B) :- #(N, 1), french([A, B, C, D, E]);
```

The ok query unifies with the head of this rule and then asks the rule's remaining structures to prove themselves. The evaluation #(N, 1) numbers the rule so that you can see which rule produces which result. The structure french([A, B, C, D, E]) unifies with the first fact of the program. The ok rule succeeds, and the query prints

```
N = 1.0, A = dark, B = full
```

The second ok rule is

```
ok(N, A, B) :- #(N, 2), french([E, D, C, B, A]);
```

This rule shows that there is nothing special about where A and B appear in the list. When the query proves itself with this rule, it prints

```
N = 2.0, A = continental, B = viennese
```

The third ok rule says

```
ok(N, A, B) :- #(N, 3), french([A | B]);
```

This rule defines its list using a vertical bar. The variable A unifies with the head of the synonym list, and B unifies with the tail. The query successfully proves itself using this rule, displaying:

```
N = 3.0, A = dark, B = [full, high, viennese, continental]
```

The fourth ok rule declares

```
ok(N, A, B) :- #(N, 4), french([C, D, E | [A, B]]);
```

Here, the rule uses a list that starts with three elements (C, D, and E) and concludes with another list. The concluding list contains exactly two elements: A and B. When this rule proves itself, C, D, and E unify with dark, full, and high. This leaves [A, B] to unify with the remainder of the synonym list, which is [viennese, continental]. This rule succeeds, and the query prints

```
N = 4.0, A = viennese, B = continental
```

The fifth (and final successful) rule specifies

```
ok(N, A, B) :- #(N, 5), french([C, D, E | [A | B]]);
```

This is identical to the fourth rule except in the specification of the tail list, which sets up B as the tail of a list. As before, this rule proves itself by unifying with the french rule, unifying C, D, and E as in the fourth ok rule. This leaves [A | B] to unify with the remainder of the list, [viennese, continental]. Now, A unifies with the head (viennese) of this list, and B unifies with the tail of this list. The tail of a list is always itself a list, and in this case the tail is [continental]. After this proof succeeds, the query displays its variables as

```
N = 5.0, A = viennese, B = [continental]
```

The other ok rules cannot successfully prove themselves. The rule that unifies N with -1 fails because its french structure contains five terms rather than a single list. The rule that unifies N with -2 fails because its list can match only other lists that contain exactly two elements.

13.9.1 Dot Notation

Internally, the logic engine stores lists as structures with a dot (".") as a functor and with two terms, the second of which is always a list. If you run into problems getting a list to behave as you would expect, it can help to write the list using this dot notation. For example, you can enter a fact about favorite lizards as either

```
favs([monitor, gilaMonster, iguana]);
```

or

```
favs(.(monitor, .(gilaMonster, .(iguana, []))));
```

In the latter notation, each "dot" structure is a structure with two terms. In each case, the second term is a list, including the innermost structure whose second term is an empty list. With either of these facts in a program, you can issue a query as either

```
favs([J, K, L])
```

or

```
favs(.(J, .(K, .(L, []))))
```

With the fact written in either notation and with the query written in either notation, the variables J, K, and L will unify with the lizards in the fact. The bracket notation is shorter than the dot notation, but the dot notation can help illuminate how list unification works.

13.10 List Applications

The combination of the list data structure and the ability to define recursive rules allows you to create several highly reusable algorithms. All the Logikus programs in this chapter are included in this book's CD in .txt files. You can open these files with any editor and copy and paste them into your own programs.

13.10.1 Member

The member program is probably the most fundamental and most reused algorithm in logic programming. The program (from file member.txt) is

```
member(X, [X | Rest]);
member(X, [Y | Rest]) :- member(X, Rest);
```

Figure 13.7 shows this program in use.

A high-level description of the member program is that an element is a member of a list if it heads the list or if it is a member of the tail of the list. A closer analysis of the logic of the member program is as follows.

The first rule states that a variable is a member of a list if it heads the list. When the query in the example proves itself, it unifies with the first rule of the program. This results in success, with the variable in the query unifying with the first element of the list, spassky.

Figure 13.7 The member program. The query uses the classic logic program member to extract chess champs of the late 20th century from a list.

When the query tries to find another proof, it asks the first rule for another proof, but there is none. The query then unifies with the second rule and tries to prove it by proving its second structure, which is member(X, Rest). This structure proves itself in exactly the same way the query structure did. It uses the first rule to find the head of Rest and the second rule to find members of the list after its head. This recurses until the list is empty, and both rules fail.

13.10.2 Prefix

A prefix of a list is another list whose elements equal the initial elements of the first list. For example, [] and [merlin] are two prefixes of

```
[merlin, prospero, gandalf, harry]
```

The following program finds all the prefixes of a list:

```
prefix([], List);
prefix([X | Rest1], [X | Rest2]) :-
    prefix(Rest1, Rest2);
```

Figure 13.8 shows a query that applies this program to a list of wizards.

The second rule of prefix declares that one list is a prefix of another if their heads are the same (X) and the first list's tail is a prefix of the second list's tail.

13.10.3 Suffix

The suffix algorithm uses the same concepts as the prefix algorithm.

```
/* usage: suffix(SuffixList, LongerList) */

suffix(List, List);
suffix(List1, [X | Rest]) :- suffix(List1, Rest);
```

13.10.4 Permutation

One list is a *permutation* of another list if it contains the same elements in any order. Figure 13.9 shows a permutation algorithm applied to a list of errands.

The file permutation.txt includes the select algorithm, whose rules are

```
select(X, [X | Rest], Rest);
select(X, [Y | Rest1], [Y | Rest2]) :-
    select(X, Rest1, Rest2);
```

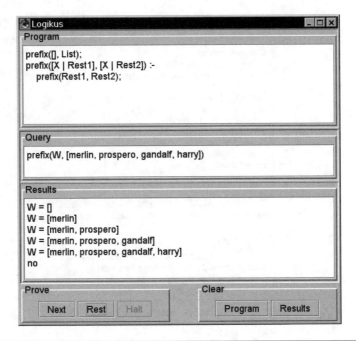

Figure 13.8 The prefix program. The query asks for all prefixes of a list of wizards.

These rules separate a list into two parts: an element extracted from the list, and the remainder of the list. The select algorithm works by declaring that X is a selectable element of a list if X heads the list or if X is selectable from the tail of the list.

Here is the permutation algorithm:

```
permutation(InList, [H | OutRest]) :-
    select(H, InList, InOther),
    permutation(InOther, OutRest);
permutation([], []);
```

This algorithm declares that an output list is a permutation of an input list if the output is an element of the input, followed by a permutation of the remainder of the input. This rule recurses, finding permutations of an ever-smaller list, until finally it asks whether an empty list is a permutation of itself, which the second rule supports.

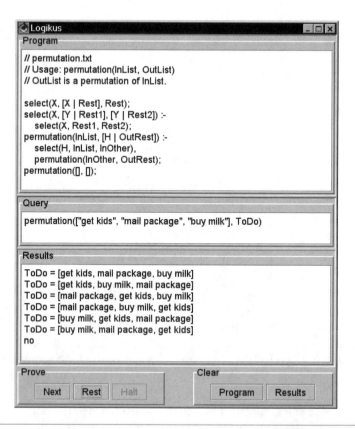

Figure 13.9   A permutation algorithm. The query uses the `permutation` algorithm to find possible sequences for completing a list of errands.

13.11 Modeling Transitive and Symmetric Relations

A *transitive* relation is a relation such as "taller," where a pair of relations can imply a third relation. For example, if Alan is taller than Britta, and Britta is taller than Chuck, then Alan is taller than Chuck. This kind of relation differs from, say, "owes a favor to," which is not transitive. If Alan owes Britta and Britta owes Chuck, Alan may or may not owe Chuck. The "owes a favor to" relation is not transitive.

A common transitive relation is "in." If A is in B and B is in C, then A is in C. This is true, for example, of boxes and geographical places. It is tempting to write, for transitive relations, a rule such as the following:

```
in(A, C) :- in(A, B), in(B, C); // wrong
```

If this rule is in a program, a query such as in(box1, X) will loop. When the rule tries to prove the first structure in its body, in(A = box1, B), this structure finds the rule again. Because B is unbound at this point, the rule tries to prove itself again in the same way, and the program loops indefinitely.

One way to model transitive relations is to distinguish between something being "directly in" and something being "transitively in" something else. For example, Figure 13.10 models the relations of a few geographic areas. This program uses the functor in to signify that one place is directly in another, and uses within to model that one place is either directly or indirectly in another place.

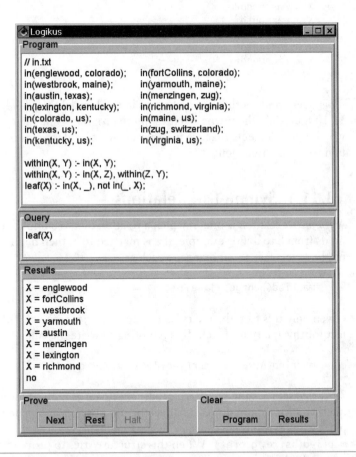

Figure 13.10 The in program. The idea of "in" is a transitive relation, so if Menzingen is in Zug and Zug is in Switzerland, then Menzingen must be in Switzerland. The query here finds every known place that contains no other place.

With this program in place, a query of

```
within(X, us)
```

produces these results:

```
X = colorado
X = maine
X = texas
X = kentucky
X = virginia
X = englewood
X = fortCollins
X = westbrook
X = yarmouth
X = austin
X = lexington
X = richmond
no
```

This query finds both cities and states in the United States. The query in Figure 13.10 finds only the towns or cities in the program. The query uses the leaf rule, which finds elements that are in other elements and screens out elements that contain some other element.

13.11.1 Symmetric Relations

A *symmetric* relation is one in which a relation of a to b implies that the same relation holds from b to a. For example, if a is married to b, then b must be married to a. You might have a fact about marriage such as:

```
married(george, jane);
```

Given only this fact, the query married(jane, george) will fail because there is no fact for this query to match. It is tempting to write the rule:

```
married(A, B) :- married(B, A); // wrong
```

This rule satisfies the query married(jane, george), but it loops for other types of queries, such a query for two names that do not appear in a married fact. For example, the query married(george, astro) finds the married rule and tries to prove married(astro, george). When this structure tries to prove itself, it finds the married rule again and tries to prove married(george, astro). This proof will go on happily ever after.

The solution is to introduce another relation to query:

```
couple(A, B) :- married(A, B);
couple(A, B) :- married(B, A);
```

A query to the couple rules cannot loop because both rules refer to married facts. For example, if a program contains the couple rules and the single fact that george is married to jane, then a request for the rest of the proofs of

```
couple(jane, X)
```

displays

```
X = george
no
```

The query

```
couple(george, astro)
```

displays simply

```
no
```

13.12 Example Applications

You can combine facts, rules, and lists into logic programs that solve complex problems. Rules add much more power and complexity to a logic program than facts do. A program with ten rules may take an hour or more for a human reader to comprehend. A well-written logic program may be much harder to understand than a well-written Java program. In part, this is because most developers have more experience with procedural programming elements than with recursive programming. It may also be that recursive programming is simply harder to comprehend than procedural programming.

13.12.1 An Authorization Program

Here is a program that models privileges in a semiconductor fabrication facility:

```
priv(jim, operate, sputter);
priv(jim, operate, implant);
priv(janie, supervise, sputter);
priv(rivki, operate, photo);
priv(bill, supervise, photo);
```

```
teammates(P1, P2) :-
    priv(P1, _, Machine),
    priv(P2, _, Machine),
    !=(P1, P2);
```

The priv facts in this program allow various queries about which person the program authorizes to perform which operations on which machine. The teammates rule finds people who can work on the same machine. For example, the query

```
teammates(jim, T)
```

produces the results

```
T = janie
no
```

You encounter a problem if you ask for all teammates with the query

```
teammates(P1, P2)
```

This query produces these results:

```
P1 = jim, P2 = janie
P1 = janie, P2 = jim
P1 = rivki, P2 = bill
P1 = bill, P2 = rivki
no
```

The problem is that the results show every pair twice. You can address this problem by adding a comparison to the query:

```
teammates(P1, P2), <(P1, P2)
```

Now the query asks to see only teammates with the workers' names in alphabetical order:

```
P1 = janie, P2 = jim
P1 = bill, P2 = rivki
no
```

If you think this is a common query, you can add it to the program as a rule:

```
orderedTeammates(P1, P2) :- teammates(P1, P2), <(P1, P2);
```

Storing a useful query as a rule is an effective approach to building a logic program iteratively. As you add rules, you should reexamine how the rules interact. For example, the orderedTeammates rule will force a not-equals comparison followed by a less-than comparison. You might accept this inefficiency, but it is important to create collections of rules that work together to form a complete logical model.

13.12.2 Epidemic

An *epidemic* occurs when a problem is transmitted through contact between objects. The word usually applies to human disease, but it also applies to computer viruses and may apply to factory problems. For example, semiconductor fabs often fire many wafers together in a single run of an oven. If a wafer emits a contaminant that sticks to other wafers, those wafers may go on to contaminate any other wafers that future firings expose them to.

A common example of an epidemic is the spread of a kissing disease through a high school. Imagine that a local epidemiologist (perhaps the principal) has traced an outbreak of symptoms to a single infected person and a lot of kissing. The following program models the epidemic:

```
kiss(jill,   james,  0321);
kiss(julian, jill,   0405);
kiss(jill,   jasper, 0412);
kiss(james,  jenni,  0420);
kiss(julian, judy,   0508);
kiss(jed,    judy,   0614);

kissed(Student1, Student2, Date) :-
    kiss(Student1, Student2, Date);

kissed(Student1, Student2, Date) :-
    kiss(Student2, Student1, Date);

infected(julian, 0307);


exposed(Student, Date) :-
    infected(Student, Date1),
    >(Date, Date1);

exposed(Student2, Date2) :-
    kissed(Student2, Student1, Date1),
    >(Date2, Date1),
    exposed(Student1, Date1);
```

This program models kissing as a symmetric relation, so the fact

```
kiss(jill,   james,  0321);
```

implies both that Jill kissed James and that James kissed Jill. The date format records this event as occurring on March 21. The program models the symmetric nature of kissing with the `kissed` rules:

```
kissed(Student1, Student2, Date) :-
    kiss(Student1, Student2, Date);

kissed(Student1, Student2, Date) :-
    kiss(Student2, Student1, Date);
```

The program notes that Julian is known to have been infected as of March 7:

```
infected(julian, 0307);
```

The first exposed rule says a that student counts as having been exposed on a given date if he or she is known to have been infected before that date:

```
exposed(Student, Date) :-
    infected(Student, Date1),
    >(Date, Date1);
```

The second `exposed` rule says that a student was exposed on a given date if the student has kissed another student on a prior date, and if the other student had been exposed at the time.

```
exposed(Student2, Date2) :-
    kissed(Student2, Student1, Date1),
    >(Date2, Date1),
    exposed(Student1, Date1);
```

If it is now June 15, the epidemiologist can enter the query

```
exposed(Student, 0615)
```

with the results

```
Student = julian
Student = jed
Student = jill
Student = jasper
Student = judy
no
```

Note that James has been spared because his kiss with Jill preceded her kiss with the infected Julian. His luck spread to Jenni, who kissed James after the onset of the epidemic but happened to kiss an unexposed student. All other students have been exposed, and that is not surprising because this was, after all, an epidemic.

13.12.3 Generate and Test

Some problems have many possible solutions, along with a way to score or validate the strength of each solution. For example, a basketball coach might consider all possible starting lineups against a known lineup of the competing coach's team. If the coach can model a matchup based on height, skill, and other factors, he or she can compare every possible permutation of a starting lineup to find the best match. In other cases, each permutation may be either acceptable or unacceptable. Logic puzzles, for example, typically have only one acceptable answer. Consider the following problem:

Each of four martial arts students has a different specialty. From the following clues, can you determine each student's full name and her special skill?

1. Ms. Ellis (whose instructor is Mr. Caldwell), Amy, and Ms. Fowler are all martial arts students.

2. Sparring isn't the specialty of either Carla or Dianne.

3. Neither the shoot fighting expert nor the pressure point fighter is named Fowler.

4. Children's techniques aren't the specialty of Dianne (whose instructor is Ms. Sherman).

5. Amy, who disdains pressure point fighting, isn't Ms. Goodrich.

6. Betti and Ms. Fowler are roommates.

7. Ms. Hightower avoids sparring because of its point scoring nature.

To solve this problem with a logic program, you must generate all permutations of first-name/last-name/specialty and verify each permutation against the clues. The following program achieves this:

```
// karate.txt

geneval(Solution) :-
    generate(Solution),
    evaluate(Solution);

// generate all possible solutions
select(X, [X | Rest], Rest);
select(X, [Y | Rest1], [Y | Rest2]) :-
    select(X, Rest1, Rest2);

permutation(InList, [H | OutRest]) :-
    select(H, InList, InOther),
    permutation(InOther, OutRest);
permutation([], []);
```

```
generate(Solution) :-
    permutation(
        [ellis, fowler, goodrich, hightower],
        LastNames),

    permutation(
        [sparring, shootFighting, pressurePoints,
         childrens],
        Specialties),

    associate(
        [amy, betti, carla, dianne],
        LastNames,
        Specialties,
        Solution);

// "associate" combines three lists into one list of
// students with three attributes

associate(
    [FirstName | Frest],
    [LastName | Lrest],
    [Specialty | Srest],
    [student(FirstName, LastName, Specialty) |
     StudentsRest])

    :- associate(
        Frest,
        Lrest,
        Srest,
        StudentsRest);

associate([], [], [], []);

// "evaluate" takes a list of "student" structures, and
// succeeds if all the criteria are met.

member(X, [X | Rest]);
member(X, [Y | Rest]) :- member(X, Rest);

evaluate(Solution) :-
    // Clue 1
    not member(student(amy, ellis, _), Solution),
    not member(student(amy, fowler, _), Solution),

    // Clue 2
    not member(student(carla, _, sparring), Solution),
    not member(student(dianne, _, sparring), Solution),

    // Clue 3
    not member(student(_, fowler, shootFighting), Solution),
    not member(student(_, fowler, pressurePoints),
                Solution),
```

```
// Clue 4
not member(student(dianne, _, childrens), Solution),

// Clue 5
not member(student(amy, goodrich, _), Solution),
not member(student(amy, _, pressurePoints), Solution),

// Clue 6
not member(student(betti, fowler, _), Solution),

// Clue 7
not member(student(_, hightower, sparring), Solution),

// Clue 4, 1
not member(student(dianne, ellis, _), Solution);
```

The program generates permutations of each of three lists, containing first names, last names, and karate specialties. The `generate` rule *associates* these three lists by building a list of `student` structures that contains a student's first name, last name, and specialty. The `Solution` variable contains a prospective solution—namely, a list of `student` structures. The `evaluate` rule checks to see whether a prospective solution runs afoul of any of the clues. The `geneval` rule early in the program generates and evaluates all possible solutions. Querying this rule with

```
geneval(Solution)
```

produces the output

```
Solution =
    [student(amy, hightower, shootFighting),
     student(betti, ellis, sparring),
     student(carla, fowler, childrens),
     student(dianne, goodrich, pressurePoints)]
```

This is the only solution that passes the gauntlet of clues. Amy Hightower is the shoot fighting expert; Betti Ellis is the sparring specialist; Carla Fowler's forte is children's techniques, and Dianne Goodrich concentrates on pressure points.

13.12.4 Generate and Test in Java

The solution to the karate puzzle is complex, in part because of the inherent complexity of the problem, and in part because of the complexity of logic programming in Logikus. The package `sjm.examples.karate` solves the karate puzzle using Java. It uses classes from `sjm.combinatorics`, which has utilities for generating permutations.

If you compare the Logikus and Java solutions, you may find that one or the other seems more straightforward. A key question is whether logic puzzles are more easily

solved in a logic language than in an object-oriented language. Of course, the
Logikus solution *is* a Java solution in that Logikus is built from Java.

13.12.5 Altitude Bands

Suppose that you want to visit a collection of cities in order of their elevation so that
you can gradually acclimatize to the deficiency of oxygen at higher altitudes. To
establish your itinerary you want to iterate over ranges, or *bands* of altitude, finding
the cities in each band.

Here is a general algorithm for iteration:

```
for(X, X, Upper) :- <= (X, Upper);
for(X, Lower, Upper) :-
    <(Lower, Upper),
    #(LowerPlusOne, Lower + 1),
    for(X, LowerPlusOne, Upper);
```

If you enter these rules as a Logikus program and enter the query

```
for(X, 1, 20)
```

the Results area will display

```
X = 1.0
X = 2.0
X = 3.0
// ...
X = 19.0
X = 20.0
no
```

When the query first proves itself, it unifies with the first rule, which causes X to
unify with 1. The first rule can prove itself only once, so when the query wants a second proof, it unifies with the second rule.

When the query unifies with the second rule, the variable Lower unifies with 1 and
the variable Upper unifies with 20. To prove itself, the rule first verifies that Lower
is less than Upper. The rule then uses an evaluation that unifies LowerPlusOne with
the value of Lower + 1. Here the evaluation is effectively an assignment because
LowerPlusOne is unbound when the evaluation begins. The rule then looks for a
proof of for(X, 2, 20). This structure finds the first rule in the program and unifies
X with 2. The flow of the proof continues until the lower bound is no longer less than
the upper bound.

You can incorporate a version of the "for" algorithm in a program that increments altitudes by 1,000 feet to find cities sorted by altitude band:

```
// travel.txt

city(abilene, 1718);
city("addis ababa", 8000);
city(denver, 5280);
city(flagstaff, 6970);
city(jacksonville, 8);
city(leadville, 10200);
city(madrid, 1305);
city(richmond, 19);
city(spokane, 1909);
city(wichita, 1305);
highCity(Name) :- city(Name, Alt), >(Alt, 5000);

for(I, I, Upper) :- <= (I, Upper);
for(I, Lower, Upper) :-
    <(Lower, Upper),
    #(LowerPlus, Lower + 1000),
    for(I, LowerPlus, Upper);

travel(AltBand, Name) :-
    for (AltBand, 1000, 20000),
    city(Name, Alt),
    >(Alt, AltBand - 1000),
    <= (Alt, AltBand);
```

Querying this program with

```
travel(AltBand, X)
```

prints

```
AltBand = 1000.0, X = jacksonville
AltBand = 1000.0, X = richmond
AltBand = 2000.0, X = abilene
AltBand = 2000.0, X = madrid
AltBand = 2000.0, X = spokane
AltBand = 2000.0, X = wichita
AltBand = 6000.0, X = denver
AltBand = 7000.0, X = flagstaff
AltBand = 8000.0, X = addis ababa
AltBand = 11000.0, X = leadville
no
```

13.13 Summary

Logic programming lets you model a problem in terms of relations. Thinking about the relations in a problem is fundamentally different from thinking about objects. To show this difference, you can try asking seasoned Java developers this question: How would you model, in Java, the fact that Aristotle is taller than Plato if you do not know either man's height?

In Logikus, the answer is

```
taller(aristotle, plato)
```

In Java, the answer is more elusive, and many developers find that they simply cannot arrive at a solution. Interestingly, for such stymied developers, it simplifies the problem to modify the relationship so that Aristotle *manages* Plato.

There are no problems Logikus can solve that Java cannot solve. There are, however, many problems that are more easily solved in a logic language than in an object-oriented language. For example, it takes many more lines to model the `taller` relation in Java than in Logikus. Any problem that is oriented around modeling relations or rules can be more readily rendered in Logikus than in Java.

CHAPTER 14

Parsing a Logic Language

Chapter 13 explains logic programming, giving examples in the Logikus programming language. This chapter explains how to construct a Logikus parser.

14.1 Building a Logic Language Environment

A logic language lets a user compose a logic program and pose queries against the program. Figure 14.1 shows the elements of a logic programming environment.

Logic languages need an engine to do the work of determining which facts and rules can prove a user's query. The code for the engine used by Logikus lies within the package sjm.engine. You can write Java programs that directly manipulate the engine classes. The package sjm.examples.engine has examples that show how to exercise various features of the engine. The problem with accessing the engine directly from Java is that the code is more voluminous and more complicated than

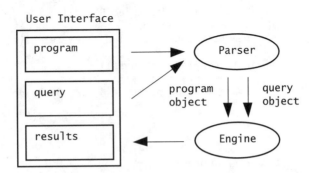

Figure 14.1 The elements of a logic programming environment. In a logic programming environment, the user supplies both the program and a query. The environment parses these and uses a logic engine to prove the query against the program.

equivalent Logikus code. For example, here is a program that shows how to create the bachelor program of Chapter 13:

```
package sjm.examples.engine;

import sjm.engine.*;

/**
 * Show a <code>Not</code> object in action.
 */
public class ShowNot {

public static void main(String[] args) {

    Program p = new Program();

    // bachelor(X) :- male(X), not married(X);

    Variable x = new Variable("X");
    Structure s0 = new Structure("bachelor", new Term[]{x});
    Structure s1 = new Structure("male", new Term[]{x});
    Structure s2 = new Not("married", new Term[]{x});
    Rule r0 = new Rule(new Structure[]{s0, s1, s2});
    p.addAxiom(r0);

    // married(jim)

    p.addAxiom(new Fact("married", "jim"));

    // male(jeremy); male(jim);

    p.addAxiom(new Fact("male", "jeremy"));
    p.addAxiom(new Fact("male", "jim"));

    System.out.println(p);

    Variable b = new Variable("B");
    Query q = new Query(p,
        new Structure("bachelor", new Term[]{b}));

    while (q.canFindNextProof()) {
        System.out.println();
        System.out.println(b + " is a bachelor");
    }
  }
}
```

Running this program prints

```
bachelor(X) :- male(X), not married(X);
married(jim);
```

```
male(jeremy);
male(jim);

jeremy is a bachelor
```

The Java program constructs and displays a `Program` object and constructs and issues a `Query` object against this program. The `Program` object displays itself as text that a Logikus parser could correctly interpret. Logikus is effectively a facade that makes it easy to use the engine.

Assemblers for a Logikus parser create objects from the classes in `sjm.engine`. The tasks for building a Logikus parser are the same fundamental tasks as for the other languages in this book:

- Write a grammar.

- Write the assemblers that build a Logikus axiom.

- Generate a parser from the grammar, plugging in the assemblers.

14.2 A Logikus Grammar

The building blocks of Logikus programs are structures and variables. A typical structure has a string as its functor and has terms enclosed in parentheses. For now, let's sketch a grammar that will recognize a structure such as

```
starred(jamesCagney, "Mister Roberts", Year)
```

The following grammar gives a first draft for recognizing Logikus structures and variables:

```
structure     = functor ('(' commaList(term) ')' | Empty);
functor       = LowercaseWord | QuotedString;
term          = structure | variable;
variable      = UppercaseWord;
commaList(p)  = p (',' p)*;
```

Note that the functor of a structure cannot be an uppercase word. Logikus shares this feature with Prolog; users need not and cannot declare variables. A string that begins with an uppercase letter is a variable, and a string that begins with a lowercase letter is a functor.

A Logikus program is a series of axioms terminated by semicolons. For example, Logikus must recognize the following three axioms:

```
customer("Jasmine Jones", 2093);

order(2093, "Brimful", 2);

q (Name, Type) :- customer(Name, CustomerNum),
    order(CustomerNum, Type, Pounds);
```

Here is an initial draft of a grammar for Logikus axioms:

```
axiom   = structure (ruleDef | Empty);
ruleDef = ":-" commaList(structure);
```

The grammar so far defines a fairly comprehensive logic language, but it does not yet provide for all the features of Logikus. In particular, you need to broaden the concept of the composition of a rule. Rules in Logikus are series of *conditions*, and a normal structure is only one type of condition. Other conditions you wish to allow are lists, comparisons, negations, and evaluations. For example, Logikus must recognize this rule:

```
travel(AltBand, Name) :-
    for (AltBand, 1000, 20000),
    city(Name, Alt),
    >(Alt, AltBand - 1000),
    <= (Alt, AltBand);
```

Logikus allows any combination of arithmetic operators and parentheses in its expressions. To capture this in the grammar, you can extend the definition of axioms as follows:

```
axiom      = structure (ruleDef | Empty);
structure  = functor ('(' commaList(term) ')' | Empty);
functor    = LowercaseWord | QuotedString;
term       = structure | variable;
variable   = UppercaseWord;

ruleDef    = ":-" commaList(condition);

condition  = structure | evaluation | comparison;

evaluation =      '#' '(' arg ',' arg ')';
comparison = operator '(' arg ',' arg ')';
arg        = expression | functor;
operator   = '<' | '>' | '=' | "<=" | ">=" | "!=" ;

expression = phrase ('+' phrase | '-' phrase)*;
phrase     = factor ('*' factor | '/' factor)*;
factor     = '(' expression ')' | Num | variable;

commaList(p) = p (',' p)*;
```

The evaluation rule recognizes any string of the form #(arg, arg), such as #(LowerPlus, Lower + 1000). The expressions allowed by evaluations and comparisons draw on the grammar developed in Chapter 7, "Parsing Arithmetic." One difference is that Logikus evaluations and comparisons work with either strings or numbers. For example, >(tyrannosaurus, triceratops) is a valid Logikus comparison.

Another valid condition is the not condition. You can extend the grammar with

```
condition = structure | evaluation | comparison | not;
not       = "not" structure;
```

Logikus also supports lists. A list is a pair of brackets that may or may not have contents. The nonempty contents of a list are a series of terms separated by commas. A list may follow these terms with a vertical bar and a tail, which must be either another list or a variable. The following grammar rules succinctly state these principles:

```
list         = '[' (listContents | Empty) ']';
listContents = commaList(term) listTail;
listTail     = ('|' (variable | list)) | Empty;
```

These rules refer to term, which we said earlier was either a structure or variable.

You need to widen this to

```
term = structure | Num | list | variable;
```

You also need to allow anonymous variables, and that means

```
variable = UppercaseWord | '_';
```

Finally, you need to allow a single dot as a valid functor for a structure. This specifically allows the manual construction of lists, such as

```
test(.(A, .(B, .(C, []))))
```

To allow the dot functor, you extend the functor rule

```
functor = '.' | LowercaseWord | QuotedString;
```

Here is the complete grammar for a Logikus axiom:

```
axiom     = structure (ruleDef | Empty);
structure = functor ('(' commaList(term) ')' | Empty);
functor   = '.' | LowercaseWord | QuotedString;
term      = structure | Num | list | variable;
variable  = UppercaseWord | '_';
```

```
ruleDef       = ":-" commaList(condition);

condition     = structure | not | evaluation | comparison |
                list;

not           = "not" structure;

evaluation    =      '#' '(' arg ',' arg ')';
comparison    = operator '(' arg ',' arg ')';
arg           = expression | functor;
operator      = '<' | '>' | '=' | "<=" | ">=" | "!=";

expression    = phrase ('+' phrase | '-' phrase)*;
phrase        = factor ('*' factor | '/' factor)*;
factor        = '(' expression ')' | Num | variable;

list          = '[' (listContents | Empty) ']';
listContents = commaList(term) listTail;
listTail      = ('|' (variable | list)) | Empty;

commaList(p) = p (',' p)*;
```

14.2.1 Comments in Logikus

The preceding grammar recognizes Logikus axioms, but it does not allow for comments. In fact, you want to define the Logikus language to allow comments both within and between axioms. You can keep the grammar simple if you allow for an understanding that you will, in practice, rely on a tokenizer to screen out comments. The implementation of Logikus in sjm.examples.logic uses a default Tokenizer object from sjm.parse.tokens. This class by default allows // comments, which comment out characters to the end of a line, and /**/ comments, which comment out their contents. See Section 9.7, "Tokenizer States," for an explanation of how Tokenizer handles comments.

14.2.2 Logikus Programs

The grammar developed in Section 14.2 recognizes Logikus axioms but not entire Logikus programs. You could extend the grammar to observe that a program is a semicolon-separated series of axioms, but it is more efficient to use a simple text-processing class to separate the input into axioms and then apply a parser to each axiom. The class TokenStringSource in sjm.parse.tokens parses a Logikus program string into statements. This simplifies the work of constructing the parser, and it reduces the amount of work the parser must perform.

Knowing that you need to build a parser for just Logikus axioms, you can generate the parser almost directly from the grammar. The parser, however, needs assemblers to build Structure objects, Variable objects, and the other components that can be composed into a Program object.

14.3 Logikus Assemblers

From one point of view, Logikus is a computer language that lets its user model a problem in terms of facts and rules. Another perspective of Logikus is that it is only a thin skin over a logic engine, specifically the engine in sjm.engine. A review of the assemblers in sjm.examples.logic confirms the view that Logikus is quite close to the logic engine. Each of the assemblers in Figure 14.2 pushes an object from one of the classes in sjm.engine.

Assembler placement is sometimes obvious. Evaluations and comparisons, for example, see their text and call on a corresponding assembler to build a corresponding engine object. The notes in Figure 14.3 refer to assembler placements that are more subtle.

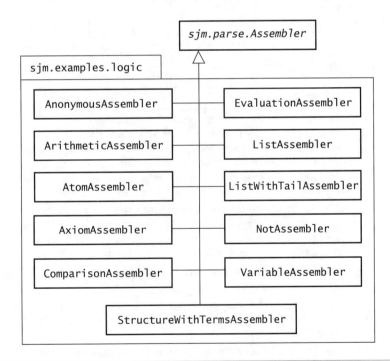

Figure 14.2   Logikus assemblers. The Logikus parser in sjm.examples.logic uses 11 assemblers, which collaborate in composing axioms from text that the parser recognizes.

Parser	Assembler	Note
arg()	AtomAssembler()	1
axiom()	AxiomAssembler()	
comparison()	ComparisonAssembler()	
evaluation()	EvaluationAssembler()	
list()	ListAssembler()	2
listTail()	ListWithTailAssembler() or ListAssembler()	3
not()	NotAssembler()	
num()	AtomAssembler()	
query()	AxiomAssembler()	4
structure()	AtomAssembler(), or StructureWithTermsAssembler()	5
variable()	new VariableAssembler() or new AnonymousAssembler()	6
Math		
divideFactor()	ArithmeticAssembler('/')	
minusPhrase()	ArithmeticAssembler('-')	
plusPhrase()	ArithmeticAssembler('+')	
timesFactor()	ArithmeticAssembler('*')	

1. The arg() subparser recognizes an expression or a functor. The functor() subparser appears twice in the grammar; in the arg rule and the structure rule. When a functor is the beginning of a structure, we need no assembler action. The structure() subparser takes the functor token from the stack when the structure() subparser completes its match. The arg() subparser must always leave a comparison term on the stack and assigns an AtomAssembler to its functor subparser.

2. The list() subparser uses a ListAssembler only if the textual list is empty. In all other cases, it defers to listTail() to properly process the list.

3. The listTail() subparser uses either a ListWithTailAssembler or a ListAssembler depending on whether the input list has a tail.

4. A query, like a rule, is a composition of a series of structures, and so it reuses the AxiomAssembler class.

5. If an input structure completes with no terms, structure() uses an AtomAssembler. Otherwise, structure() uses StructureWithTermsAssembler to build a Structure object with terms.

6. The variable() subparser uses a VariableAssembler object if it sees an uppercase word and an AnonymousAssembler object if it sees an underscore.

Figure 14.3 Logikus Assembler Placement. This table shows the assembler or assemblers that Logikus subparsers employ.

The "Parser" column in Figure 14.3 refers to methods of the class `LogikusParser` in `sjm.examples.logic`. These methods correspond to rules from the Logikus grammar developed earlier in this chapter. The notes in Figure 14.3 refer to assembler placements that merit explanation.

A parser for Logikus follows directly from its grammar along with a knowledge of where to place the parser's assemblers. The `start()` method of class `LogikusParser` in package `sjm.examples.logic` provides a parser for Logikus.

14.4 The Logikus Interactive Development Environment

When you develop a computer language, you must also develop a way for your users to access it. Package `sjm.examples.logic` includes the class `LogikusIde`, which provides an interactive development environment for creating and querying Logikus programs. Chapter 13, "Logic Programming," shows this IDE many times. This class is one of five classes that collaborate to make the Logikus language available to a user, as Figure 14.4 shows.

The classes `LogikusIDE` and `LogikusMediator` work as a pair to create a Swing interface for Logikus programming. The IDE class contains methods that create Swing components, such as `programArea()` and `proveNextButton()`. The mediator class follows the *mediator* pattern [Gamma et al.] and contains methods that respond to Swing events. Components such as the **Rest** button in the IDE register the mediator as their event listener. The mediator uses `LogikusFacade` to simplify its use of the `Logikus` parser. Figure 14.5 shows a typical message sequence.

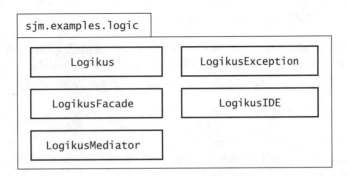

Figure 14.4 Collaborating classes connect a user to the language. The classes shown work together to make the Logikus language available to a user.

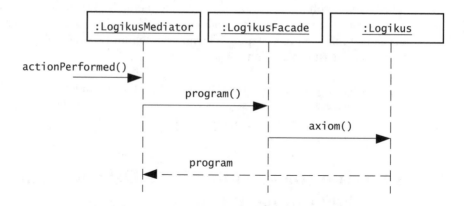

Figure 14.5 A typical message sequence. When the user clicks the **Rest** button on the IDE, the mediator, which is listening for button events, receives an `actionPerformed()` message. The mediator uses a facade, which in turns uses a parser, to convert the text to an object of class `Program`.

When a user clicks a button in the Logikus IDE, the button notifies its listener, which is a `LogikusMediator` object. The mediator determines which action the user took and responds accordingly. If the program text has changed, the mediator parses the text of both the program and the query. Instead of working directly with a `Logikus` parser object, the mediator uses an object of class `LogikusFacade`.

14.4.1 A Facade for Logikus

The intent of the *facade* pattern [Gamma et al.] is to provide an interface that makes a subsystem easier to use. The `LogikusFacade` class simplifies the parsing of a Logikus program by breaking it into separate axioms and using a `Logikus` parser object to parse each axiom. The facade also provides a method for parsing a query, and it handles exceptions that the parser may throw.

The `Logikus` parser class uses `Track` objects in place of `Sequence` objects in many of its subparsers. A `Track` object is identical to a `Sequence` object except that it throws an exception if a sequence begins but does not conclude. For example, feeding the query

```
city(denver,,5280)
```

to a `Logikus` parser causes the parser to throw a `TrackException`. The mediator catches this and displays:

```
After   : city ( denver ,
Expected: term
Found   : ,
```

The facade also throws informative exceptions when it detects problems. For example, a query that begins with an uppercase letter is invalid. The facade checks for this common error and throws a corresponding exception. Entering the query

```
City(denver, 5280)
```

results in the IDE message

```
> Uppercase City indicates a variable and cannot begin a query.
```

The facade sees the problem with the capital letter and throws a `LogikusException`. The mediator catches this exception (and any other exception) and displays the message's text.

14.5 Summary

Instruction on programming in Logikus (or any other logic language) could easily fill a semester course. It is striking, then, that the grammar for the language contains just 20 rules. The grammar rules translate to fewer than 250 Java statements in `LogikusParser.java`. Language development lets you make a small amount of code go a long way.

The difficulty of learning Logikus derives not from a complex grammar but rather from the fact that Logikus addresses concepts orthogonal to Java. Java emphasizes modeling through objects, whereas Logikus emphasizes modeling through relations, facts, and rules.

Businesses have become increasingly aware that the one aspect of development that they cannot address with frameworks or off-the-shelf software is business *logic*. Thus, object-oriented development may become the province of framework developers, with application developers concentrating on developing business logic. Given this trend, it is well worth considering bringing rules to the surface of a system and employing a logic programming language such as Logikus.

CHAPTER 15

Parsing a Query Language

This chapter shows how to create a parser for a query language. A query language parser translates textual queries into calls to an engine. Commercial databases send queries to an engine that comes with the database product. Instead of using a commercial engine, this chapter uses the logic engine developed in Chapter 12. The engine proves the query against a data source and returns successful proofs as the result of the query. For its examples this chapter uses Jaql, a query language created for this book.

15.1 The Role of Query Languages

Query languages, particularly SQL (Structured Query Language), represent a powerful force in applied computer science. Few businesses operate without a database, and every commercial database includes some form of a query language for retrieving data. The basic idea of SQL is that a query language empowers users to pose questions about data that no developer has foreseen. When you develop your own query language, you provide your users with this ability. Users of your language can derive new results without writing Java, and indeed without feeling as if they are "programming" at all.

The object that makes query languages possible is an engine. An engine knows how to answer a query, and it knows how to look through a collection of data. The groundwork for creating a query language includes acquiring an engine, making your data accessible to the engine, and writing a parser to translate your users' textual queries into engine queries. To provide your users access to the engine's power, you can package access to your parser in a user interface. When your user enters a query, you parse the query, feed the query to the engine, and display the engine results. An engine plus a query language is one of the most powerful tools you can provide your user.

To create new query languages, you do not need a database. What you need is an engine, and the one in `sjm.engine` may suffice for your purposes. If you need a stronger engine, you can improve the code in `sjm.engine` or acquire an engine in some other way. With an engine in hand, you can create a query language parser and provide your users with the ability to issue ad hoc queries, posing questions about whatever objects are important in your domain.

15.2 A Sample Database

Query language examples must query something, and so this chapter needs a sample data set. For its data, this chapter uses an object model from a gourmet potato chip company that is just starting out and has only a few customers. As Figure 15.1 shows, the package `sjm.examples.chips` contains the chip data as an object model.

The `ChipBase` class contains a complete object model of customers and their orders for chips. Figure 15.2 shows the `ChipBase` static methods that return these three classes of object.

`ChipBase.chip()` returns a dictionary of all the types of chips the company supplies. This dictionary uses the `ChipID` as a key, something that allows an axiom source to retrieve chips by ID.

The `ChipBase.customer()` method returns `Customer` objects in a `Dictionary` keyed by `CustomerID`. The `ChipBase.order()` method returns `Order` objects as a `Vector`, without any key information.

Figures 15.3, 15.4, and 15.5 show the object model as it would appear in a set of tables.

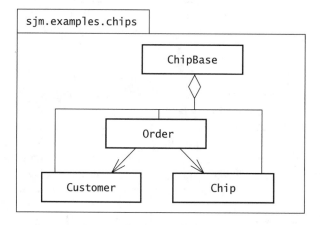

Figure 15.1 The `sjm.examples.chips` package. This package contains an object model of customers and their chip orders.

```
┌─────────────────────────────────┐
│            ChipBase             │
├─────────────────────────────────┤
│ +chip():Dictionary              │
│ +customer():Dictionary          │
│ +order():Vector                 │
└─────────────────────────────────┘
```

Figure 15.2 The ChipBase database. This class returns a dictionary of chips keyed by chip ID, a dictionary of customers keyed by customer ID, and an unkeyed vector of orders.

ChipID	ChipName	PricePerBag	Ounces	Oil
1001	Carson City Silver Dollars	8.95	12	Safflower
1002	Coyote Crenellations	9.95	12	Coconut
1003	Four Corner Crispitos	8.95	12	Coconut
1004	Jim Bob's Jumbo BBQ	12.95	16	Safflower
1007	Saddle Horns	9.95	10	Sunflower

Figure 15.3 A chip table. The types of chips a company offers.

CustomerID	ChipID	BagsPerMonth
11156	1001	2
11156	1004	1
11158	1007	4
12116	1002	2
12116	1003	2
12122	1004	2
12122	1007	2

Figure 15.4 An order table. Standing monthly customer orders for bags of chips.

CustomerID	LastName	FirstName
11156	Hasskins	Hank
11158	Shumacher	Carol
12116	Zeldis	Kim
12122	Houston	Jim

Figure 15.5 A customer table. Customer ID and name.

The data in these tables is accessible through static methods on the `ChipBase` class.

To make this data available to the logic engine in `sjm.engine`, you must create `Fact` objects from this data, load them into a `Program` object, and query this program. The class `ChipSource` in `sjm.examples.query` provides this service, creating a `Program` object with the data from the preceding figures. You can print this program with this statement:

```
package sjm.examples.query;

import sjm.engine.*;

/**
 * This class shows the chip facts that
 * <code>ChipSource</code> makes available.
 */
public class ShowChipSource {

public static void main(String[] args) {
    System.out.println(ChipSource.program());
}
}
```

Running this program prints the following:

```
chip(1007, Saddle Horns, 9.95, 10.0, Sunflower);
chip(1004, Jim Bob's Jumbo BBQ, 12.95, 16.0, Safflower);
chip(1003, Four Corner Crispitos, 8.95, 12.0, Coconut);
chip(1002, Coyote Crenellations, 9.95, 12.0, Coconut);
chip(1001, Carson City Silver Dollars, 8.95, 12.0,
    Safflower);
customer(12116, Zeldis, Kim);
customer(11158, Shumacher, Carol);
customer(11156, Hasskins, Hank);
customer(12122, Houston, Jim);
order(11156, 1001, 2);
order(11156, 1004, 1);
```

```
order(11158, 1007, 4);
order(12116, 1002, 2);
order(12116, 1003, 2);
order(12122, 1004, 2);
order(12122, 1007, 2);
```

15.2.1 Facts, Objects, and Rows

Converting objects into facts falls under the topic of *object/relational mapping*. One object in an object model usually represents one object in a problem domain, such as a machine or a customer. A logic program models the domain object as one fact, and a relational database models the domain object as one row in a database table. Java objects that represent domain objects are objects of the same class; all the rows of a relational table are, of course, members of the same table.

Java instances are tightly bound to Java classes, and relational table rows are tightly bound to tables. The affiliation of facts in a program to related facts is much looser. The role of a Java class or relational table appears in a logic program as the collection of structures in a logic program that have the same functor and the same number of terms. The number of terms in a structure is its *arity*. Figure 15.6 shows the correspondences of modeling elements in Java, relational databases, and logic programming.

Here is one fact from the chip data source:

```
chip(1004, "Jim Bob's Jumbo BBQ", 12.95, 16, "Safflower")
```

You could model this information as any of the following:

- One object of class `Chip`
- One row in a chip table in a relational database
- One fact in a logic program with functor "chip" and with 5 terms

Java	Relational Database	Logic Program
Class	Table	Functor/arity
Object	Row	Fact
Attribute	Column Name	Position

Figure 15.6 Modeling correspondences. The fields of object-oriented programming, relational programming, and logic programming use different words for similar concepts.

Java as well as relational databases give names and types to object attributes. Logic engines such as the one in sjm.engine are much more lax in how they define object attributes. A logic engine relies on all facts with the functor chip and arity 5 having their attributes in the same position. A logic engine query for a type of chip matches a query with functor chip and arity 5 against all facts with this same functor and arity. We return to the topic of issuing queries in Section 15.5, "Translating User Queries to Engine Queries," after a look at Jaql.

15.3 Jaql

To provide a running example of query language programming, this chapter introduces Jaql, a general-purpose query language similar to SQL. The name Jaql is an acronym for "just another query language."

This section shows examples of Jaql queries and their results against the chip company's data. If you like, you can run the sample program and try your own queries. Using the files on the CD, run the Jaql environment:

```
> java sjm.examples.query.JaqlUe
```

The JaqlUe class starts up a UE (user environment), as Figure 15.7 shows.

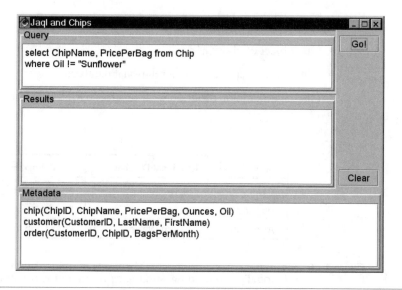

Figure 15.7 An environment for Jaql queries. This user environment accepts queries, applies them against a potato chip database, and shows the results.

Although Jaql is a general-purpose language, this UE always applies the queries it receives against the chip company's data. When the UE starts, it preloads a sample query, as Figure 15.7 shows. This query is an example of a valid query against the chip data. The bottom panel in the UE shows the *metadata* of the chip database. Metadata is data about data, specifically about the layout of the database. Displaying metadata in the UE gives the user clues about how to form valid queries. Each line of metadata shows, effectively, one table and the column names for that table. The sample `select` query chooses two columns from the `Chip` table, and it limits the results with a `where` clause.

Figure 15.8 shows the result of pressing the **Go!** button, which executes the query.

Pressing **Go!** asks the UE to parse the user query into a Java query that the engine in `sjm.engine` understands. The UE feeds the engine the query and displays the results.

15.3.1 Jaql Syntax

A Jaql query contains

- The word `select`
- A list of variables
- The word `from`

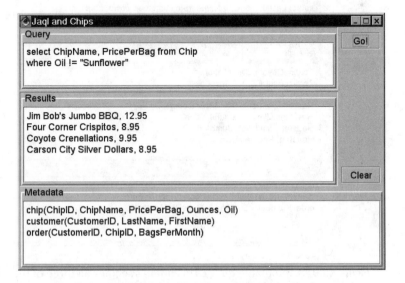

Figure 15.8 Query results. Pressing the **Go!** button executes the query.

- A list of class names
- Optionally, a where clause

A where clause contains the word where followed by a series of comparisons. A comparison applies one of these operators

$$< \quad > \quad = \quad <= \quad >= \quad !=$$

to two arguments, which may be variables, quoted strings, or mathematical expressions.

15.3.2 Jaql Joins

In Jaql, a query that specifies more than one table implies a *join* on columns that have the same name. Joining means that any variable that appears in two or more tables must take on the same value in a successful query. Figure 15.9 shows an example.

The query in Figure 15.9 uses the three tables customer, order, and chip. Jaql joins customer and order on CustomerID. Jaql first finds a customer from the customer table and then looks for an order from the order table that has the same value of CustomerID. Finding such an order, Jaql then looks for a chip from the chip table that

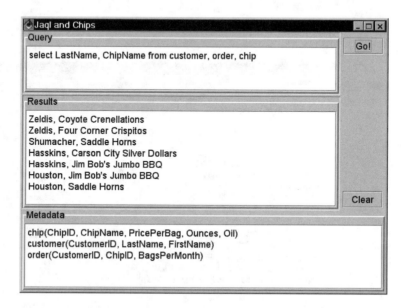

Figure 15.9 A multitable query. This query specifies all three of the tables in the chip database. Jaql automatically joins these tables on their common column names.

has the same ChipID as the order. The results show a list of customers and the types of chips they have on order.

15.3.3 Jaql Expressions

Jaql allows mathematical expressions to appear in where clauses and select parameters. Figure 15.10 shows an example.

The query in Figure 15.10 multiplies the bags per month by the price per bag for a type of chip. Such mathematical expressions can use any combination of multiplication, division, addition, subtraction, and parentheses. These expressions can occur either as select parameters or in where clauses. Note that in a comparison, a string to compare to must appear in quotes. Also note that Jaql ignores case when looking for column and table names. For example, *order* and *Order* both refer to the order table.

15.4 Building a Query Language Environment

Figure 15.11 shows the elements of a query language.

The motivation for a query language begins with an object model and a desire to let a user issue ad hoc questions about the data in the model. The engine expects queries

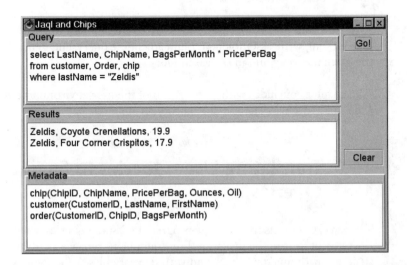

Figure 15.10   Jaql expressions. This query uses a mathematical expression as a select parameter to calculate the total amount of money a customer spends each month on a type of chip.

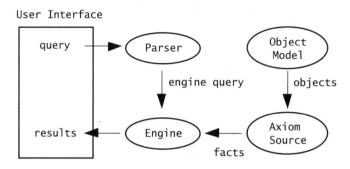

Figure 15.11   The elements of a query language. A user interface for a query language passes a textual query to a parser, which translates the text into an engine query. The user interface asks the engine to prove the query, something it does by drawing on facts that come from an object model.

to arrive as query objects, so you need a strategy for translating a `select` statement into an engine query. The following section covers translating user queries to engine queries.

As the parser works through the user's textual query, the parser will discover parts of an engine query. You need a *builder* to help store progress in building the engine query. As you build, you use a *speller* object to verify that the query refers only to table names and variable names that occur in the object model. A pair of sections covers a query builder and a speller.

After covering these supporting classes, this chapter describes how to write a grammar for Jaql, write assemblers to build an engine query, and generate the parser from the grammar, plugging in the assemblers.

The chapter concludes with a discussion of the user environment, focusing on the UE's ability to help the user solve problems in incorrect queries.

15.5 Translating User Queries to Engine Queries

You can extract facts from a logic program by issuing queries whose structures match the types of facts in the program. For example, to retrieve chip facts you can create a structure with functor "chip" and with five variables. When you write a query language for a commercial database engine, the ability to query any table is probably already built into the engine. Because you are using a logic engine here, you must create a query method for each class of fact in the program. Your parser will rely on these query structures when it translates a user query into an engine query. Figure 15.12 shows the query methods for ChipSource.

For each class in the object model, ChipSource has a static method that produces a query for objects of that class. Here is the code for ChipSource.queryChip():

```
/*
 * Returns a query that matches chip facts.
 */
public static Structure queryChip() {
    return new Structure("chip", new Term[]{
        new Variable("ChipID"),
        new Variable("ChipName"),
        new Variable("Price"),
        new Variable("Ounces"),
        new Variable("Oil")});
}
```

This method creates a structure that prints itself as

```
chip(ChipID, ChipName, Price, Ounces, Oil)
```

This structure can unify with a chip fact, which unifies each variable in the query structure with its corresponding value in the fact. When you build a query language parser, you create assemblers that use query structures to extract the values of facts. The query methods for customer and order are similar. With these elements in place, you can formulate a translation strategy for user queries.

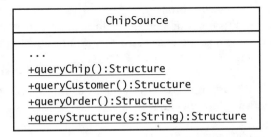

Figure 15.12   The ChipSource query methods. ChipSource contains protected methods that produce query structures for each class in the object model. These methods support the public queryStructure() method, which returns a query structure given the object's class name.

You want to let a user enter a Jaql query such as

```
select CustomerLast, BagsPerMonth from Customer, Order
where BagsPerMonth > 2
```

To achieve this, you must parse the text and create a `Query` object that

- Has a query structure for each named class

- Has a comparison structure for each `where` clause

- Selects only the named variables to return to the user

If you ignore for now the user's request for only some of the variables, the engine query that you want is

```
customer(CustomerID, LastName, FirstName),
order(CustomerID, ChipID, BagsPerMonth),
>(BagsPerMonth, 2)
```

This translation simply replaces each class that the user query names with the query template for that class, and it converts the `where` clause into a comparison format that the engine can understand. This translation relies on the *natural join* of like-named variables in the query structures.

15.5.1 Natural Joins

In the example, the engine query forces a natural join on the variable `CustomerID`, which appears in both query structures. When the query proves itself, the `customer` structure in the query unifies with one of the customer facts in the `Program` object. After each successful unification of the `customer` structure, the query tries to unify its `order` structure with order facts. All the structures in a query share the same variable scope, so at this point in a proof the `order` structure's `CustomerID` variable is unified with a value. Thus, the `order` structure will be able to unify only with order facts for that customer.

Occasionally, joining variables by name is limiting. For example, consider a Logikus program with the genealogical data

```
parent(henry, peter);
parent(peter, bridget);
```

To find grandparents, children, and grandchildren, you could issue the query

```
parent(Grandparent, Child), parent(Child, Grandchild)
```

This query will find

```
Grandparent = henry, Child = peter, Grandchild = bridget
```

You cannot translate this Logikus program and query into Jaql because Jaql does not provide for naming variables within a fact. There is no way to retrieve parent facts so that the first term is in one case a Grandparent and in a another case a Child. You can overcome this limitation by extending the syntax of Jaql to allow naming variables, but this book does not take up that challenge.

15.5.2 Where Clauses

When the query is able to unify with customer and order facts, the last structure in the query applies the where clause. A where clause is a comparison, and the query language parser must translate the user input to comparisons that the engine can process.

For example, the query clause

```
where BagsPerMonth > 2
```

translates to the engine structure

```
>(BagsPerMonth, 2)
```

15.5.3 Projection

Limiting the variables the user wants to see introduces the topic of *projection*. Projection is a matter of specifying which variables are interesting to the user. For example, consider again the select statement

```
select CustomerLast, BagsPerMonth from Customer, Order
where BagsPerMonth > 2
```

As this query executes, it establishes values for all the variables in Customer and Order. However, the query asks to see results for only CustomerLast and BagsPerMonth. An intuitive way to achieve this result in the engine is to introduce a rule whose head has only the variables you want:

```
q(CustomerLast, BagsPerMonth) :-
    customer(CustomerID, LastName, FirstName),
    order(CustomerID, ChipID, BagsPerMonth),
    >(BagsPerMonth, 2)
```

You can add this rule to the engine and create a query:

```
q(CustomerLast, BagsPerMonth)
```

This query unifies with the head of the rule, the rule proves itself, and the variables in q unify with the proof values. This approach is effective, but in practice you can use a shortcut. To limit the query results to only CustomerLast and BagsPerMonth, you need not add a rule to the engine. It is simpler to prepend the q structure to the query and prove the tail of the query. You create the query as

```
q(CustomerLast, BagsPerMonth),
customer(CustomerID, LastName, FirstName),
order(CustomerID, ChipID, BagsPerMonth),
>(BagsPerMonth, 2)
```

You cannot prove this query because there is no q fact in the program. However, the tail of the query can prove itself as before if the tail consists of all the structures after the first, head structure q. The trick to reducing the variables seen by the user is to introduce a head structure that contains only the interesting variables, prove the tail of the query, and show the user the variables in the head structure. These variables will unify with successful results as before.

15.6 A Query Builder

As a parser parses a user's query, the parser sees select terms, class names, and where clause comparisons. After all these pieces are parsed, you can build a Query object that is a translation of the user's input.

The *builder* pattern applies when "the algorithm for creating a complex object should be independent of the parts that make up the object and how they are assembled" [Gamma et al.]. You use a builder to collect the various aspects of a query and then ask the builder for a query after parsing all the input text. Figure 15.13 shows the QueryBuilder class.

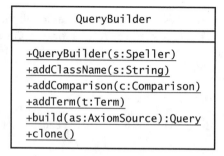

Figure 15.13   The QueryBuilder class. A QueryBuilder object collects information about a desired query and then builds the query on demand.

The constructor for `QueryBuilder` takes a `Speller` object, described in the next section. The speller lets the `QueryBuilder` correct the spelling of class names; a `QueryBuilder` throws a runtime exception if a class name is unknown to the speller.

15.7 A Speller

You want the user environment for chip queries to be helpful when the user enters an unknown table name or variable name. You also want the UE to allow the user to enter queries in any combination of uppercase and lowercase, although the engine is case-sensitive. You can use a *speller* to achieve these aims.

One technique for maintaining a preferred spelling of known words is to keep a dictionary whose key/value pairs are composed of a known word spelled in all lowercase, followed by the preferred spelling of the word. For example, such a dictionary would contain

```
customerid -> CustomerID
```

This lets the UE accept `customerid` as a valid variable name. This dictionary is also a registry of known names, so the UE will detect, for example, that `CustId` is not merely misspelled but also an unknown variable name.

As Figure 15.14 shows, this chapter uses a `Speller` interface and a `ChipSpeller` implementation of it to support the proper spelling of class and variable names.

The constructor for `ChipSpeller` calls the two load methods. The `loadClassNames()` method adds each class name from the `Chip` object model into the `ChipSpeller` object's dictionary of class names. The `loadVariableNames()` method uses the query templates from `ChipSource` to detect the variable names in the object model.

Given any capitalization of a class name or variable name, a `ChipSpeller` object can look up the proper capitalization. It does this by converting the given spelling to all lowercase and then looking up this string in the appropriate dictionary.

15.8 Jaql Grammar

You can define a grammar for Jaql using a top-down approach, starting with the grammar

```
select = "select" variables "from" classNames optionalWhere;
```

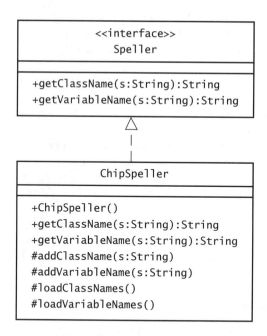

Figure 15.14 The ChipSpeller class. This class records the proper capitalization in the spelling of all class names and variable names in the Chip object model.

If your users are familiar with SQL, the words *select* and *from* will be familiar to them. For your own query language, you can use other words such as *show* or *present*. As a language designer, you should determine the keywords of your language according to the effect they will have on your users.

As a first cut, you can model variables and classNames as repetitions of words, separated by commas:

```
select        = "select" variables "from" classNames
                optionalWhere;
variables     = commaList(variable);
variable      = Word;
classNames    = commaList(className);
className     = Word;
optionalWhere = empty | "where" comparisons;
comparisons   = commaList(comparison);
commaList(p)  = p (',' p)*;
```

Now let's enhance this grammar to allow more interesting terms in the select list. For example, let's allow the user to select a discounted price, such as

```
select PricePerBag * 0.9 from chip where PricePerBag > 10
```

You can allow this by allowing a `selectTerm` to be an expression involving numbers, words, and variables. You can write the grammar as follows:

```
select        = "select" selectTerms "from" classNames
                optionalWhere;
selectTerms   = commaList(selectTerm);
selectTerm    = expression;
variable      = Word;
classNames    = commaList(className);
className     = Word;
optionalWhere = empty | "where" comparisons;
comparisons   = commaList(comparison);
commaList(p)  = p (',' p)*;
```

This grammar now relies on some other source for `expression` and for `comparison`. A grammar to supply these subparsers is similar to the arithmetic grammar presented in Chapter 7, "Parsing Arithmetic":

```
comparison = arg operator arg;
arg        = expression | QuotedString;
expression = term ('+' term | '-' term)*;
term       = factor ('*' factor | '/' factor)*;
factor     = '(' expression ')' | Num | variable;
variable   = Word;
operator   = "<" | ">" | "=" | "<=" | ">=" | "!=";
```

The Jaql grammar has no knowledge of chip company data, so the language is fairly reusable. The work it would take to use Jaql on other object models is primarily the creation of fact and query conversion methods specific to each new object model.

To help simplify the Jaql parser, the package `sjm.examples.query` has a separate parser for comparisons and uses it in the Jaql parser. This reduces the size of the parser class that implements the grammar. It also demonstrates the flexibility you have in how you store the objects that can be composed into a parser.

15.9 Creating the Jaql Parser

The code for the parsers (`ComparisonParser` and `JaqlParser`) is in each case almost a direct translation of the grammars, following the rules in Section 3.6 "Translating a Grammar to Code." Both parsers require a `Speller` instance variable and a constructor that accepts a speller. A `JaqlParser` object passes its speller to a `ComparisonParser` object, which uses the speller when it sees a variable name.

Other than spelling, the only addition to make to `ComparisonParser` and `JaqlParser` in `sjm.examples.query` is to plug in their assemblers.

15.10 Jaql Assemblers

When you parse a user's query, you want to create a Query object as a result. To achieve this, you set the initial assembly's target to be a QueryBuilder object. This builder collects information as you parse the user's query. You need assemblers to capture select terms, class names, and comparisons. To handle expressions, you need assemblers for arithmetic operations and variables. Finally, you need an assembler that exchanges a token on an assembly's stack with an atom that has the token's value as its functor. Altogether, the Jaql parser uses six assemblers, as Figure 15.15 shows.

The comparison parser must use an assembler when it sees an arithmetic expression, a word, a comparison, or a variable. Most of these assemblers process elements on the stack. For example, the arithmetic assembler pops two arithmetic operands, builds an ArithmeticOperator object from them, and pushes this object. The ComparisonParser class in sjm.examples.query reuses the AtomAssembler and ArithmeticAssembler classes from sjm.examples.logic.

The assembler for variables pops a token from the stack, extracts its string, and pushes a Variable object of that name. This assembler also looks up the variable name in a ChipSpeller object (which the builder carries) and throws a runtime exception if the variable name is unknown.

The assemblers for comparisons, select terms, and class names update a query builder. They expect that the target of the assembly the parser is working on will be

Parser Class	Method	... uses Assembler
ComparisonParser	plusTerm(), minusTerm(), timesFactor(), divideFactor()	ArithmeticAssembler
ComparisonParser	arg()	AtomAssembler (on QuotedString)
ComparisonParser	factor()	AtomAssembler (on Num)
ComparisonParser	comparison()	ComparisonAssembler
ComparisonParser	variable()	VariableAssembler
Jaql	className()	ClassNameAssembler
Jaql	selectTerm()	SelectTermAssembler

Figure 15.15 Jaql assemblers. The Jaql parser uses six assemblers that help it build an engine query from a user's textual query. Jaql offloads much of its work to a separate comparison parser.

a `QueryBuilder` object. For example, the class name assembler informs the query builder that the given name is a class name to select from:

```
package sjm.examples.query;

import sjm.parse.*;
import sjm.parse.tokens.*;
import sjm.engine.*;

/**
 * Pops a class name, and informs a QueryBuilder that this
 * is a class to select from.
 */
public class ClassNameAssembler extends Assembler {

public void workOn(Assembly a) {
    QueryBuilder b = (QueryBuilder) a.getTarget();
    Token t = (Token) a.pop();
    b.addClassName(t.sval());
}
}
```

The code for all the assemblers and the Jaql and Comparison parsers is on the CD in package `sjm.examples.query`.

15.11 The Jaql User Environment

The role of a query language is to take a user query and produce results. You can create a simple graphical user environment where users of your language can develop queries, issue them, and see the results. The heart of such an environment has two text areas: one for user queries and one for results. The environment also needs a button to tell the environment to execute the query and a second button to clear the result area. The sample code for this package includes the class `JaqlUe`, which provides an interactive user environment for applying Jaql queries to the Chip data model. The code for this user interface is tangential to the subject of writing parsers, but all the code is on the CD included with this book.

The code in `sjm.examples.query` separates its handling of user interaction into two classes: `JaqlUe` and `JaqlMediator`. The `JaqlUe` class is responsible for the creation of Swing components. It also contains the `main()` method that launches the user interface. The `JaqlMediator` class controls the interaction of the Swing components. This class implements `ActionListener`, and it defines the action method that executes when the user presses the **Go!** button, as Figure 15.16 shows.

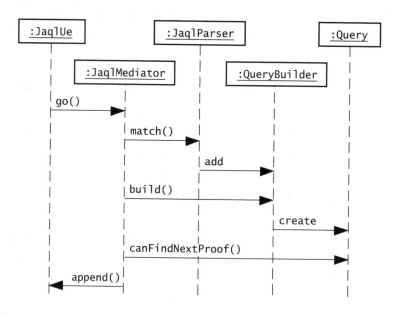

Figure 15.16 A Jaql user environment sequence. The objects in this diagram collaborate to recognize a user's text query and create a corresponding Query object.

When the user clicks the **Go!** button, a `JaqlMediator` object receives notification that action is required. The mediator uses a `JaqlParser` object to parse the user's query. As the parse proceeds, the parser adds select terms, class names, and comparisons to a `QueryBuilder` object.

After the parse, the mediator asks the builder to build, passing it a `ChipSource` object as a source of axioms. The builder creates and returns a `Query` object. The mediator asks this object for proofs and appends the results to the results area in the user environment.

15.11.1 Exception Handling

When the user presses the **Go!** button, the mediator constructs a `QueryBuilder` object, passing it a `ChipSpeller` object to use for spell checking. The spell check relies on the exception handling of `JaqlMediator` to display the proper error message. When the Jaql parser sees a class name, its `ClassNameAssembler` object passes the class name to the `QueryBuilder` object. The query builder checks for a class of this name using the `ChipSpeller` object, throwing an `UnrecognizedClassException` if the entered class name is unknown. The `JaqlMediator.actionPerformed()` method catches this exception and appends it to the output text area.

15.11.2 Tracks

Chapter 11, "Extending the Parser Toolkit," explains how Track objects throw a runtime exception when a sequence begins but does not complete. The use of tracks in lieu of normal sequences greatly aids a user who is struggling to enter a proper query.

The select sequence and the three comma-separated lists in the Jaql parser use tracks to help diagnose the source of input errors. For example, if the user forgets the word from,

```
select ChipName, PricePerBag
chip where Oil = "Coconut"
```

The user environment prints

```
After    : select ChipName , PricePerBag
Expected: from
Found    : chip
```

15.11.3 Handling Abject Failure

Tracks work only after the track begins. If the user enters text that the Jaql parser cannot parse at all, the JaqlMediator object detects the failure. In this case, the mediator expresses the problem that it cannot parse the input. For example, if the user enters

```
How do I use this?
```

the JaqlMediator object displays

```
Cannot parse input text.
```

15.12 Summary

Few of the challenges of creating a query language lie in writing the parser. The first challenge is that you must have an engine that can prove a query. For this, you can use the engine in sjm.engine, or you can write your own or find one from another source. An interesting project would be to use an engine from a commercial database, although database vendors typically do not make their engines easily accessible.

Once you have an engine, developing a practical query language requires you to engineer a scheme for feeding the engine. First, you must be able to translate a user query into an engine. This requires writing your parser, its associated assemblers, and typically a query builder. You also need query structures for each class in the object model. You can write these by hand, as in the examples in this chapter, or you can explore the automatic approach using Java's reflection capabilities.

In addition to feeding the engine a query, you must develop an approach to feeding the engine facts. For a small object model, you can load all the data from your object model into a single `Program` object. For a midsize or larger object model, you need to limit the conversion of facts. For example, given the query

```
chip(1004, ChipName, PricePerBag, Ounces, Oil)
```

a smart axiom source returns just one chip type, the one whose ID is 1004. An axiom source can also use indexing and caching to reduce the number of facts it creates and feeds to an engine.

Tying a query language to an engine is hard work, but the benefits can make it worthwhile. The primary benefit is that your users can issue ad hoc queries. In a normal object-oriented system, the only way to interrogate an object model is to write a Java method that performs the query. As a developer, you have to foresee what questions your users will have about an object model, something that, history has shown, is not possible. A query language lets users decide, after the system is complete, which questions they have about the object model.

CHAPTER 16

Parsing an Imperative Language

This chapter shows how to create imperative languages, which are also called *programming* or *scripting* languages. An imperative language lets a user create a collection of commands (the program or script) that, within some context, direct the computer's actions. A parser for an imperative language translates a user's program into an executable composition of commands.

To provide a running example of how to construct an imperative language, this chapter uses Sling, a programming language created for this book. Sling allows a user to compose mathematical functions and to request plots of these functions. A Sling environment accepts Sling programs and displays a user's plots.

16.1 The Role of Imperative Languages

Java is a potent imperative language. If you need a language that precisely controls what a computer will do, Java is hard to beat. Given the prowess of Java, why would you ever create a new imperative language?

One justification for new imperative languages is simplicity. You may want to offer your users a language that they can master more quickly than Java. If your users are nonprofessionals, and especially if your users are children, you will want to provide a language that is easy to learn.

Another justification for creating a new imperative language is specificity to a context. UNIX shell script languages are excellent examples. These languages include built-in knowledge of the file structure and other features of the UNIX operating system. A UNIX shell lets users quickly learn a powerful language that controls the UNIX environment.

Many other applications call for flexible but precise control, and new application-specific languages may fill a niche. If your domain requires a flexible framework for issuing explicit commands, an imperative language may be the answer.

16.2 Sling

Sling is a programming language for specifying plots of mathematical functions, notably *slings*. A real sling is a weapon that consists of a strap about a yard long and a stone that attaches to the end of the strap. With some practice and acquired skill, you can whirl a sling over your head, release the stone at the right moment, and strike a target. A famous example of the use of a sling appears in Chapter 17 of the first book of Samuel in the Old Testament. The youthful David steps forward in a battle of champions, and with a skillful shot from his sling he slays the mighty Goliath.

The Sling programming language plots the path of a sling stone as seen from above, as it rotates around the hurler's head. Slings in the Sling programming language are mathematical objects that you can manipulate in interesting ways, such as adding them together.

16.3 Sling Programming

This section shows how to program in Sling. Playing with Sling is fun. You can start the Sling IDE with

```
> java sjm.examples.sling.SlingIde
```

16.3.1 A Basic Sling

Sling lets you plot mathematical functions by issuing plot commands. The namesake of Sling is the sling() function, which takes two arguments: the length of the sling strap, and the number of times the sling goes around (one's head). For example, to plot the path of a sling whose strap length is 1 and that travels three-quarters of a revolution, run the class SlingIde and enter the Sling program

```
plot sling(1, .75);
```

Click the **Go!** button in the IDE or press the Ctrl and G keyboard keys to make the program execute. Figure 16.1 shows the results.

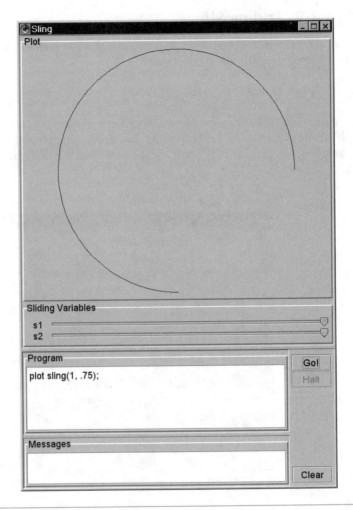

Figure 16.1 A basic sling. This plot shows the path of sling, seen from overhead. This sling has a strap length of 1 and circles the hurler's head 0.75 times.

You can plot a complete circle by setting the second argument to the sling function to 1:

```
plot sling(1, 1); // a complete circle
```

You can also specify a number greater than 1 for the number of revolutions and still get a circle:

```
plot sling(1, 3); // still a circle
```

A sling that goes around three times traces the same circle three times.

16.3.2 Adding Slings

To make the plot more interesting, you can attach a second, smaller sling to the end of the first sling using the command

```
plot sling(1, 1) + sling(.5, 5);
```

Figure 16.2 shows this plot. The smaller sling is half as long and goes around five times. If a little sling goes around five times as a larger sling goes around once, only four loops appear. It is useful to prove this by hand, but it is also fun just to play with Sling.

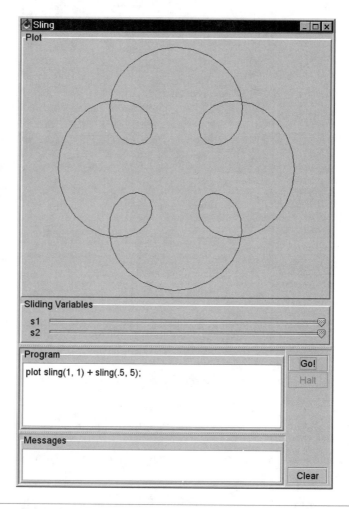

Figure 16.2 A sling with a sling on its end. In place of a stone, this sling has another sling, which has a shorter strap and is revolving more quickly.

16.3.3 Plotting Time

The Sling IDE uses the variable t to represent time, and the IDE assumes that time goes from 0 to 1 as the IDE draws the path of a sling. To let the length of your strap go from 0 to 1 as the plot draws, you can represent the length of the strap as t. For example, you can use

```
plot sling(t, 3);
```

to show a sling that lengthens from 0 to 1 as it goes around three times. Figure 16.3 shows this plot.

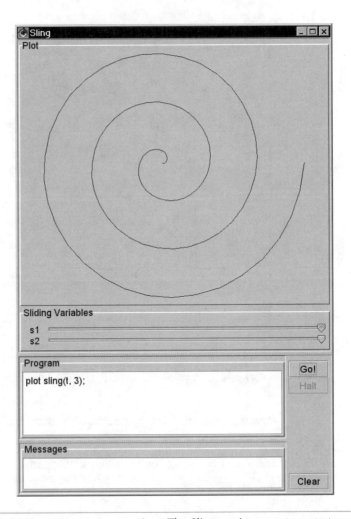

Figure 16.3   Letting out a strap over time. The Sling environment uses t to represent time and assumes that t goes from 0 to 1 as the plot completes.

16.3.4 Line Effects

By default, the Sling IDE uses 100 lines to draw its plot. If a sling moves really fast, the result can be a strobe effect that connects only a few points of the sling's actual path. Figure 16.4 shows the effect of using only 100 lines to draw a spiral that goes around 33 times.

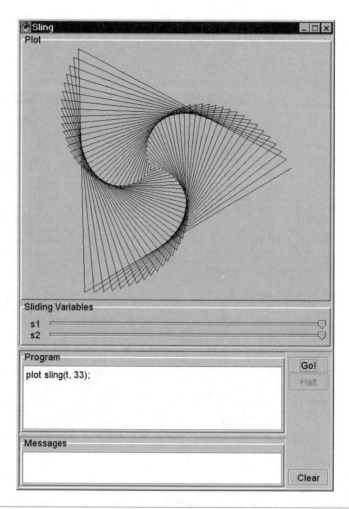

Figure 16.4 A quickly spiraling sling. When a sling moves quickly, these lines can connect only a few points on the sling's actual path.

16.3.5 Adding Lines

You can increase the number of lines in a plot by changing the value of the nLine variable. This variable establishes the number of lines in *each* plot. Figure 16.5 uses 2,000 lines to depict a rapidly spinning sling.

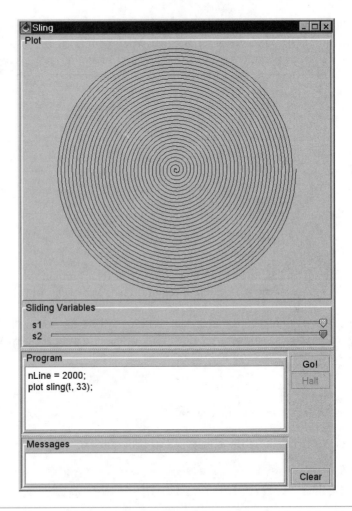

Figure 16.5 Increasing a plot's precision. By setting a value for the nLine variable, you can increase the number of lines that the Sling IDE uses.

16.3.6 Cartesian Plots

The Sling language is named for its most interesting function, but the language includes other functions that describe one- and two-dimensional functions of time, including cartesian. A Cartesian plot specifies separate functions for the x and y values of the path of a point. When you're working with one-dimensional functions, it is often useful to apply a scale() function.

The value of a scale function varies linearly from its first parameter to its second parameter as time varies from 0 to 1. You can also say that a scale value varies between its parameters "during the course of a plot." For example, to specify that x should vary from -5 to 5 during the course of a plot, you can write

```
x = scale(-5, 5);
```

The Sling programming language includes the built-in value for pi, so you might also write

```
x = scale(-pi, pi);
```

You can create y as a function of x. Here's an example:

```
y = sin(4*x);
```

The variable y holds a sin function of 4*x. Its argument goes from -4*pi to 4*pi in the course of the plot, enough for four complete cycles of the sin function.

You can tie the x and y functions together with a cartesian() function, which accepts two parameters: a source for x values and a source for y values. The complete program is

```
x = scale(-pi, pi);
y = sin(4*x);
plot cartesian(x, y);
```

Figure 16.6 shows the results of this program.

16.3.7 Cartesians as Points

Another use of the cartesian function is to model particular points, using a scale to draw a line between the points. For example, Figure 16.7 shows a net of straight lines.

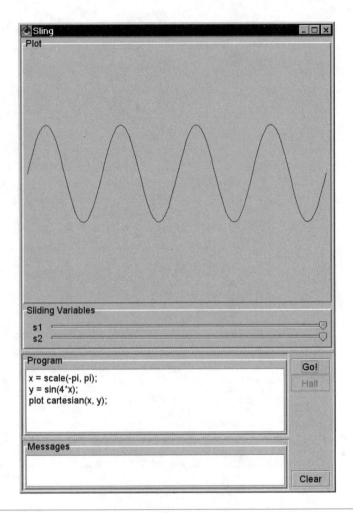

Figure 16.6 A Cartesian plot. The cartesian function lets you define the x and y values of a point separately. Here, x goes from -pi to pi as Sling makes its plot, and y is a function of x.

16.3.8 Polar Plots

The polar function in Sling is similar to the sling function, but the second argument is the angle of the sling rather than the number of rotations of the sling. Specifying the angle directly lets you make the angle of the plot constant. Consider plotting a line from the lower-left corner to the upper-right corner. The angle of this

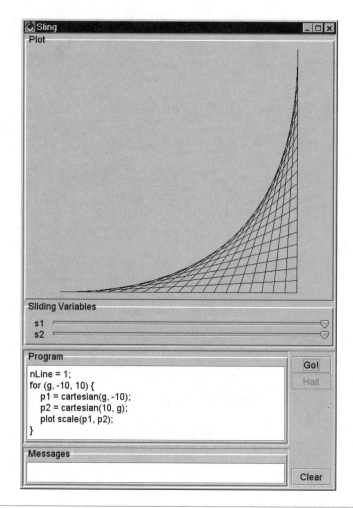

Figure 16.7   Using Cartesian functions as points. A `cartesian` function can contain a simple point, and a `scale` can create a line between a pair of such points.

line is 45 degrees, or `pi/2` radians. To appear as a line, you must let the strap out over time, so the Sling command is

```
plot polar(t, pi/4);
```

You can interpret this as, "Plot the path of a stone on a sling whose strap varies from 0 to 1 during the course of the plot and that is at a constant angle of `pi/2`."

The second argument to the `polar` function need not be a constant. An interesting effect is to let the sling strap oscillate. For example, to establish a function for an angle that makes one revolution, use the statement

```
theta = 2*pi*t;
```

Then you can make the length of the strap a constant plus a smaller length that oscillates:

```
len = 1 + .5*sin(8*theta);
```

During the course of a plot, the value `8*theta` will vary from 0 to `16*pi`, which is equal to 8 rotations. The strap length will go in and out 8 times as the plot proceeds. If you rotate (or swing) the sling a number of times that is relatively prime to the number of times you let the strap in and out, you can produce a braiding effect. For example:

```
plot polar(len, 3 * theta);
```

plots a line that goes around the origin 3 times, crossing itself many times but rejoining itself only once. Figure 16.8 shows this effect, plotting the pattern twice for esthetic effect.

The difference between the `sling` function and the `polar` function is that the `sling` function assumes that you expect the strap to rotate. The `sling` function creates a result equivalent to taking a polar function and multiplying its angle argument by `2*pi*t`. The program in Figure 16.8 is equivalent to the following version, which uses the `sling` function in lieu of the `polar` function:

```
nLine = 400;
theta = 2*pi*t;
len = 1 + .5*sin(8*theta);
plot sling(len, 3);
plot sling(len - .2, 3);
```

16.3.9 For Loops

For loops in Sling let you iterate a variable over a given range of integers. For example, Figure 16.9 uses a `for` loop to plot slings having different strap lengths.

The parameters in a `for` command are a variable and two functions. The functions can be any sling functions, but integer values are most common. The Sling environment augments integers in a `for` loop to be two-dimensional functions of time. In Figure 16.9 the environment augments the "to" and "from" values to be

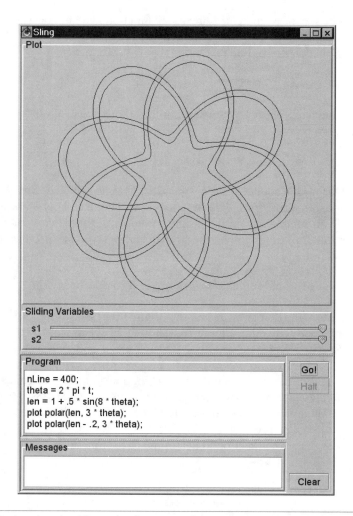

Figure 16.8 A polar plot. The polar function takes two arguments: a radius (the length of a sling strap) and the arc of the stone.

`cartesian(t, (0, 1))` and `cartesian(t, (0, 5))`. The *step* of a for loop is always `(1, 1)`.

Consider the program

```
for (c, cartesian(3, 3), cartesian(7, 7)) {
    plot c + sling(1, 1);
}
```

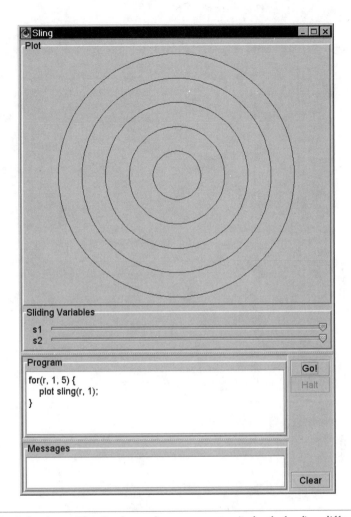

Figure 16.9 A for loop. The for loop shown executes its body for five different values of the variable r.

This program steps the variable c through the values (3, 3), (4, 4), (5, 5), (6, 6) and (7, 7), drawing a sling around each of these centers.

16.3.10 Sliders

The Sling development environment provides two sliders that let you experiment with many different variations of any program. For example, Figure 16.10 shows one of thousands of plots that result from the given program.

Figure 16.10   Sling sliders. The Sling environment redisplays the plot almost continuously as the user moves the sliders.

16.3.11 A Composite Example

You can use the Sling IDE to explain to someone new to Sling the basic idea of how Sling works. In Figure 16.11, the slider s1 controls the degree of sweep around David's head. The slider s2 controls the size of the arc.

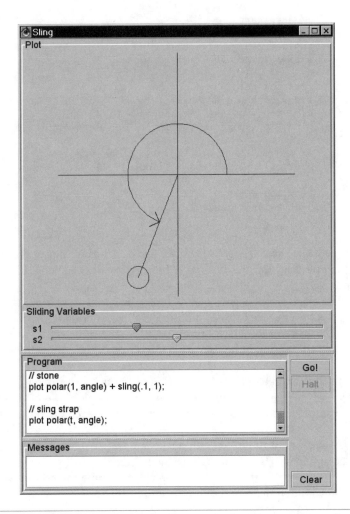

Figure 16.11 An illustration of a sling. In this screen shot, the user has pulled the slider s1 nearly three-fourths of the way from right to left. The plot animates this movement, showing the stone's rotation as the user pulls the slider.

Here is the program for Figure 16.11:

```
// crosshairs
s = scale(-1.1, 1.1);
plot cartesian(s, 0);
plot cartesian(0, s);
```

```
// arrow arc
r = s2;
angle = 2*pi * (1 - s1);
plot polar(r, angle*t);

// arrow head
tip = polar(r, angle);
plot tip + polar(.1*t, angle - pi/4);
plot tip + polar(.1*t, angle - 3/4 * pi);

// stone
plot polar(1, angle) + sling(.1, 1);

// sling strap
plot polar(t, angle);
```

The vertical and horizontal lines in the figure form *crosshairs* that identify the x and y axes. The variable s goes from -1.1 to 1.1 during the course of the plot. Two Cartesian plots lay out this line segment horizontally and vertically.

The angle variable goes from 0 to 2 * pi, as s1 goes fom 1 to 0. This arrangement gives the effect of the user pulling the sling around David's head. As the user pulls the slider from its initial, rightmost position, the stone circles around. The stone makes one full rotation if the user pulls the slider all the way to the left.

The program describes the location of the tip of the arrow's head using polar(r, angle). From this tip, the program plots two other polar functions that head off at an angle of pi/2 (90 degrees) from each other.

The center of the stone is always 1 unit away from the center of the plot at polar(1, angle). To this center, you attach a small sling function whose job is to draw the stone (the circle) in the plot. Each time the user moves the slider, you draw the whole stone, centered on the end of the strap.

For the strap, you need a straight line at the calculated angle. To effect this, imagine a ray that goes from 0 to 1 with time, heading in the angle direction. A function for this ray is polar(t, angle). If the first argument were a constant, the polar function would specify only one point and not a line to represent the strap.

This program uses a variety of techniques to compose an interactive program that illustrates the path of a sling.

16.3.12 More Plots

The idea of Sling is to have fun experimenting with your own programs and especially to play with the effects of the sliders. You can use the examples in this section to get started writing your own programs. In addition, the directory "Sling Programs" on the CD contains a few more examples.

16.3.13 The Elements of Sling

Figure 16.12 summarizes the elements of Sling.

Sling Element	Meaning
abs(x)	The absolute value of x, which is just x if x is positive and –x if x is negative.
cartesian(x, y)	The location of a stone (or point) given its x and y values.
ceil(x)	The smallest integer that is equal to or greater than x.
cos(angle)	The x component of a stone's location at the given angle.
floor(x)	The largest integer that is equal to or less than x.
pi	Shorthand for the ratio of a circle's circumference to its diameter, approximately 3.1416.
polar(radius, angle)	The location of a stone in terms of the length of a sling's strap and the angle (in radians) around the slinger's head.
random	A random number between 0 and 1.
s1	The value of the "s1" slider, which goes from 0 to 1 as the slider moves left to right.
s2	The value of the "s2" slider, which goes from 0 to 1 as the slider moves left to right.
scale(from, to)	A number that varies from "from" to "to" as time (t) varies from 0 to 1.
sin(angle)	The y component of a stone's location at the given angle.
sling(radius, nRotations)	The location of a stone in terms of the length of a sling's strap, and the number of times the stone has gone around the slinger's head.
t	The value of time, which varies from 0 to 1 as the Sling environment draws its plot.
tan(angle)	The ratio of a sling stone's y component to its x component at the given angle.

Figure 16.12 The elements of Sling. Each of these elements can appear in a plot command, and each element can serve as an argument to any other element.

16.4 Building the Sling Environment

The remainder of this chapter covers how to implement an imperative language, focusing on Sling for its examples. The internal representation of an imperative language script is a *command*. The following two sections cover

- Building commands
- Sling commands

Imperative languages often allow the user to create new functions, such as cartesian(x, sin(4*x)). A pair of sections cover

- Building runtime functions
- Sling functions

After showing you how to capture Sling commands and functions, this chapter wraps up with a discussion of the Sling target class and covers the remaining tasks for building a Sling parser:

- Write a grammar.
- Write assemblers to build Sling commands.
- Generate a Sling parser from the grammar, plugging in the assemblers.

The package sjm.examples.sling provides an environment for Sling, including a collection of classes that implement the language and make it available to a user. Figure 16.13 shows a high-level view of the sequence of methods that produce a Sling plot.

The classes in sjm.examples.sling include a user interface. Like other user interfaces in this book, the Sling environment divides user interface tasks between an IDE class and a mediator class. The IDE class organizes and displays visual Swing components, and the mediator class handles component interaction. This separation makes it easier to understand, extend, and debug the user interface.

The action buttons in the class SlingIDE register a SlingMediator object as their event listeners. When a Sling user clicks the **Go** button, the object receives an actionPerformed() call. The mediator checks the user's program to see whether the program text has changed since the last time the mediator parsed it. If it has, the mediator uses a SlingParser object to parse the text.

When a SlingParser object completes its recognition of a user's program, the result is a collection of commands on an Assembly object's stack. These commands correspond

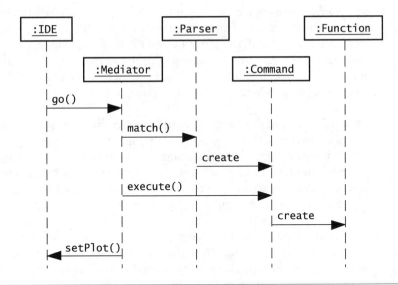

Figure 16.13   A Sling environment sequence. The objects in this diagram collaborate to recognize a user's program and create a corresponding command.

to the assignment statements and the `plot` and `for` commands of the user's program. The mediator pops these commands, builds a composite command from them, and executes the command. When `plot` commands execute, they create Sling functions and add them to a `RenderableCollection` object (not shown in Figure 16.13). After the mediator executes the command, it sends the function collection to the `SlingIDE` object's display panel, and the plot displays.

The following sections describe how to build commands and how to build runtime functions.

16.5   Building Commands

Imperative languages such as Sling let a user write a script, or program, that tells the computer what to do. When you create a parser for an imperative language, a good approach is to follow the *command* pattern [Gamma et al.]. The intent of this pattern is to encapsulate a request. The Sling parser builds a command object that contains the user's request in a Java object. An advantage of building a command from an imperative script is that this approach divides your user's task into two phases.

Users, when programming in your language, will spend much of their time trying to arrive at a syntactically correct input that your parser can recognize. Simple typographic errors as well as deeper misunderstandings about the rules of your language will usually be a significant barrier for users. It is advisable to have your program follow along with the state your user is in. First, help the user to enter syntactically correct input by issuing informative messages about why the parser cannot parse the input text. Issue no output and perform no commands until your parser successfully comprehends the user's complete input.

Once users get past the hurdle of entering input that your parser can recognize, their task is to verify that the program does the right thing. For example, a syntactically correct program for Sling might produce a picture that surprises users. Now they will struggle with the meaning, or semantics, of the program, a different struggle from that of entering recognizable input. An advisable approach is to assemble a Command object as your parser recognizes the user's request, and then execute the command.

A command for a typical imperative language script is a composition of other commands. The command that represents the entire script usually contains branching and looping commands along with commands that pertain only to the specific context of the language. Figure 16.14 shows a package of reusable commands. When you create an imperative language, you can combine these classes with your own subclasses of Command that are specific to the goals of your language.

These classes by themselves cannot create really interesting composite commands. For that you must add new commands that pertain to a context. The Sling environment adds new commands for assigning a function to a variable and for adding a function to a function collection. But to show how the commands can be composed, the next section gives a simple example that uses only the classes in sjm.imperative.

16.5.1 A Command Example

The commands in sjm.imperative allow simple input and output. Today's users typically expect graphical user interfaces for any programming language. However, you can use the PrintlnCommand and ReadCommand classes to create simple examples of composite commands.

Most of the classes in sjm.imperative rely on classes and interfaces from the package sjm.engine. Classes in the Command hierarchy must use variables that they can evaluate on demand, and the classes in sjm.engine fill this need. For example, a PrintlnCommand object can print any instance of Term. Here is a program that builds a for command and then executes the command:

```
package sjm.examples.imperative;

import sjm.engine.*;
import sjm.imperative.*;
```

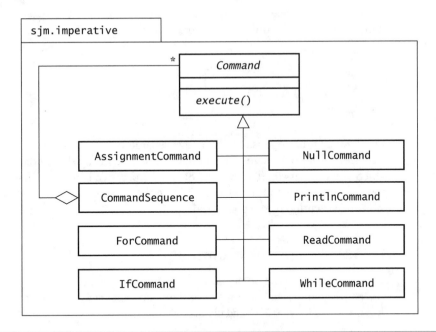

Figure 16.14 The imperative package. This package contains a collection of subclasses of the abstract Command class. Each subclass encapsulates a request that a calling object can execute at any time.

```
/**
 * This class shows a simple composition of commands from
 * <code>sjm.imperative</code>.
 */
public class ShowCommand {

public static void main(String[] args) {
    Fact go          = new Fact("go!");
    PrintlnCommand p = new PrintlnCommand(go);

    Variable i       = new Variable("i");
    ForCommand f     = new ForCommand(i, 1, 5, p);

    f.execute();
  }
}
```

This program wraps the string "go!" in a Fact because the PrintlnCommand class expects Term from sjm.engine as its argument. The Term interface allows PrintlnCommand to accept an argument that might be either a variable or a value. The main() method of ShowCommand creates a variable i and a ForCommand f. The

ForCommand object encapsulates a request to step i from 1 to 5, executing the command p each time. Running ShowCommand prints:

```
go!
go!
go!
go!
go!
```

The power of the code is this: You have separated a composite command from its execution. You can execute the command any time in any thread on any computer to which you can pass the ForCommand object. Imperative language parsers can use the power of the command pattern to separate the parsing of a composite command from the execution of the command.

16.5.2 AssignmentCommand

An AssignmentCommand object class holds an object of class Evaluation from sjm.engine, and executes it upon receiving an execute() command. Figure 16.15 shows the AssignmentCommand class.

The AssignmentCommand class makes it possible to store an assignment for later execution. An AssignmentCommand object can appear inside another command, where it can be executed repeatedly. For example, the following program composes a ForCommand object that has an AssignmentCommand object as its body:

```
package sjm.examples.imperative;

import sjm.engine.*;
import sjm.imperative.*;

/**
 * This class provides an example of the assignment command.
 *
 * The <code>main</code> method of this class creates
 * a variable "x" and pre-assigns it the value 0. Then the
```

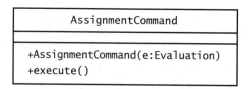

Figure 16.15 The AssignmentCommand class. An AssignmentCommand object holds an Assignment object, which it executes in response to the execute() method.

```
 * method creates a "for" command that encapsulates:
 *
 * <blockquote><pre>
 *
 *      for (int i = 1; i <= 4; i++) {
 *          x = x * 10 + 1;
 *      }
 *
 * </pre></blockquote>
 *
 * The method executes the "for" command, leaving x with the
 * value 1111.0.
 */
public class ShowAssignmentCommand {

public static void main(String[] args) {
    Variable x = new Variable("x");
    x.unify(new NumberFact(0));

    // *(x, 10.0)
    ArithmeticOperator op1 =
        new ArithmeticOperator('*', x, new NumberFact(10));

    // +(*(x, 10.0), 1.0)
    ArithmeticOperator op2 =
        new ArithmeticOperator('+', op1, new NumberFact(1));

    // #(x, +(*(x, 10.0), 1.0))
    AssignmentCommand ac =
        new AssignmentCommand(new Evaluation(x, op2));

    ForCommand f =
        new ForCommand(new Variable("i"), 1, 4, ac);

    f.execute();
    System.out.println(x);
}
}
```

Running this program prints the following:

```
1111.0
```

The program creates the variable x and initializes its value to 1. This initialization is outside any command object, although the program might equivalently establish the initialization as another AssignmentCommand. The program establishes two operators: one that multiplies x by 10 and another one that adds 1 to the first operator. The program creates an AssignmentCommand object that effectively stores the request x = x * 10 + 1;. The program places the assignment command in a for command, executes it, and displays the value of x.

16.5.3 CommandSequence

This class contains a *sequence* of other commands, which is a basic building block of composition. Looping and branching commands such as if, while, and for can execute a CommandSequence object that contains any number of other commands. Figure 16.16 shows the CommandSequence class.

16.5.4 ForCommand

A ForCommand object executes some other command in a loop, iterating a given variable from a from value to a to value. Figure 16.17 shows ForCommand.

The ForCommand class retains four parameters that the constructors receive or establish. These parameters are a setup command, a condition, an end command, and a body command. The execute() method executes a for loop, essentially executing

```
for (setup; condition; endCommand){
    bodyCommand;
}
```

16.5.5 IfCommand

This command mimics a normal if statement, such as

```
if (x > 7) {
    // body to execute if condition is true
} else {
    // body to execute if condition is false
}
```

Figure 16.18 shows the IfCommand class.

```
┌─────────────────────────────────┐
│      CommandSequence            │
├─────────────────────────────────┤
│                                 │
├─────────────────────────────────┤
│ +CommandSequence()              │
│ +addCommand(c:Command)          │
│ +commands():Vector              │
│ +execute()                      │
└─────────────────────────────────┘
```

Figure 16.16   The CommandSequence class. This class provides the basic ability to create a command as a sequence of other commands.

```
+---------------------------------------+
|              ForCommand               |
+---------------------------------------+
+---------------------------------------+
| +ForCommand(                          |
|     setupCommand:Command,             |
|     condition:BooleanTerm,            |
|     endCommand:Command,               |
|     bodyCommand:Command)              |
| +ForCommand(                          |
|     setupCommand:Variable,            |
|     from:double,                      |
|     to:double,                        |
|     step:double,                      |
|     command:Command)                  |
| +ForCommand(                          |
|     setupCommand:Variable,            |
|     from:int,                         |
|     to:int,                           |
|     command:Command)                  |
| +execute()                            |
+---------------------------------------+
```

Figure 16.17   The ForCommand class. Most of the flexibility in the ForCommand class comes from its variety of constructors. The first constructor is fundamental; the other constructors use the first to construct a for command that iterates a given variable between two values.

```
+---------------------------------------+
|              IfCommand                |
+---------------------------------------+
+---------------------------------------+
| +IfCommand(                           |
|     condition:BooleanTerm,            |
|     ifCommand:Command)                |
| +IfCommand(                           |
|     condition:BooleanTerm,            |
|     ifCommand:Command,                |
|     elseCommand:Command)              |
| +execute()                            |
+---------------------------------------+
```

Figure 16.18   The IfCommand class. When asked to execute(), an IfCommand object evaluates its condition and then asks either its ifCommand or elseCommand to execute.

16.5.6 NullCommand

This command does nothing, and that can provide exactly the right effect in some cases. For example, an if command with no given else uses a NullCommand object for its else command.

16.5.7 PrintlnCommand

This command, when executed, prints the value of a term provided in the constructor. This object can be either a structure (usually a fact) or a variable. Figure 16.19 shows the PrintlnCommand class.

```
┌─────────────────────────────────┐
│         PrintlnCommand          │
├─────────────────────────────────┤
│                                 │
├─────────────────────────────────┤
│ +PrintlnCommand(term:Term)      │
│ +PrintlnCommand(               │
│     term:Term,                  │
│     out:PrintWriter)            │
│ +execute()                      │
└─────────────────────────────────┘
```

Figure 16.19 The PrintlnCommand class. The second constructor in the figure allows the creator to specify the output stream; the default output stream is System.out.

16.5.8 ReadCommand

This command, when executed, reads a string and assigns it to a supplied variable. Figure 16.20 shows the ReadCommand class.

16.5.9 WhileCommand

A WhileCommand object mimics a normal while loop, executing a given command in a loop as long as some condition holds true. Figure 16.21 shows WhileCommand.

16.5.10 Commands Summary

Command classes let you compose a request and execute it later. This is important to parsers because it is advantageous to parse a user's program first to verify that the program is syntactically correct. Another advantage of constructing a composite

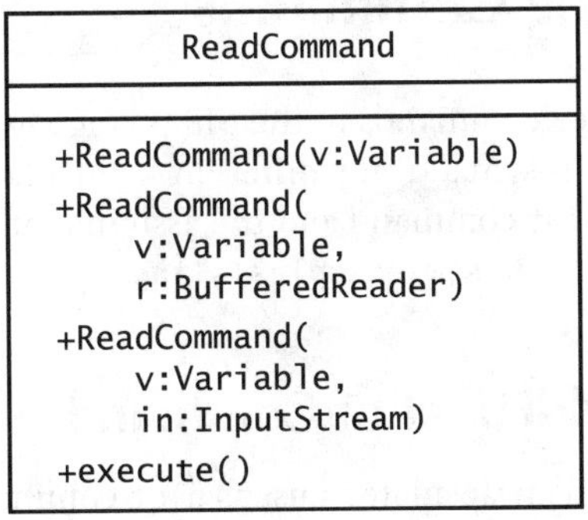

```
                    ReadCommand

        +ReadCommand(v:Variable)
        +ReadCommand(
            v:Variable,
            r:BufferedReader)
        +ReadCommand(
            v:Variable,
            in:InputStream)
        +execute()
```

Figure 16.20   The ReadCommand class. A ReadCommand object encapsulates a request to accept input from a given source, which defaults to System.in.

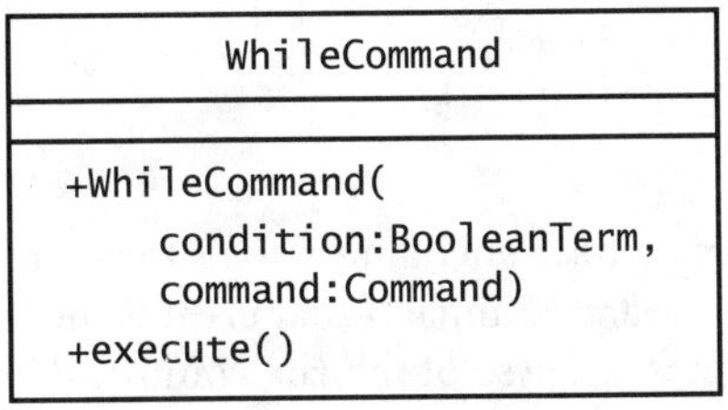

```
                    WhileCommand

        +WhileCommand(
            condition:BooleanTerm,
            command:Command)
        +execute()
```

Figure 16.21   The WhileCommand class. A WhileCommand, when asked to execute(), checks its condition, executes its command, and repeats this loop as long as the condition's value is true.

command that encapsulates a user's program is that you may need to execute the program many times.

The Sling development environment parses a user's program into a command only when the program changes. The environment reexecutes the command each time a slider moves without reparsing the program text. If your language includes variable elements that may change after a user's program is parsed, it is especially important to build a composite command and reexecute it when the variables change.

The commands described in this section are only the beginning. You will almost always add new subclasses of Command to support imperative elements and functions that are relevant to your application.

16.6 Sling Commands

There are three commands in the Sling language: plot, assignment, and for. The for command is syntactically different from a Java for command, but its function is similar. The plot command and the assignment command need application-specific implementations in sjm.examples.sling.

16.6.1 AddFunctionCommand

This command encapsulates a user's plot command. Internally, the Sling parser does not actually start drawing when it parses a plot command. Rather, the parser uses an assembler to place an AddFunctionCommand object on an assembly's stack. Figure 16.22 shows AddFunctionCommand.

Consider the program

```
for (r, 3, 5) {
    plot sling(r, 1);
}
```

When the Sling parser encounters the plot command, it creates and stacks an AddFunctionCommand command that creates the function sling(r, 1). When the parser completes its parse of the for command, it creates a ForCommand object whose body command is the AddFunctionCommand command.

After parsing, the mediator executes the ForCommand object, which in turn repeatedly executes the AddFunctionCommand command. When this command executes, it evaluates the function, creating a plottable function that does not contain variables.

```
┌─────────────────────────────────────────────┐
│              AddFunctionCommand               │
├─────────────────────────────────────────────┤
│                                               │
├─────────────────────────────────────────────┤
│ +AddFunctionCommand(                          │
│       renderables:RenderableCollection,       │
│       f:SlingFunction,                        │
│       nLine:Variable)                         │
│ +execute()                                    │
└─────────────────────────────────────────────┘
```

Figure 16.22 The AddFunctionCommand class. An AddFunctionCommand object holds a SlingFunction object that it evaluates and adds to a collection when the command executes.

The `AddFunctionCommand` object in the `for` loop executes three times and adds three plottable functions to a function collection. These functions are `sling(3, 1)`, `sling(4, 1)`, and `sling(5, 1)`.

16.6.2 AssignFunctionCommand

An `AssignFunctionCommand` object, when executed, evaluates a function and sets it as the value of a variable. Figure 16.23 shows `AssignFunctionCommand`.

Consider the Sling program

```
for (base, 7, 10) {
    r = base + 3*sin(7*2*pi*t);
    plot sling(r, 3);
}
```

The Sling parser builds a `ForCommand` object representing this program. When this command executes, it executes its body four times. Each time the body executes, it evaluates

```
base + 3*sin(7*2*pi*t)
```

and assigns the value to the variable r. Each time the `plot` command executes, it evaluates its function, using the then-current value of r, so that four different functions accumulate. After the `for` loop executes, the mediator plots the four functions.

```
┌─────────────────────────────────────┐
│        AssignFunctionCommand         │
├─────────────────────────────────────┤
│                                      │
├─────────────────────────────────────┤
│ +AssignFunctionCommand(              │
│       v:Variable,                    │
│       f:SlingFunction)               │
│ +execute()                           │
└─────────────────────────────────────┘
```

Figure 16.23   The `AssignFunctionCommand` class. When an `AssignFunctionCommand` object executes, it evaluates its function and assigns this value to its variable.

16.7 Building Runtime Functions

When you create an imperative language, you often want to provide your users the ability to compose functions in your language. For example, Sling allows a user to type an expression such as abs(sin(2*pi*t)). One way to represent this function is as a new method—say, absSin2PiT()—that accepts a variable t and returns Math.abs(Math.sin(2*Math.PI*t)). The Sling environment does not create a new method but rather creates an object that represents this new function.

16.7.1 Function Wrapping

The desire to create new functions while a parser is running creates a paradox: You want to create a new method at runtime, but you must know all method names at compile time. A resolution to this paradox is as follows:

- Design principle 1: Represent each known function with a class that implements the method f().

The package sjm.examples.sling includes a hierarchy of function classes that implement f(), as Figure 16.24 shows.

Each class in the hierarchy in Figure 16.24 provides a known function. The one exception is Variable, which we discuss shortly.

A simpler example might be a string language, which could use classes such as Trim and LowerCase to provide string functions. The package sjm.examples.string contains a collection of classes that subclass an abstract class StringFunction. This abstract class has an abstract method f(), which Trim, LowerCase, and other subclasses implement. Figure 16.25 shows the function hierarchy in sjm.examples.string.

The method signatures of StringFunction.f() and SlingFunction.f() are different because they are hierarchies of string and mathematical functions, respectively. Each function subclass in these hierarchies implements f() according to the superclass's signature, and each class applies a function that corresponds to its name.

To implement the Trim class, for example, you might think of writing f() as

```
String f(String s) {
    return s.trim();
}
```

This is the right idea in that Trim is implementing a standard interface in a way that supports the function that the name Trim implies. However, this implementation does not allow a Trim object to wrap itself around another function. You must set up

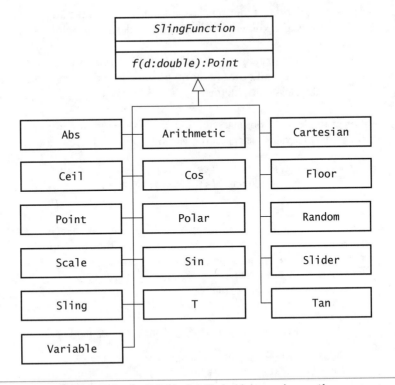

Figure 16.24 The SlingFunction hierarchy. Each of these classes (from sjm.examples.sling) implements the function f(), applying a function that corresponds to the class name.

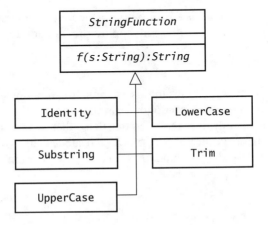

Figure 16.25 The StringFunction hierarchy. Each of these classes (from sjm.examples.string) implements the function f(), applying a function that corresponds to the class name.

Trim and any other function class so that it follows the *decorator* pattern [Gamma et al.], which is also known as *wrapping*. The design principle is as follows:

- Design principle 2: Write f() for each function class so that wraps its function around other function objects. Require that these objects be supplied to the class constructor.

For example, the Trim class accepts in its constructor another StringFunction object that the constructor saves as the variable source. Here is the method Trim.f():

```
public String f(String s) {
    return source.f(s).trim();
}
```

This method applies String.trim() to the result of source.f(s). In other words, the Trim class wraps a trim() function around another function. Consider an instance of Trim with a source that is an instance of LowerCase:

```
package sjm.examples.string;

/**
 * Create and use a string function at runtime.
 */
public class ShowStringFunction {
public static void main(String[] args) {
    StringFunction func = new Trim(new LowerCase());
    System.out.println(
        ">" + func.f(" TAKE IT EASY ") + "<");
}
}
```

This program creates a func object, which represents the new function trim(lower(s)). The program applies the function to a string and prints

```
>take it easy<
```

Like the string functions in this example, the functions in Sling implement the design principles this section has discussed so far. The package sjm.examples.sling includes a family of function classes that subclass an abstract SlingFunction class. Each subclass implements f(), and each subclass has a constructor that accepts other functions that the new function wraps. Before examining these implementations, let's address principles for datatypes.

16.7.2 Umbrella Types

The signature of the common function `f()` depends on the domain of your functions. As the previous examples show, the signature of `f()` for classes in `sjm.examples.string` is

```
String f(String s)
```

String functions accept and return strings.

In the Sling environment, the input argument to `f()` is always time, which you define as varying from 0 to 1 as a plot unfolds. Time is a number, and the parameter signature of `f()` is `f(double t)`.

You might think that functions in Sling would have different types of return values. For example, you might expect two-dimensional functions, such as `cartesian`, `polar`, and `sling` functions, to have `f(t)` return a point (something they do, in fact). You might also expect the mathematical functions `abs`, `sin`, `cos`, `ceil`, and `floor` to have `f(t)` return a single number. In fact, these functions and all functions in `sjm.examples.sling` return a point as the value of `f()`.

To provide an environment that does not require a user to declare variable datatypes, it is useful to declare at a design level that everything is an instance of some overarching, or *umbrella*, type. In addition to `cartesian`, `polar`, and `sling`, *all* the functions in the `sling` package are two-dimensional functions of time. This practice simplifies development and reduces chances for errors in implementing the environment. For example, because everything in Sling is a two-dimensional function of time, the following Sling expression is well defined:

```
sling(1, 1) + sin(8*pi*t)
```

If the `sling` function returned a `Point` object and the `sin` function returned a single number, the arithmetic function would have to have some way to coerce the two types to be compatible for addition. Sling avoids this problem by following this principle:

- Design principle 3: Define the signature of `f()` to be broad enough to encompass all the functions in a language.

In Sling, the signature of `f()` is

```
Point f(double t)
```

This third design principle is optional. When you implement your own languages, you may decide to allow different return types of functions. The difficulty of such an approach is that managing the interplay of different types will permeate your environment. Using a single return type moves the problem of datatype coercion to function constructors. This requires the following corollary:

- Design principle 3.1: Establish policies for widening all datatypes to fill the return value of f().

Sling implements this principle with the following policy:

- In Sling, any function class that would naturally return a single number y will instead return a Point object (t, y).

Sling functions insert time as the x value of single-valued functions. For example, the mathematical sin function returns a single number. If you call that number y, then Sin.f(t) returns the Point object (t, y). This policy is more useful than, say, just inserting 0 as the x value, because using time as the default x dimension has desirable effects. For example, the program

```
plot sin(2*pi*t);
```

plots a sin-wave because this program is equivalent to

```
plot cartesian(t, sin(2*pi*t));
```

The policy of inserting time as the x component moves the coercion of types away from arithmetic and other areas where different types might come together. The problem of coercion is pushed to the function constructors, where a simple policy defines how functions are widened to the broadest possible type.

16.7.3 Runtime Functions in Sling

The design principles of this section determine the code for SlingFunction subclasses. For example, the code in Sin.java (with comments removed) is as follows:

```
package sjm.examples.sling;

public class Sin extends SlingFunction {

public Sin(Function source) {
    super(source);
}

public Point f(double t) {
    return new Point(t, Math.sin(source[0].f(t).y));
}
}
```

This code exemplifies all of the design principles for Sling functions:

- Design principle 1: Sin implements the common function f().

- Design principle 2: Sin provides a constructor that accepts another function as its source. The SlingFunction superclass stores the source function in an array because a function may have more than one source. The source function for a Sin object is thus available as source[0]. The f() method calculates and uses the source function's value at time t.

- Design principle 3: The source function, like any function, returns a point as a function of t. The method Sin.f() ignores the x value of this point, wrapping Math.sin() around the y value of the source function's point. The y value for f() to return is thus Math.sin(source[0].f(t).y). The mathematical sin function is a single number, and so f() returns a Point with t as its x value.

By following these principles, the functions in sjm.examples.sling meet the objectives of allowing runtime composition of functions and of using an umbrella type.

16.7.4 Execution Phases

To create a working environment for your language, you must parse a program into a command object and then execute the object. The Sling environment includes a third phase for drawing a program's functions. The phases of the Sling environment are as follows:

1. Parse the user's program, building a command object that represents the program.

2. Execute the command, creating the collection of functions requested by the user's program.

3. Draw the functions.

For example, consider the Sling program

```
for (r, 1, 4) {
    plot sling(r, 1) + sling(s1, 5);
}
```

This program uses the value of the first slider, s1. When a user types this program and clicks **Go!**, a Sling parser object parses the text and builds a composite command that represents the program. Next, the environment executes the command. Each pass through the for loop creates one new function to plot. The plottable functions are

```
+(sling(1, 1), sling(s1, 5))

+(sling(2, 1), sling(s1, 5))

+(sling(3, 1), sling(s1, 5))

+(sling(4, 1), sling(s1, 5))
```

At this point, the Sling environment has four function objects to plot. After creating these functions, the environment plots them using the current value of the slider s1. Each time the slider moves, the environment plots the functions again—without re-parsing the text and without reexecuting the command. To let the display keep up with a slider's movement, it is important that the Sling environment replot the functions for each new slider value without reexecuting the command.

The variable r and the slider s1 in the preceding program may look similar to a user, but they have different roles in the Sling environment. The slider s1 refers to the value of the slider in the Sling user interface, and this reference persists even after the command executes and creates the command's functions. When the environment draws a program's functions, it looks up the current value of the slider. The variable r does not survive to the function-plotting phase. Variables melt away as the command executes. The for command in the preceding program uses the variable r. As the for command executes, it evaluates r and bakes the value of r into the functions that the plot command creates.

Functions in Sling and in most imperative languages must be able to contain variables and to evaluate themselves. For example, the function

```
+(sling(r, 1), sling(s1, 5)) // object 1
```

must be able to evaluate itself to create a corresponding but unvarying function. If the value of r is 3 (for example) at the moment of evaluation, the function must create a new version of itself as

```
+(sling(3, 1), sling(s1, 5)) // object 2
```

There is a difference between these two objects. The first object may contain variables; the second may not. However, the second object is so similar to the first object that you can use a prototyping strategy.

16.7.5 Prototyping

The idea of the *prototype* pattern [Gamma et al.] is to specify the kind of object to create using a prototypical instance. Every function in Sling needs three similar types of object: assemblers, terms, and functions. You might think that you need to create a

SlingAssembler class, a SlingTerm class, and a SlingFunction class. With this approach, you would also have to create a SinAssembler class, a SinTerm class, and a SinFunction class. In addition, you would need three similar classes for each function that the Sling language supports. However, you can do without these classes by applying the prototype pattern.

The package sjm.examples.sling implements each function of the Sling language with a single class. For example, the only class in sjm.examples.sling that relates to the sin function is the class Sin, which extends SlingFunction. Similarly, the only class that relates to the sling function is the class Sling. The Sling environment uses one instance of this class as an assembler, uses other instances for each sling term in a Sling program, and uses other instances each time a sling term evaluates into a sling function. To see the different roles that a Sling object can play, it is useful to count the number of assembler, term, and function objects in a sample program. Consider the program

```
for (r, 1, 4) {
    plot sling(r, 1) + sling(s1, 5);
}
```

To execute this program, the Sling environment uses 11 copies of a Sling object: one for the assembler, two for terms, and eight for the plottable functions. Ten of these objects are copies (that is, clones) of the initial object that the environment uses as an assembler.

When the Sling parser parses a program, it uses a FunctionAssembler object as the assembler for all Sling functions, including sin, cos, ..., and sling. The constructor for FunctionAssembler requires a SlingFunction object; the assembler uses this object as a prototype. For example, the Sling parser associates an assembler with the sling() function; this assembler is a FunctionAssembler object that has a Sling object as its prototypical function.

Each time the parser sees a sling() function, the parser asks a FunctionAssembler object to "work on" the assembly that the parser is parsing. The assembler pops arguments from the stack to use as the new object's source functions. The number of arguments the assembler pops is equal to the number of source functions the prototype has. For example, a prototype for the sling() function has two source functions, so a FunctionAssembler object that uses this prototype pops two arguments as sources. The assembler then makes a copy of its prototype, sets the copy's sources to be the popped functions, and stacks the new object.

When the parser is finished with the preceding program, it will have created one Sling object to use as an assembler, and two copies of this object to act as terms in a command.

The Sling environment then asks the command that represents the user's program to execute. When the plot command executes, it evaluates the function it is plotting. During evaluation, the sling terms copy themselves.

For example, on the second pass of the for loop, sling(r, 1) term copies itself and sets the copy's source function to be the value of r, which is 2. The sling(s1, 5) term also copies itself, although this is not strictly necessary because this term has no variables to evaluate. Each pass of the for loop creates a new sum that includes two new instances of Sling.

After the command representing the user's program executes, the mediator sends its plottable functions to a SlingPanel object. The SlingPanel class, a subclass of JPanel, knows how to plot SlingFunction objects.

16.7.6 Function Evaluation

All functions other than variables evaluate themselves in the same way, deferring to SlingFunction.eval():

```
public SlingFunction eval() {
    SlingFunction f = fresh();
    for (int i = 0; i < source.length; i++) {
        f.source[i] = source[i].eval();
    }
    return f;
}
```

This method creates a copy of the object using fresh(), which is a clone() method that does not clone the object's source functions. The eval() method establishes the new object's sources as evaluations of the receiving object's sources.

Design principle 2 requires that you compose functions from functions. To allow variables in the composition of a function, variables themselves must be functions. The Variable class is the only subclass of SlingFunction that overrides eval(), using

```
public SlingFunction eval() {
    if (source[0] == null) {
        throw new UnassignedVariableException(
            "> Program uses " + name + " before assigning " +
            "it a value.");
    }
    return source[0].eval();
}
```

Variables expect to hold some function at evaluation time. For example, the following assignment can work only if x has a value at the time the assignment command executes:

```
y = sin(x);
```

In the Sling environment, an AssignFunctionCommand object represents this statement. The command holds the variable y and a function object that represents sin(x). When the command executes, it evaluates sin(x). If the variable x has no value, Variable.eval() throws an exception. Otherwise, the evaluation completes successfully, and the assignment command sets the value of y to the value of sin(x).

16.8 Sling Functions

In the source code for the function classes in the SlingFunction hierarchy, the design principles show through. They are as follows:

- Represent each known function with a class that implements the method f().

- Write f() for each function class so that it wraps its function around other function objects. Require that these objects be supplied to the class constructor.

- Define the signature of f() to be Point f(double t).

- For any base function that would naturally return a single number y, return new Point(t, y), where t is the input parameter to f().

The classes in this hierarchy also provide the ability to create unvariable functions from variable functions by evaluating their sources. The Variable class and the hierarchy superclass SlingFunction are the only classes that actually implement methods that support evaluation.

16.8.1 SlingFunction

This class is at the top of the hierarchy of functions (see Figure 16.26).

Class SlingFunction defines f() as an abstract method and defines eval() for evaluating a function into an unvariable form.

```
┌─────────────────────────────────┐
│         SlingFunction           │
├─────────────────────────────────┤
│                                 │
├─────────────────────────────────┤
│   f(d:double):Point             │
│   eval():SlingFunction          │
│   fresh():SlingFunction         │
└─────────────────────────────────┘
```

Figure 16.26 The SlingFunction class. This class defines, for a large number of sub-classes, the methods for evaluating and copying a function.

16.8.2 Abs, Ceil, Cos, Floor, Sin, and Tan

Each of these Sling functions wraps a routine from class Math in java.lang. Each of these functions normally takes a single number and returns a single number. To follow the Sling environment design principles, each function must find its input number by evaluating its source at a given time and then extracting the y component. The Sling functions pass this number to the appropriate Math method and get back a single number. The Sling functions augment this number, using time as the x component, to create a two-dimensional point. For example, Abs.f(t) contains the statement

```
return new Point(t, Math.abs(source[0].f(t).y));
```

The other functions in the title of this section operate in the same way, each using a different function from Math.

16.8.3 Arithmetic

This class wraps an arithmetic function around two source functions. The Arithmetic class's constructor requires a char (to indicate an operator), and two source functions. The operator must be "+", "-", "/", "*", or "%"; otherwise, f(t) of this object will always be the point (0, 0).

The value of an arithmetic function at time t is the value of the operator applied to the source functions at time t. For example, evaluating the arithmetic sum

```
f1 + f2
```

at time t creates the point

```
(f1(t).x + f2(t).x, f1(t).y + f2(t).y)
```

16.8.4 Cartesian

This class combines the y component of each of two source functions to form a new two-dimensional function. This allows functions that are normally one-dimensional to combine into a two-dimensional function.

For example, both sin and cos are normally one-dimensional functions, returning a single number for any given value. The classes Sin and Cos store their results in the y dimension of a function, augmenting any particular point with t as the x value. Objects of the Cartesian class ignore the x component of each source function. The y component of the first source function becomes the x component of the Cartesian function, and the y component of the second function becomes the y component of the Cartesian function.

Consider the following program, which plots a circle:

```
theta = 2*pi*t;
x = cos(theta);
y = sin(theta);
plot cartesian(x, y);
```

The design principles at play in sjm.examples.sling augment the x and y functions so that they are effectively cartesian(t, cos(theta)) and cartesian(t, sin(theta)). The program recombines the y components of these functions into a new cartesian with an x value of cos(theta) and a y value of sin(theta).

16.8.5 Point

Objects of this class store two numbers that effectively determine a point in two-dimensional space.

16.8.6 Polar

This class represents the location of a sling stone in terms of the length of a sling's strap and the angle (in radians) around the slinger's head. The constructor accepts two source functions. The y component of the first function represents the length of the strap, and the y component of the second function represents the strap's angle.

When you whirl a sling, the stone's path covers 2*pi radians of arc as the stone makes one revolution. The arc varies from 0 to 2*pi, starting in the positive x direction and rotating counterclockwise. You can use the variable r to represent the strap's length, and the variable theta to represent the strap's angle. At any point in time, then, the stone's position is

```
polar(r, theta)
```

This is equivalent to

```
cartesian(r * cos(theta), r * sin(theta))
```

because the cos and sin functions represent the x and y components of a stone's path. Thus, the implementation of Polar.f() is

```
public Point f(double t) {
    double r = source[0].f(t).y;
    double theta = source[1].f(t).y;
    return new Point(
        r * Math.cos(theta), r * Math.sin(theta));
}
```

16.8.7 Random

Objects of this class return a random number between 0 and 1 when asked for their value. Here is the implementation of Random.f():

```
public Point f(double t) {
    return new Point(t, Math.random());
}
```

16.8.8 Scale

A Scale function varies between two limits. As a plot unfolds, time varies from 0 to 1. When time is 0, the value of a Scale object is the value of its first limit. When time is 1, the value of a Scale object is the value of its second limit. For example, the Sling program

```
plot scale(cartesian(-1, -1), cartesian(1, 1));
```

plots a 45-degree line from the lower-left corner to the upper-right corner.

16.8.9 Sling

This class represents the location of a sling stone in terms of the length of a sling's strap and the speed of the stone's rotation around the slinger's head.

The constructor accepts two source functions. The y component of the first function represents the length of the strap, and the y component of the second function represents the stone's angular speed. A speed of 1 represents one full rotation that occurs during the course of a plot. Here is the implementation of Sling.f():

```
public Point f(double t) {
    double r = source[0].f(t).y;
    double speed = source[1].f(t).y;
    double theta = Math.PI * 2 * speed * t;
    return new Point(
        r * Math.cos(theta), r * Math.sin(theta));
}
```

16.8.10 Slider

This class holds a Swing JSlider component, returning the slider's value in its f(t) call. The slider, which this class's constructor requires, should vary from 0 to 100. This class divides that value by 100 so that the slider effectively varies from 0 to 1. The y component of the return value of f(t) ignores time and depends only on the slider value. Like all one-dimensional functions, however, this function uses time as the x component of the value it returns.

16.8.11 T

This class represents time, which the Sling environment defines to vary from 0 to 1 as a plot unfolds. Here is the implementation of T.f():

```
public Point f(double t) {
    return new Point(t, t);
}
```

16.8.12 Variable

A variable is a named place that can store another function. The Variable class is a subclass of SlingFunction, which allows functions to compose themselves from other functions. During the execution phase, term objects evaluate themselves into function objects that do not contain variables. It is an error to ask a variable for f(t) because this function applies only in the drawing phase. Here is the implementation of Variable.f(t):

```
public Point f(double t) {
    throw new InternalError();
}
```

16.9 Sling Target

As a Sling parser recognizes an input program, it must build a composite command that represents the program. `Assembler` subclasses do the work of building this command, sharing certain objects during parsing. The assemblers use a target object to contain the common objects the assemblers need while parsing a Sling program. The target is a single object of class `SlingTarget` containing a *scope*, two sliders, and a `RenderableCollection` object. The assemblers update the target and leave one or more `Command` objects on the assembly's stack. Figure 16.27 shows the `SlingTarget` class.

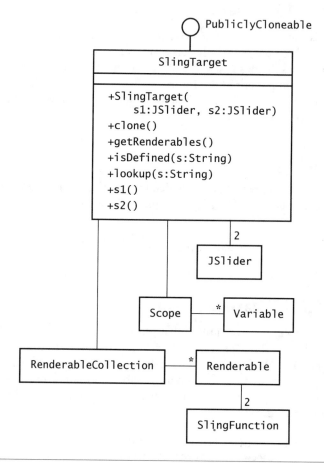

Figure 16.27   The `SlingTarget` class. An instance of `SlingTarget` holds objects that the environment's assemblers refer to while constructing a command that represents a user's program.

A `SlingTarget` is created by a mediator when the user enters a program and clicks the **Go!** button. The classes in `sjm.examples.sling` divide the task of providing an interactive development environment into two parts. The `SlingIDE` class has all the user interface components, and the `SlingMediator` class handles all the component interactions. When the user clicks **Go!**, the mediator checks that the program text has changed since any previous parse. If the text is new, the mediator creates a new `SlingTarget` object by feeding the `SlingTarget` constructor the two sliders from the user interface. Assemblers refer to these sliders whenever the user's program references s1 or s2. In addition to the sliders, a new target object starts with an empty `RenderableCollection` object and an empty `Scope`.

A target's `Scope` object is a dictionary of variables, and a target's `RenderableCollection` object is a collection of plottable functions. A `Renderable` object combines two Sling functions: One is the function to plot (or render), and the other one represents the number of lines to use in the plot.

The `RenderableCollection` object remains empty throughout the parsing phase. When the parser sees a `plot` command, a `PlotAssembler` object pulls the `RenderableCollection` object from the target and uses it to create an `AddFunctionCommand`. When the mediator executes the command during the execution phase, the command adds a function to the `RenderableCollection` object.

Consider the Sling program

```
nLine = 5;
plot sling(1, 1);
plot sling(1, 2);
```

When the parser parses a `plot` command, the parser first uses an assembler to stack the `sling` function, and then the parser asks a `PlotAssembler` to work on the assembly. The assembler pops the function, looks up the target's `RenderableCollection` object and nLine variable, and uses the function, the number of lines, and the collection to create a new `AddFunctionCommand`. The sample program plots two functions, each of which appears in the target's `RenderableCollection` object after the `AddFunctionCommand` object executes.

After a parser completes its parse of a user's program, the target itself is no longer useful. Its purpose is to act as a central storage place for the scope, sliders, and function collection that the parser builds. The Sling environment's various assemblers wire the target's contents to commands that the assemblers leave on the assembly's stack.

16.10 A Sling Grammar

A Sling program is a series of statements:

```
statements = statement statement*;
```

These statements may be either assignment statements, for statements, or plot statements:

```
statement     = assignment | forStatement | plotStatement;
assignment    = variable '=' expression ';' ;
plotStatement = "plot" expression ';';
forStatement  =
    "for" '(' variable ',' expression ',' expression  ')'
    '{' statements '}';
```

A variable is any unreserved word; the reserved words in Sling are the elements shown in Figure 16.12.

```
variable = Word;
```

Expressions in Sling allow for normal arithmetic manipulation:

```
expression        = term (plusTerm | minusTerm)*;
plusTerm          = '+' term;
minusTerm         = '-' term;
term              = element (timesElement | divideElement |
                           remainderElement)*;

timesElement      = '*' element;
divideElement     = '/' element;
remainderElement  = '%' element;
element           = '(' expression ')' | baseElement |
                    negative;

negative          = '-' baseElement;
```

The base elements of Sling are those in Figure 16.12 plus numbers and variables:

```
baseElement = Num | "pi" | "s1" | "s2" | variable |
    noArgs("random")    |
    noArgs("t")         |
    oneArg("abs")       |
    oneArg("ceil")      |
    oneArg("cos")       |
    oneArg("floor")     |
    oneArg("sin")       |
    oneArg("tan")       |
    twoArgs("polar")    |
    twoArgs("cartesian") |
```

```
        twoArgs("scale")      |
        twoArgs("sling");

noArgs(i)  = i;
oneArg(i)  = i '(' expression ')';
twoArgs(i) = i '(' expression ',' expression ')';
```

16.11 Sling Assemblers

The Sling parser needs assemblers for each of its allowable commands and for each base element of the language. The base elements include numbers, variables, pi, the sliders s1 and s2, negation, and the Sling functions. A single function assembler suffices to assemble all the different types of functions in Sling except for scale.

The scale function requires a special assembler because internally a Scale object takes five parameters in its constructor, and the Sling language allows for only two arguments in the scale function. The Sling parser always sets the first three parameters of a Scale object to 0, t, 1.

The three command assemblers needed by the environment are for the plot command, assignment command, and for command. Figure 16.28 shows the Sling assemblers.

Figure 16.29 shows the placement of assemblers in a Sling parser.

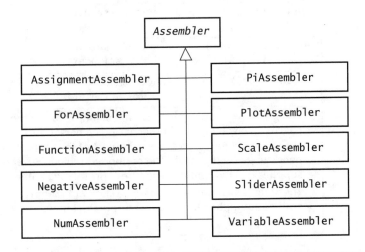

Figure 16.28 Assemblers for Sling. There is one assembler for each command, and one for each basic element of Sling. The FunctionAssembler greatly reduces the number of assemblers because it can assemble any kind of function.

Parser	Assembler	Note
assignment()	AssignmentAssembler()	
forStatement()	ForAssembler()	
negative()	NegativeAssembler()	
num()	NumAssembler()	
pi()	PiAssembler()	
plotStatement()	PlotAssembler()	
s1()	SliderAssembler(1)	
s2()	SliderAssembler(2)	
scale()	ScaleAssembler()	
variable()	VariableAssembler()	
Functions		1
noArgs(name, f)	FunctionAssembler(f)	
oneArg(name, f)	FunctionAssembler(f)	
twoArgs(name, f)	FunctionAssembler(f)	
Math		2
divideElement()	FunctionAssembler(new Arithmetic('/'))	
minusTerm()	FunctionAssembler(new Arithmetic('-'))	
plusTerm()	FunctionAssembler(new Arithmetic('+'))	
remainderElement()	FunctionAssembler(new Arithmetic('%'))	
timesElement()	FunctionAssembler(new Arithmetic('*'))	

1. The grammar shows only the name of a function in the routines noArgs(), oneArg(), and twoArgs(). The parser must send a second argument, namely a prototypical object of the class of function that needs to go on the stack. The method SlingParser.baseElement() supplies the arg routines with these prototypical objects.
2. The Sling environment uses a single class, Arithmetic, to represent all arithmetic functions and passes an operator telling which specific function to apply.

Figure 16.29   Sling assembler placement. This table shows the assembler that each Sling subparser employs.

16.11.1 AssignmentAssembler

This assembler pops a function and a variable, constructs an `AssignFunctionCommand` from these terms, and pushes the command. For example, after parsing

```
y = sin(x);
```

this assembler expects the variable y and the function `sin(x)` to be on the stack, and it constructs an assignment command from these objects.

16.11.2 ForAssembler

This assembler builds a `for` command from elements on the stack, which should be a variable, a `from` function, a `to` function, a "{" token, and a series of commands. This class uses the curly brace as a fence, popping commands above it and creating a composite from these commands. This composite command is the body of the `for` loop. This assembler pops the `from` and `to` functions and the variable, constructs a `ForCommand` object, and pushes it.

16.11.3 FunctionAssembler

This assembler uses information from a prototypical function object received in a constructor to guide the construction of a new function.

The constructor for this class requires a `SlingFunction` object that serves as a prototype. The prototype specifies the type of function to assemble and how many source functions this type needs. When this assembler works on an assembly, it pops as many functions to use as sources as the number of sources in the prototype. This assembler then creates a copy of the prototype, uses the popped sources as the copy's source functions, and pushes the copy.

16.11.4 NegativeAssembler

This assembler pops the assembly and pushes a new function that multiplies this function by –1.

16.11.5 NumAssembler

This assembler pops a number token and pushes a number function. A design principle for the `sjm.examples.sling` package is that "everything" is a two-dimensional function of time. Thus, if the stack contains, say, a token that is only the number 3, this assembler pushes a new Cartesian function (t, (0, 3)).

16.11.6 PiAssembler

This assembler pushes the function `cartesian(t, (0, pi))`.

16.11.7 PlotAssembler

This class expects the target of an assembly to contain a `RenderableCollection` object, which is a collection of evaluatable Sling functions. This assembler pops a function, builds an `AddFunctionCommand` from the target and this function, and pushes the command.

16.11.8 ScaleAssembler

This class augments the stack with default scale arguments and then uses a `FunctionAssembler` with a `Scale` object to work on the assembly.

A scale requires five source functions: aFrom, a, aTo, bFrom, and bTo. These functions allow a mapping between two coordinate systems. The Sling language accepts only two arguments in a `scale` function: bFrom and bTo. Internally, the Sling parser defaults the "a" system to be time. For example, the Sling language function

        scale(-pi, pi)

implies the internal scale function

        scale(0, t, 1, -pi, pi).

The `ScaleAssembler` class pushes the arguments (0, t, 1) onto the stack and then uses a normal `Scale` object to work on the assembly.

16.11.9 SliderAssembler

This class uses one of the sliders in an assembly's target to create a `Slider` function and pushes this function. The class expects the assembly's target to contain a `SlingTarget` object, which holds references to two `JSlider` objects. This class's constructor determines which slider to ask for. When an object of this class works on an assembly, it gets the slider component from the target, creates a `Slider` function with it, and pushes this function.

16.11.10 VariableAssembler

This class expects an assembly's target to be a `SlingTarget` object. The target has a scope, which is a collection of variables organized by name. When this assembler works on an assembly, it pops a name from the stack, looks up a variable in the scope using the name, and pushes the variable onto the stack. This lookup creates the variable in the scope if the scope does not already contain a variable of that name.

16.12 A Sling Parser

You can create a Sling parser almost directly from the Sling grammar. You must supplement the parser with the assemblers, as Section 16.11 shows. You also must add logic for reserved words.

16.12.1 Reserved Words

In Sling, you want to allow variable definition, but you do not want to allow confusion about whether pi, s1, and s2, for example, are variables or built-in expressions. You do not want to allow

```
s1 = 42; // wrong
```

In fact, entering this line as a program in the Sling development environment will elicit this message:

```
> s1 is a reserved word
```

The strategy that `SlingParser` uses to reserve words is to modify the standard tokenizer to return specified words as a different type of token. The parser uses the class `WordOrReservedState` developed in Chapter 11, "Extending the Parser Toolkit," to replace the normal word state in the `Tokenizer` class. The `SlingParser` class has a `tokenizer()` method that diverts characters that begin words to a `WordOrReservedState` object. Most of the subparsers in `SlingParser` reserve a word from the Sling language by calling `SlingParser.reserve()`. This method adds a word to the `WordOrReservedState` object and establishes the sought word as a `ReservedLiteral` rather than a normal `Literal` parser. A `ReservedLiteral` parser matches only a particular word, and it expects the token type to indicate a reserved word.

When the Sling parser tries to match s1 = 42;, the parser fails completely because s1 will tokenize as a reserved word, and nothing in the language allows a reserved word to begin an assignment statement. The Sling mediator checks for this common problem, notes that the parser cannot get past the s1 token, and issues the message that s1 is a reserved word.

16.12.2 Assembler Placement

Figure 16.29 shows where the assemblers plug in. As the first note to the table describes, the `noArgs()`, `oneArg()`, and `twoArgs()` methods need to know both the name of the function to match and a prototype of the function. For example, the baseElement subparser uses the following code to add recognition of a sling function:

```
baseElement.add(twoArg("sling", new Sling()));
```

The twoArg() method uses the function prototype to plug in the appropriate function assembler:

```
protected Parser twoArg(String name, SlingFunction f) {
    Track t = new Track(name);
    t.add(reserve(name));
    t.add(lParen());
    t.add(expression());
    t.add(comma());
    t.add(expression());
    t.add(rParen());
    t.setAssembler(new FunctionAssembler(f));
    return t;
}
```

With strategies in place for reserved words and function prototypes, you can follow the guidelines in Section 3.6, "Translating a Grammar to Code," to create the parser.

16.13 Summary

Imperative languages tell a computer what to do, giving the computer a script or program of operations to follow. If you need an imperative language, Java may be the best answer. Java is far more powerful than any language in this book, and it is easy to overestimate the complexity of learning Java. A good rule of thumb is this: If your users will spend more than 300 hours developing expertise in a language, perhaps the language for them to learn is Java. On the other hand, for many applications a smaller and more easily learned language will fit nicely.

When you create a new imperative language, a good strategy is to have your parser create a composite command that represents your user's program. This approach separates the parsing phase from the execution phase, and that mirrors the state of your users. Users tweak programs until they are recognizable, and then they focus on what happens when the program executes.

When your users need the flexibility of programming in their business or learning environment and they do not have time to learn Java, a new imperative language may be the perfect solution.

CHAPTER 17

Directions

T his chapter gives advice on further study and points out some directions to explore with the languages you create.

17.1 Get Started

You may wish that you could skip the basics and move immediately to advanced topics. Teachers typically resist this and urge students to start at the beginning. If you are amenable to that sort of advice, there are a few steps you should take.

17.1.1 Get the Most Out of This Book

If you have not yet tried out the software in this book, do so. Get the software loaded on your machine, and play with it. You should be able to get the Sling environment running in less than an hour; Section 16.3, "Sling Programming," tells how.

In addition to getting the software to run, you should experiment with extending and modifying the software. Get the ShowHello class in sjm.examples.preface to run, as as described in the "Hello World" section in the Preface. Then try creating a new language and writing a parser for it. A language like the coffee language in Chapter 5, "Parsing Data Languages," is a good place to start.

17.1.2 Other Essential Reading

In addition to this book, there are a few books that every software developer should read. You will never regret reading these:

- *The Java Programming Language* [Arnold and Gosling]
- *Design Patterns* [Gamma et al.]
- *The Unified Modeling Language User Guide* [Booch et al.]

Of the many advances in recent decades, these three technologies (at least) are here to stay. If you are not conversant in Java, design patterns, and the UML, you should read these books.

17.2 Keep Going

When you begin to master the tools and techniques this book describes, you can advance in many directions that are open to new discoveries.

17.2.1 Create New Languages for Your Colleagues

Empowering those around you with a new query language or a special shell that you tailor to their domain is motivating and rewarding.

17.2.2 Create New Languages for Children

There are surprisingly few computer languages for children. Surely we can expect that a great language for twelve-year-olds is different from a great language for six-year-olds. There are, of course, many other differences that call for a range of languages to be available for children. Choose a niche and fill it.

We need to teach children to program computers because natural languages such as English and languages usable by computers are here to stay. For decades to come, we will continue to need to compromise between the power of natural language and the limits of computer understanding. Until computers achieve human-level intelligence, we will need to teach people to program computers.

17.2.3 Explore Languages as Human Interfaces

The advent of graphical user interfaces makes it easy to forget that textual interfaces, especially computer languages, play a major role in how humans and computers interact. Many environments include a combination of human and textual interface. For example, spreadsheets are mostly graphical, but they typically accept formulas as text. The Sling environment also blends a textual and a graphical interface. Can you change the Sling toy to become entirely graphical? What is the ideal mix of text and widgets?

17.2.4 Improve Languages as Receptacles for Human Thought

Part of the strength of object-oriented languages is that they simplify translation from how we think about the world to how we write computer programs. We think and program, at least in part, in terms of objects. The philosophy of how humans categorize their observations into a model of reality is *ontology*. To learn more about ontology, a wonderful resource is *The Oxford Companion to Philosophy* [Honderich].

Although it is nice that we have a good mapping from real objects to objects in Java, the mapping is incomplete. In particular, real objects vary with time, but today's object-oriented languages offer little support for temporal modeling. For example, the basic temporal notion that a physical object can be in only one place at one time is not built into Java. In addition, assignment statements obliterate any previous value instead of remembering it, as a human would. Can you write an imperative language that comprehends the natural temporality of objects?

In addition to (temporal) objects, a simple view of our mental model of reality must include some idea of relations. We know, for example, that if mushrooms cost more than peppers, then peppers must cost less than mushrooms. The symmetry of this relation is much easier to model in Logikus and Prolog than in Java. If you want to learn more about relational modeling and logic programming, two excellent resources are *The Art of Prolog* [Sterling and Shapiro] and *Prolog Programming in Depth* [Covington et al.].

Logikus augments the ontological power of Java by adding support for the modeling of relations. However, Logikus does not comprehend the notion of transitivity. For example, if mushrooms are costlier than peppers, then radishes cannot cost more than mushrooms and cost less than peppers. But Logikus does not detect that the following program breaks the transitivity of the `costlier` relation:

```
costlier(mushrooms, peppers);
costlier(peppers, radishes);
costlier(radishes, mushrooms);
```

Can you create a language that supersedes Logikus by allowing a user to specify that `costlier` is a transitive relation? Our languages become more useful when they become better receptacles for our mental models of the world. The ontological power of languages beckons exploration.

17.2.5 Choose Your Own Direction

This chapter gives a few glimpses into the vista of opportunity that lies before you. The best computer language for you to write is the one that motivates you. Choose a direction and pursue it. The future is in your hands.

UML Twice Distilled

This appendix briefly explains the features of the Unified Modeling Language (UML) that this book uses.

The UML[*] provides conventional notation that this book applies to illustrate the design of object-oriented systems. Although the UML is not overly complex, developers commonly underestimate the richness of its features. The figures in this book go beyond the simple modeling of classes but still use less than half of the features available in the UML. For a rapid introduction to most of the features of the UML, read *UML Distilled* [Fowler and Scott]. For a more thorough review, read *The Unified Modeling Language User Guide* [Booch et al.]. By learning to use standard nomenclatures and notations, developers learn to communicate at a design level, making us all more productive.

A.1 Classes

Figure A.1 applies some of the UML features for illustrating classes.

In Figure A.1, note the following.

- A package appears as the name of the package in a rectangle left-aligned with a larger box that may show classes and interfaces. Figure A.1 shows a portion of the `sjm.parse` package.

- A class appears as the name of a class centered in a rectangle. Figure A.1 shows three classes: `Assembler`, `Assembly`, and `Repetition`.

---

[*] This book follows the precedent set by the UML's creators in referring to the standard as "the" UML.

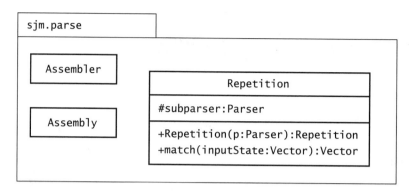

Figure A.1 Classes. Note that there is no guarantee that a UML diagram portrays every element of a package or class. The amount of detail in a diagram depends on the objective of the illustrator.

- A diagram may show a class's instance variables and methods in rectangles beneath the class name. Class Repetition has an instance variable subparser, of type Parser. This class also has (at least) one constructor and (at least) one method, match().

- Instance variable declarations appear as the name of the variable followed by a colon and the type of the variable, as in subparser:Parser.

- Variables in method signatures also appear as the name of the variable followed by a colon and the type of the variable.

- A diagram that shows a method such as match() may also show the method's signature in the parentheses after the name. A colon and the return type of the method may follow this.

- A class diagram may indicate that an instance variable or a method is protected by preceding it with a pound sign (#). A plus sign (+) indicates that a variable or method is public.

- A diagram may indicate that an instance variable is static (and thus has class scope) by underlining it. (Figure A.1 does not show this feature.)

A.2 Class Relationships

Figure A.2 shows a few of the UML's features for modeling class relationships.

In Figure A.2, note the following.

- A diagram may show a class name or method name in italics to indicate that the class or method is abstract.
- A large, open arrowhead points to a class's superclass.
- A line between classes indicates that instances of the classes are connected in some way. Most commonly, a line on a class diagram means that one class has an instance variable that refers to the other class. The classes `Alternation` and `Sequence`, for example, use a `Vector` variable that `CollectionParser` declares to hold collections of other parsers.
- An asterisk (*) indicates that zero or more instances of an object of a class may be connected to objects of an associated class. For example, a `Sequence` object has a reference to zero or more `Parser` objects.
- A multiplicity indicator, such as `0..1`, indicates how many connections may appear between objects. For example, a `Parser` object can have zero or one associated `Assembler` objects.

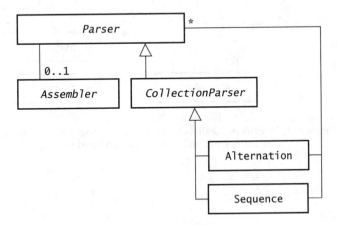

Figure A.2 Class relations. Various lines between classes indicate relationships between objects of the classes.

A.3 Interfaces

Figure A.3 shows the basic features for illustrating interfaces.

In Figure A.3, note the following.

- A diagram can show that a class implements an interface by showing a line and circle (a "lollipop") and the name of the interface. The `Assembly` class, for example, implements the `Enumeration` and `PubliclyCloneable` interfaces.

- A diagram can also show an interface by placing the text `<<interface>>` and the name of the interface in a rectangle, as Figure A.3 shows. In this approach, a diagram can show that a class implements the interface using a dashed line and a large, open arrowhead.

- When showing a class relationship, a diagram can emphasize that objects of one class are aggregations of objects of another class by adding a diamond to the connecting line. Figure A.3 indicates that a structure is an aggregation of terms, which may be variables or other structures.

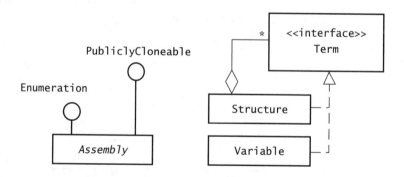

Figure A.3　Interfaces. Unless there is other structural information that you want to illustrate, you can use a simple line and circle to show that a class implements an interface.

A.4 Objects

An object diagram illustrates specific instances of classes, as Figure A.4 shows.

In Figure A.4, note the following.

- An object typically appears as a colon followed by the name of the class, all underlined, in a rectangle. For example, :Repetition indicates an object of the Repetition class.
- A diagram can point out the name of a variable that references an object by prepending the name, as in good:Sequence.
- A line between objects indicates that one object has a reference to another.

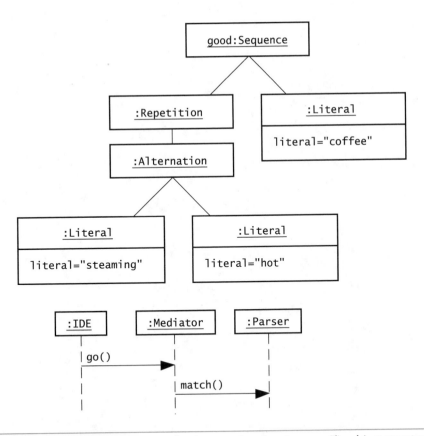

Figure A.4 Objects. The UML provides features for showing specific object structures and interactions.

- An object diagram can show the value of an instance variable, as with the :Literal objects in Figure A.4.

- A diagram can show a sequence of objects sending messages to other objects, as the lower part of Figure A.4 shows. The order of messages is top to bottom, and the dashed lines indicate the existence of the object over time.

References

Aho, Alfred V., Ravi Sethi, and Jeffrey D. Ullman. 1986. *Compilers: Principles, Techniques and Tools*. Reading, MA: Addison-Wesley.

Arnold, Ken, and James Gosling. 1998. *The Java Programming Language*, 2d ed. Reading, MA: Addison-Wesley.

Beck, Kent. 2000. *Extreme Programming Explained*. Boston, MA: Addison-Wesley.

Booch, Grady, James Rumbaugh, and Ivar Jacobsen. 1999. *The Unified Modeling Language User Guide*. Boston, MA: Addison-Wesley.

Covington, Michael A., Donald Nute, and Andre Vellino. 1997. *Prolog Programming in Depth*. Upper Saddle River, NJ: Prentice Hall.

Flanagan, David. 1997. *Java in a Nutshell*, 2d ed. Sebastapol, CA: O'Reilly.

Fowler, Martin, and Kendall Scott. 2000. *UML Distilled*, 2d ed. Boston, MA: Addison-Wesley.

Gamma, Erich, Richard Helm, Ralph Johnson, and John Vlissides. *Design Patterns*. 1995. Reading, MA: Addison-Wesley.

Honderich, Ted, ed. 1995. *The Oxford Companion to Philosophy*. New York: Oxford University Press.

Hopcroft, John E., and Jeffrey D. Ullman. 1979. *Introduction to Automata Theory, Languages and Computation*. Reading, MA: Addison-Wesley.

Slonneger, Ken, and Barry Kurtz. 1995. *Formal Syntax and Semantics of Programming Languages*. Reading, MA: Addison-Wesley.

Sterling, Leon, and Ehud Shapiro. 1994. *The Art of Prolog*, 2d ed. Cambridge, MA: The MIT Press.

Index

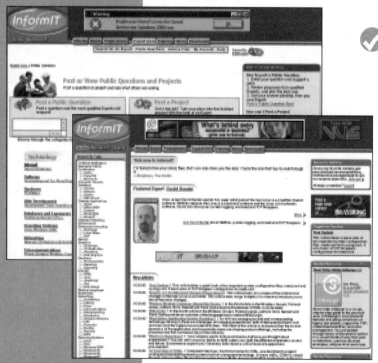 

Register
Your Book
at www.aw.com/cseng/register

You may be eligible to receive:

- Advance notice of forthcoming editions of the book
- Related book recommendations
- Chapter excerpts and supplements of forthcoming titles
- Information about special contests and promotions throughout the year
- Notices and reminders about author appearances, tradeshows, and online chats with special guests

Contact us

If you are interested in writing a book or reviewing manuscripts prior to publication, please write to us at:

Editorial Department
Addison-Wesley Professional
75 Arlington Street, Suite 300
Boston, MA 02116 USA
Email: AWPro@aw.com

Visit us on the Web: http://www.aw.com/cseng

CD-ROM Warranty

Addison-Wesley Professional warrants the enclosed disc to be free of defects in materials and faulty workmanship under normal use for a period of ninety days after purchase. If a defect is discovered in the disc during this warranty period, a replacement disc can be obtained at no charge by sending the defective disc, postage prepaid, with proof of purchase to:

Editorial Department
Addison-Wesley Professional
Pearson Technology Group
75 Arlington Street, Suite 300
Boston, MA 02116

e-mail: AWPro@awl.com

After the 90-day period, a replacement will be sent upon receipt of the defective disc and a check or money order for $10.00, payable to Addison-Wesley Professional.

Addison-Wesley Professional and the author make no warranty or representation, either expressed or implied, with respect to this software, its quality, performance, merchantability, or fitness for a particular purpose. In no event will the author or Addison-Wesley Professional, its distributors, or dealers be liable for direct, indirect, special, incidental, or consequential damages arising out of the use or inability to use the software. The exclusion of implied warranties is not permitted in some states. Therefore, the above exclusion may not apply to you. This warranty provides you with specific legal rights. There may be other rights that you may have that vary from state to state.

http://www.awl.com/cseng/titles/0-201-71962-2